A TRUFFAUT NOTEBOOK

Jean-Pierre Léaud and François Truffaut on the set of *Love on the Run* (1979).

A TRUFFAUT NOTEBOOK

SAM SOLECKI

McGill-Queen's University Press
Montreal & Kingston • London • Chicago

© McGill-Queen's University Press 2015
ISBN 978-0-7735-4624-0 (cloth)
ISBN 978-0-7735-9798-3 (ePDF)
ISBN 978-0-7735-9799-0 (ePUB)

Legal deposit fourth quarter 2015
Bibliothèque nationale du Québec

Printed in Canada on acid-free paper

McGill-Queen's University Press acknowledges the support of the Canada Council for the Arts for our publishing program. We also acknowledge the financial support of the Government of Canada through the Canada Book Fund for our publishing activities.

Library and Archives Canada Cataloguing in Publication

Solecki, Sam, 1946–, author
A Truffaut notebook / Sam Solecki.

Includes bibliographical references and index.
Issued in print and electronic formats.
ISBN 978-0-7735-4624-0 (bound). – ISBN 978-0-7735-9798-3 (ePDF).–
ISBN 978-0-7735-9799-0 (ePUB)

1. Truffaut, François – Criticism and interpretation. I. Title.

PN1998.3.T78S64 2015   791.4302'33092   C2015-904023-X   C2015-904024-8

To Karen Mulhallen and Rick Powers

CONTENTS

xi Acknowledgments

3   The Films of François Truffaut

5   Chronology

9   Why Truffaut?

22 In His Own Words I

23 Roland Lévy and Roland Truffaut

26 Early Films: François and Sam

31 The Godfather: André Bazin (1918–1958)

36 1 January 1954: "A Certain Tendency in French Cinema"

41 *The Mischief Makers* (1957): Some Boys and a Girl on a Bicycle

44 Films Truffaut Didn't Make I

48 Some Titles for *The 400 Blows* (1959)

50 Making Films Together: A Letter to the Cast and Crew of *The Last Metro* (21 January 1980)

53 *The 400 Blows*: A Life on Film

62 Jean-Pierre Léaud with Truffaut, Jean-Luc Godard, and Bernardo Bertolucci

69 Robert Lachenay (1930–2005): The Best Friend and the Ancillary Life

72   Sacha Guitry (1885–1957): *Le Roman d'un tricheur* and *The 400 Blows*

75   *Shoot the Piano Player* (1960): All You Need Is Love

80   *Shoot the Piano Player* and a Debt to the Past

82   Truffaut's *Breathless* and Jean-Luc Godard's

84   A Posthumous Questionnaire (January 2015)

90   Truffaut in His Letters

95   *Jules and Jim* (1961): When We Speak of Freedom and Love and Death

104 Eric Rohmer's *La Collectionneuse* (1967) and *Jules and Jim*

107 Julian Barnes's *Talking It Over* (1991) and *Jules and Jim*

109 Salman Rushdie's *The Ground beneath Her Feet* (1999) and *Jules and Jim*

112 Truffaut in and out of His Time

114 Carlos Saura on *The Soft Skin* (1964), Obliquely

116 The Auteur and the Empty Room

119 Meeting Jeanne Moreau in Venice

124 Truffaut Looks back to Godard: *Fahrenheit 451* (1966) and *Alphaville* (1965)

125 *Fahrenheit 451* and Truffaut's English

128 *The Bride Wore Black* (1967)

131 Jacques Demy, Catherine Deneuve, Françoise Dorléac, and Truffaut

134 *Stolen Kisses* (1968): A Debt to Marcel Proust or Anatole France

136 David Thomson's *Mississippi Mermaid* (1969)

138 *Fahrenheit 451* (1966), *Week-end* (1967), *The Wild Child* (1969): A Dialogue?

142 Maurice Pialat's Wild Child: *L'Enfance nue* (1968)

144 Woody Allen's *Deconstructing Harry* (1997) and Antoine Doinel

146 Patrice Leconte's *The Girl on the Bridge* (1999)

148	"François, My Boy" and "Mr Hitchcock"
153	Truffaut's Typewriters
156	The Ending of *Two English Girls* (1971)
161	*Two English Girls*, *Agora* (2009), and Seeing Red on the Screen
164	Truffaut, Godard, and *Timbres*
166	Truffaut's Afterlife: *The Diving Bell and the Butterfly* (2007)
168	*Johnny Guitar* (1954): Bad Faith in Truffaut and David Thomson
171	A Title Quiz
172	Creativity and Accidents
176	*Day for Night* (1973): The Family Movie
180	*Day for Night*, Wes Anderson, and American Express
183	*8 1/2* (1963), *Day for Night* (1973), *Stardust Memories* (1980), *Nine* (2009)
185	Pauline Kael, Wim Wenders, and Truffaut
190	Truffaut, Adam Zagajewski, and the Fate of Spirit
191	Truffaut in *The Squid and the Whale* (2005)
194	Truffaut and Paul Léautaud (1872–1956)
199	Montmartre and "Certification"
201	*The Story of Adèle H.* (1975): Truffaut's Feminism
206	Truffaut and Deneuve in *The Story of Adèle H.*
209	A Dream: *The Story of Adèle H.* and Elle
211	*Small Change* (1976) and Renoir's *The River* (1951)
214	An Aged Man Is But a Paltry Thing
217	Ingmar Bergman, *Cavaleur*
220	Fame: Daphne Moon, Niles Crane, and a Truffaut Film
221	*The Man Who Loved Women* (1977): Truffaut and Don Juan
224	João César Monteiro's *A Comédia de Deus* (1995): The Man Who Loved Girls
226	Leslie Caron

229 Suzanne Schiffman (1929–2001)
232 Trufard and Godfaut: Resemblances
234 Balthus (1908–2001)
236 Film Names: Who Remembers Michel Poiccard and Patricia Franchini?
241 *The Green Room* (1978): The Man Who Loved One Woman
250 A Short History of "Dummies": Luis Buñuel, Truffaut, and Oskar Kokoschka
255 The Sentence that Sticks
258 Pauline Kael's Farewell to Truffaut and Godard
261 Paul Schrader's Tears
263 *The Last Metro* (1980): François Truffaut-Lévy
269 Subtitles and Voices
271 Roberto Rossellini (1906–1977): The Italian Godfather
274 *The Woman Next Door* (1981): "Neither with you nor without you"
278 Fanny Marguerite Judith Ardant
280 François and Sam: Some Favourite Films
281 A Godard Dream (26 June 2011)
284 *Le Journal d'Alphonse*: A Doinel Sequel
288 In His Own Words II
289 Truffaut's Afterlife: *Amélie* (2001)
292 Antoine de Baecque's *Two in the Wave* (2010)
295 Unfinished Business: Films Truffaut Didn't Make II
299 The Grave in Montmartre
302 Last Words
303 Notes
319 Bibliography
331 Index

ACKNOWLEDGMENTS

This book's dialogue with those who have written about François Truffaut, the New Wave, and film in general will be obvious to anyone who reads even a few pages. I am particularly indebted to Antoine de Baecque and Serge Toubiana's biography of Truffaut, de Baecque's equally impressive life of Godard, and his edition (with Arnaud Guigue) of *Le Dictionnaire Truffaut*. Truffaut's own editions and compilations of his screenplays and essays have also been indispensable as have the volumes assembled by Gilles Jacob and Claude de Givray (*Correspondence 1945–1984*), Dominique Rabourdin (*Truffaut by Truffaut*), Anne Gillain (*Le Cinéma selon François Truffaut*), Wheeler Winston Dixon (*The Early Film Criticism of François Truffaut*), and Ronald Bergan (*François Truffaut Interviews*). Pauline Kael, Stanley Kauffmann, and David Thomson have helped me think about film in roughly the same way that Robert Hughes, Arthur Danto, and Julian Bell have taught me about art: all write with a fierce intelligence and are nothing if not critical. I also want to thank the readers for MQUP and Claude Lalumière, my copyeditor, who made many useful suggestions; more importantly, they read the manuscript in the spirit I hoped it would be read. A special thank you to my editors Mark Abley and Ryan Van Huijstee, who saw the book through from the first lap to the last.

Closer to home, I owe a long-standing debt to Edward Costigan, who introduced me to foreign films half a century ago. More recent encouragement came from my children, Vanessa and André; my colleagues and friends Tom Adamowski, Rick Greene, Tamara Trojanowska, Peter Harris, Greig Henderson, Alexander Leggatt, Barrie Hayne, Henry Auster, Andrea Werner-Thaler, Gale Moore, Philip Sohm, Howard Engel, Judy

Stoffman, Katherine Ashenberg, Elias Polizoes, Fred Gerson (d.), Lynd Forguson (d.), Emmet Robbins (d.), Krystyna Sieciechowicz (d.), Josef Skvorecky (d.), who loved movies – writing them, acting in them, and talking about them – and J.M. Cameron (d.), who agreed with Truffaut that films should be in black and white; Ursula Bialas, with whom I watched movies for twenty years; Michael Ondaatje; Roberto Dante Martella, who screens classic Italian films daily in his Toronto restaurant *Grano* and who owns a *La Dolce Vita* poster signed by Mastroianni; and Laura and Sandro Forconi, Audrey McDonagh, Susan Addario, Mylissa Falkner, Robert Imlay, Gillian Northgrave, Robin Roger, Guy and Alberta Nokes, and Anne Michaels.

Some parts of the book first appeared in "L'Histoire de François T.: Truffaut's Films" (*Brick*, no. 44); "The Avenging Angel of the New Wave: A review of *Correspondence 1945–1984*" (*Globe and Mail*, 12 January 1991); *Ragas of Longing: The Poetry of Michael Ondaatje* (University of Toronto Press, 2003); "From a Truffaut Notebook" (*Descant*, summer 2011); and as a departmental lecture at the University of Toronto (2003) and a seminar at University College in the University of Toronto (2008). Translations from French texts unavailable in English are my own.

Photographs are courtesy of TIFF Film Reference Library and Photofest, except the photograph of Truffaut's grave, which is my own. The cartoon by Matthew Diffee is courtesy of *The New Yorker* / Condé Nast.

Sam Solecki, Toronto

A TRUFFAUT NOTEBOOK

Delacroix was passionately in love with passion,
and coldly determined to seek the means of expressing
passion in the most visible way.

CHARLES BAUDELAIRE

—

Film was his salvation, because in film everything has a
meaning. Life is chaotic but in cinema you can stop time.
François used to say, "Those who love life, love cinema."
That's for sure.

FANNY ARDANT

—

If it is hard to be categorical about exactly when the old
order was swept away, the death of François Truffaut on
21 October 1984 offers a symbolic milestone …
A certain tendency of the French cinema had died.

CHARLES DRAZIN

—

THE FILMS OF FRANÇOIS TRUFFAUT

1954	*Une Visite (A Visit)*
1957	*Les Mistons (The Mischief Makers)*
1958	*Une Histoire d'eau (The History of Water)*
1959	*Les Quatre Cents Coups (The 400 Blows)*
1960	*Tirez sur le Pianiste (Shoot the Piano Player)*
1961	*Jules et Jim (Jules and Jim)*
1962	*Antoine et Colette*
1964	*La Peau douce (The Soft Skin)*
1967	*La Mariée était en noir (The Bride Wore Black)*
1968	*Baisers volés (Stolen Kisses)*
1969	*La Sirène du Mississippi (Mississippi Mermaid)*
1969	*L'Enfant sauvage (The Wild Child)*
1970	*Domicile conjugale (Bed and Board)*
1971	*Les Deux Anglaises et le continent (Two English Girls)*
1972	*Une Belle Fille comme moi (Such a Gorgeous Kid like Me)*
1973	*La Nuit Américaine (Day for Night)*
1975	*L'Histoire d'Adèle H. (The Story of Adèle H.)*
1976	*L'Argent de poche (Small Change)*
1977	*L'Homme qui aimait les femmes (The Man Who Loved Women)*
1978	*La Chambre verte (The Green Room)*
1979	*L'Amour en fuite (Love on the Run)*
1980	*Le Dernier Métro (The Last Metro)*
1981	*La Femme d'à côté (The Woman Next Door)*
1983	*Vivement Dimanche! (Confidentially Yours)*

CHRONOLOGY

1932 François Roland Truffaut is born on 6 February in Paris to Janine de Monferrand and Roland Lévy. The two don't marry because her family opposes marriage to a Jew. When Janine marries Roland Truffaut two years later, he gives the boy his name.
FT lives with his maternal grandmother for most of the decade. When he rejoins his parents, they live at 33 rue de Navarin in the 9th arrondissement.

1943 FT meets Robert Lachenay, his best friend for the next two decades. Both are scamps and film buffs. FT begins to keep notes on the films he sees.

1946 FT drops out of school, runs away from home, and works at odd jobs.

1948 FT begins writing letters to movie magazines and founds a film club. On 30 November he meets André Bazin, a teacher and increasingly influential film critic, who over the next few months becomes a surrogate father. Their very close relationship lasts until Bazin's death on 11 November 1958. In December Truffaut's father puts him in a detention centre as a result of thefts and unpaid loans. Also in December, in *L'Écran Français,* Bazin publishes "In Defense of the Avant-Garde," a call for "whatever in the cinema expands the possibilities of the medium."

1949 Bazin secures an early release for FT from detention in March and helps him get a job at the magazine *Travail et Culture.* FT meets Jean-Luc Godard, Susan Klochendler (later Schiffman), and other film enthusiasts.

1950 FT enlists in the army in December and is sent to Germany. When he is jailed for desertion, Bazin helps him return to civilian life. FT attempts suicide in July in reaction to a failed love affair. He begins writing reviews and articles for various magazines while living for two years with Janine and André Bazin. In August 1950 Bazin publishes "Soviet Cinema and the Myth of Stalin" in *Les Lettres Françaises*.

1951 Bazin and Jacques Doniol-Valcroze found *Cahiers du Cinéma*, the most influential European film journal of the next two decades. The first issue appears in April.

1953 FT writes his first article for the March issue of *Cahiers*. Most of the others who will form the French New Wave are also associated with the magazine during the decade.

1954 In January FT publishes "Une Certaine Tendance du cinéma français," probably the most controversial and influential film article of its time. He films the short *Une Visite* with Jacques Rivette behind the camera.

1955 FT publishes the story "Antoine and the Orphan Girl" in *La Parisienne*; it is Antoine's first appearance in his work. (As Antoine Doinel the character later becomes Truffaut's alter-ego in five films.)

1956 FT becomes an assistant to Roberto Rossellini during a fallow creative period in the Italian director's life.

1957 FT sets up the production company Les Films du Carrosse (after Jean Renoir's film) and makes the short film *Les Mistons* starring Bernadette Lafont. He marries Madeleine Morgenstern on 29 October 1957.

1958 FT shoots *Une Histoire d'eau* with Godard as co-director. Bazin dies on 11 November, one day after FT begins shooting *The 400 Blows*. He dedicates the film to him.

1959 Henri-Pierre Roché dies on 9 April. FT admires his novels *Jules and Jim* and *Two English Girls and the Continent*. He had told the writer of his plans to film the first. Laura Truffaut is born. *The 400 Blows*, starring Jean-Pierre Léaud, wins the prize for best direction at Cannes. FT is famous overnight and the New Wave is hot.

1960 *Shoot the Piano Player* (Charles Aznavour). Godard films *Breathless* with Jean-Paul Belmondo and Jean Seberg.

1961 *Jules and Jim* (Jeanne Moreau, Oskar Werner). Eva Truffaut is born.
1962 FT films the short *Antoine and Colette* (Léaud, Marie-France Pisier) in one week as an episode for *Love at Twenty*.
1963 Jean Cocteau, an early supporter, dies on the same day as Edith Piaf, 11 October.
1964 *The Soft Skin* (Françoise Dorléac, Jean Desailly). Madeleine and FT separate in February.
1965 FT and Madeleine divorce in December.
1966 FT publishes *Le Cinéma selon Hitchcock* (the English edition, *Hitchcock*, appears a year later). He shoots *Fahrenheit 451* in England with Julie Christie and Werner.
1967 *The Bride Wore Black* (Jeanne Moreau).
1968 *Stolen Kisses* (Léaud, Claude Jade). His mother dies. FT hires a private detective to find his biological father.
1969 *Mississippi Mermaid* (Catherine Deneuve, Jean-Paul Belmondo). FT plays the lead adult role in *The Wild Child*. Suzanne Schiffman begins working regularly with him.
1970 *Bed and Board*, the third instalment in the Doinel series. FT publishes *Les Aventures d'Antoine Doinel*. He lives with Deneuve until she leaves him on 22 December. The breakup results in a lengthy depression.
1971 FT films *Two English Girls* with Léaud, Kika Markham, and Stacey Tendeter. He edits and writes a preface for Bazin's book on Renoir (later, he will be involved in three further volumes of Bazin's criticism).
1972 *Such a Gorgeous Kid like Me* (Lafont).
1973 FT receives an Oscar for Best Foreign Film for *Day for Night* (Jacqueline Bisset, Jean-Pierre Aumont, FT). He breaks off relations with Godard in a reply to a letter attacking the film and himself.
1975 *The Story of Adèle H.* (Isabelle Adjani); *Small Change*. FT publishes *The Films in My Life*.
1976 FT makes his debut in American film as the scientist Claude Lacombe in Steven Spielberg's *Close Encounters of the Third Kind*.
1977 *The Man Who Loved Women* (Charles Denner). Rossellini dies.
1978 FT stars in *The Green Room*.

1979 *Love on the Run* (Léaud, Pisier), the last Doinel film. Jean Renoir dies.
1980 *The Last Metro*, FT's biggest hit, wins 10 Césars. It stars Deneuve and Gérard Depardieu. He refuses Godard's invitation to come for a New Wave reunion in Switzerland. Hitchcock and Sartre die.
1981 FT refuses the Legion of Honour and the Directorship of the *Cinémathèque Française* on the grounds that he wants to remain independent.
1981 *The Woman Next Door* (Gérard Depardieu, Fanny Ardant).
1983 *Confidentially Yours* (Ardant, Jean-Louis Trintignant). FT completes a new edition of the Hitchcock book. He collapses during the summer and is operated on for a brain tumour on 12 September. Josephine, his daughter with Ardant, is born later in the month.
1984 FT dies 21 October and is buried in Montmartre Cemetery: Avenue Berlioz, division 27, line 2, plot 77. It is a short walk from Stendhal's grave and near the neighbourhood of his youth.

WHY TRUFFAUT?

> My religion is film. I believe in Charlie Chaplin.
> FRANÇOIS TRUFFAUT[1]
> —

For two decades before his death in 1984, François Truffaut was one of the most recognizable faces of France and contemporary French culture. He was never in the same league as Brigitte Bardot but, then, no one was, not even Jean-Paul Sartre. Truffaut established himself as a name with knowledgeable filmgoers as well as with those aware of things French by three films that helped change the course of modern cinema – *The 400 Blows* (1959), *Shoot the Piano Player* (1960), and *Jules and Jim* (1961). Together with the brilliantly innovative early work of his friend Jean-Luc Godard, these were at the heart of the movement that came to be known as the French New Wave (*la nouvelle vague*). Supported by the critic André Bazin and his influential journal *Cahiers du Cinéma*, it included directors as different as Claude Chabrol, Alain Resnais, Eric Rohmer, Jacques Rivette, Louis Malle, and Agnes Varda. As Renais aptly put it, "They come from everywhere, and go in many different directions."[2] More like an open club than a fraternity, the New Wave was a loosely knit group held together by *Cahiers* and a desire to make films different in style and subject from those of their French elders. Truffaut had the group's most visible public profile both because he had been a well-known film reviewer during the 1950s and because he won the prize for best director at Cannes in 1959 for *The 400 Blows*. The film's triumph at Cannes was the New Wave's breakthrough moment and gained it more publicity "at one stroke ... than all the films and articles that had preceded it."³ Truffaut was an early master of the sound bite, and he wrote with a chip on his typewriter and with a precocious and passionate knowledge of film. His later collections of articles and interviews testify to how active and effective he had been in promoting his own films as well as those of others while simultaneously helping rewrite film history from his generation's point of view. Had he failed as a filmmaker, he could easily have continued as a writer and critic: his 1964 book of interviews with Alfred Hitchcock is a modern classic, and his collected criticism is often still as electric as it was half a century ago. Truffaut has had more of his writing published in English than any other foreign director of his time, perhaps ever. The following memorable sentence from his 1958 review of *Touch of Evil* is not uncharacteristic: "Welles's physique would seem to preclude his playing Hitler, but who's to say that one day he will not force us to weep over the fate of Herman Goering."⁴ He's also at least partly responsible for our habit of distinguishing until very recently, however loosely, between "films" (made by highly regarded directors) and "movies" made by everyone else. That today this has become a distinction without a difference is suggested in recent references I have noticed to "the films" of Blake Edwards and to the latest "Bond film."

Without Truffaut's selfless work on its behalf with the media, the New Wave's spread and influence would probably have been less rapid, extensive, and influential. Publicizing his films abroad, Truffaut always took time to answer questions about the recent work of its members. For instance, more people heard the famous comment "there is cinema before Godard and cinema after Godard" from Truffaut than from Luigi Chiarini, who first said it.⁵ Although they were estranged by 1973, Godard acknowledged after Truffaut's death the important role he played in his career. Godard told an interviewer that when Truffaut died Anne-Marie Miéville, Godard's partner, commented, "Now that he's dead, nobody will protect you since he was the only one of the New Wave who was accepted by and tried, in a way, to join to establishment." Although the next question – "How did he protect you?" – goes unanswered, we can guess it from Miéville's reference to the "establishment."⁶ Truffaut had an influential rapport with a much larger audience than Godard, and he was better known and more widely respected outside France than any of his

French contemporaries. While there was never any doubt that Godard was the New Wave's resident genius and the darling of budding critical theorists, Truffaut looked after its public accounts while producing formally less challenging films with a faithful following and their own critical reputation. He was sufficiently confident in his own stature to ask rhetorically in 1967 whether "Godard is the greatest filmmaker in the world."[7] Many French films were bigger hits abroad than Truffaut's – Claude Lelouch's *A Man and a Woman*, for instance – but none of their directors had his standing with audiences, press, and critics. In other words, he was better placed than anyone to act as a mediator between his peers and the establishment. Despite the eventual breakdown of his relationship with Godard, Truffaut never turned on him in public. He continued to acknowledge Godard's importance to contemporary film even when he disagreed with his leftist politics and found his films without interest.

If Truffaut entered the establishment, he did so on his own terms as an independent filmmaker who had set up his own production company, Les Films du Carrosse, as early as 1957, two years before *The 400 Blows*. The film had both a popular and critical success, winning at Cannes just two years after the festival had banned Truffaut for criticizing it. Though several of his twenty-one films failed to find a substantial French audience, all covered their budget in the long run: his first three films had established a following he never lost. Whether based on novels or his own ideas, his body of work is united by related concerns that have their origins in his life, especially in his childhood and in his relationships with women. His comment that Welles's films "are autobiographical in a subterranean manner"[8] is also true of his own work. He is one of the last great Romantic artists, and the twenty-one films constitute a formally and thematically coherent whole whose focus, more often than not, is love as suffering and loss. I sometimes think of them as a volume in the long tradition of French writing on love, at least one book of which, Stendhal's *Love*, Truffaut knew well. Each film, whatever its genre, is an instalment in a continuing engagement with his essential themes: the lives of children, the destructive nature of love, mourning, obsession, memory, and film. His filmic fingerprint is evident in his lyricism, distinctive music and pace, romantic realism, film language, Renoirian sympathy for the subject, and signature allusions to his own films and those he admired. The ostensible story and incidental details may differ but each film's underlying emotional deep grammar and semantics are the same.

In other words, each film is a repetition with variation and change. The intense continuing focus on his own life is part of Truffaut's tacit assertion that the director is an "auteur" against influential period claims – see Roland Barthes and Michel Foucault – that the author is dead. Despite four decades of critical theory, even a cursory glance at contemporary cinema shows that the auteur is alive and well in Paris and abroad in the work of, among many others, Wes Anderson, Michael Haneke, Olivier Assayas, Catherine Breillat, Martin Scorsese, Leos Carax, Patrice Leconte, François Ozon, Quentin Tarantino, Paolo Sorrentino, and the Taviani brothers. Another sign of the term's vitality is the fact that far too many recent movies begin with the unearned tag "A Film by ..."

Truffaut's films and those of the other New Wave directors were a revelation to North American audiences. A half century later you can still hear the excitement in the early reviews and in contemporary histories of film. They carried the inescapable fascination of the new and foreign – everything un-North American – the attraction and effect of which should not be underestimated. Looking back, it's clear that the 1950s, '60s, and '70s were the heroic years of European film on this side of the Atlantic with the arrival of Ingmar Bergman, Federico Fellini, Michelangelo Antonioni, the French New Wave, the Czech New Wave, and the New German cinema. It was also the golden age of film criticism, its last hurrah before cultural commentary was kidnapped by the universities and taught a mandarin dialect accessible only to the initiated. Pauline Kael, Andrew Sarris, and Stanley Kauffmann wrote for anyone who went to the movies.

My discovery of Truffaut on coming to university in 1965 and my fascination with foreign film were representative of a segment of my generation. Over the next two decades I saw Truffaut's films as they came out. During the 1960s the restlessly inventive and much cooler Godard had as great a claim on my attention as Truffaut, who settled much more quickly into what in retrospect might be called a thematically coherent project and a more conservative curve of development. Where the present- and future-oriented Godard seemed intent on being the gravedigger of classical cinema – Alain Badiou calls him "the great director of contemporaneity"[9] – Truffaut's more modest ambition was to renew and in a sense complete a tradition within it. There is a unavoidable sense in which Godard's films, just by asserting their difference, increasingly called into question the relevance of all others. Truffaut's didn't; if anything, they invited the viewer to see them in relation to those in the history of cinema that influenced them and that they in turn influenced. As young men, both were in what might be called, following Fernando Pessoa, a state of disquiet, though the source of Truffaut's was personal and Godard's political: Truffaut loved the individual, Godard humanity; Truffaut was haunted by remorse for an unhappy past, Godard was driven by a utopian desire for social change; Truffaut wanted to continue the best work of his predecessors, Godard filmed with a "primordial ignorance of boundaries."[10] Like many others, I began to lose interest in Godard between *La Chinoise* (1967) and *Tout va bien* (1972); reports of his enthusiasm for Mao didn't help. His onscreen politics were simple-minded and the films had become dull. Godard was simply not giving me enough to keep me interested. We had begun to bore each other. Badiou's suggestion that he became "truth's traffic cop"[11] could serve as his epitaph though I doubt that all the mourners would agree on what he meant by the truth. After his astonishing creative outburst of the 1960s, Godard quickly lost much of his audience with films increasingly political, polemical, and experimental whose characters lacked affect and were more an assembly of semiotic signs than recognizable figures in a landscape. As one of his admirers put it, "movies with no commercial potential turned out to be movies that almost nobody wanted to see."[12] By the time his fascinating *Histoire(s) du cinéma* was televised in France in May 1989 it attracted "an audience too small to be measured."[13] Which is just as well since a larger ratings share would probably have left the Godardians suspicious that he was moving toward the centre.

In contrast to Godard, Truffaut was apolitical and never voted. The only public issues he cared about were the welfare of children and censorship. If Godard is among the most radical of French filmmakers, Truffaut belongs in what he wittily termed "the extreme centre."[14] On one occasion he told an interviewer, "I am definitely 'left,' but I believe that a writer can only remain honest if he keeps free of party labels."[15] On another, he said he was "leftish" ("gauchisant") rather than left. His films, like Alfred Hitchcock's and Marcel Carné's, consistently resist history and politics to create a space of freedom for the personal by means of the aesthetic, though he never uses the term. It was typical of his generosity of spirit and thoughtfulness to dedicate his 1973 Oscar for *Day for Night* to his colleagues in the art, the one "party" to which he was committed for life. It was a way of saying that he knew what he owed his predecessors and understood that his films summed up and renewed a tradition. It was his most public moment before the largest audience of his life. Less than a decade later it would be repeated on a smaller scale in Paris when *The Last Metro* won ten Césars.

The original impulse to write a book about Truffaut came in 1992 after I had published an essay about writers and writing in his films, the graphomania that often turns the screen into a page to be typewritten or written upon (in Truffaut's hand). Looking back I realize that the essay was partly a response to the end of a particularly "subterranean" relationship with Elle, a determined diarist. After writing it, I sensed that thinking about Truffaut's films had to some extent helped me to understand the wreckage. I decided to go on and find out as much as I could about Truffaut – his life, art, writing, film, film crew, milieu, and family. The best way to do this was to settle in for the long haul by watching his films, those that had influenced him and those of his contemporaries; reading his scripts and reviews; and writing a book. Truffaut echoed Renoir in insisting that films should help us live; he disliked Antonioni's because they didn't. When a slightly dubious younger colleague in my English department asked me about my credentials for writing a book about a film director, I answered by way of Geoff Dyer's straight response to a similar query about his desire to write *But Beautiful: A Book about Jazz*: "I don't have any except that I like to watch movies and I love Truffaut." I might have responded, following Eric Neuhoff's affectionate *Open Letter to François Truffaut*, that I think of myself as a type of Truffaut's ideal viewer, the one he kept in mind when writing a script, shooting a film or giving an interview. And like Neuhoff, I like him.

After several starts and stops, I abandoned work on the book in 2006, a couple of years after finishing a study of Michael Ondaatje's poetry. Despite enjoying the films and writing about them, I found it difficult to write about someone as self-conscious and articulate as Truffaut: not only did he comment freely and perceptively on his work in print, he was also remarkably self-analytical writing about himself. He confessed to taking stock of his life once a week and at the end of each year. A more disabling problem, however, was my failure to find a sufficiently elastic form that would allow me to include everything that interested me in relation to Truffaut. I had known from the start that I didn't want to write another narrowly academic overview with a master narrative shepherded over hundreds of pages. That sort of book had already been done well by several others. I also knew that I didn't want to write a book under the sign of one of the currently fashionable theoretical orthodoxies, though I was willing to use whatever I found conceptually and terminologically useful. What it really came down to is that I was reluctant to write either a book similar to the ones I had written about D.H. Lawrence (unpublished), Josef Skvorecky, Al Purdy, and Michael Ondaatje or a study inflected by contemporary critical theory and inevitably aimed at academic readers. I found a way out of the impasse during a lunch in summer 2008 with my friend Philip Sohm, an art historian. Among other subjects we talked about our admiration for Geoff Dyer's *Out of Sheer Rage*, his frenetic book about not being able to write a book about D.H. Lawrence. When I told Philip about my dead-end with Truffaut, he suggested that I go back with Dyer in mind. Geoff is inimitable, but at least Philip's suggestion started me thinking outside the box. Serendipity came into play a few weeks later. Reading Camus's *Notebooks 1942–1951* I ran across an entry in which he looks forward to writing "a hodge-podge ["petits choses au hasard"]. Everything that goes through my head."[16] I chose to interpret this as suggesting a more open-ended engagement with Truffaut in a more fragmented, inclusive, and disorderly form. After a few weeks of reading through my files and the abandoned manuscript, I decided to write in the format of what I think of as a mongrel notebook that is a multifaceted introduction to the man, his work, and the intimate relationship between the two. Among the models that came to mind are Jed Perl's *Antoine's Alphabet* (about Watteau), Roland Barthes's *Roland Barthes*, Michel Butor's *Comment écrire pour Jasper Johns*, and Dyer's *Zona*. The book combines a portrait of the artist, a dialogue with the subject, an *hommage* in the form of a selective appreciative commentary on his career, suggestions about his influence, narratives of the New Wave, and many digressions on a variety of related sometimes personal subjects including his dreams and mine. It is a book that tries to understand Truffaut on his own terms – and mine; in other words, objectively and subjectively. I assume that my implied readers agree with Kenneth Burke's comment, "The main ideal of criticism … is to use all that there is to use."[17] I have quoted Truffaut more often than I originally intended because I want readers to hear his voice side by side with mine to evoke his personality more directly. I like to imagine the reader able to hear not only Truffaut's voice but the voices of the characters in the films when they are discussed. Writing and reading about films we tend to remember the eye but not the ear.

Though the title is *A Truffaut Notebook*, the book has a form based on a chronological structure and a set of recurring concerns. The formal pillars are the longer chronologically arranged essays on the films that interest me enough to warrant substantive entries, from *The Mischief Makers* in 1957 to *The Last Metro* in 1980. The shorter variously themed entries appear within the temporal and thematic orbit of these longer ones. (To compare great with small, think how in the Sistine Chapel vault Michelangelo organizes the Prophets, Sibyls, and Ancestors of Christ around the nine main Genesis narratives.) *A Truffaut Notebook* is not quite a running argument but it passes muster as a multifaceted chronological narrative providing various perspectives and contexts for a discussion of Truffaut – sometimes observed with a zoom lens and sometimes from a distance. As in Michelangelo, almost every section is in its proper place.

If some of the entries appear eccentric, I can only plead they are there to help explain my angle of approach. Jean-Luc Godard, for instance, is an intrusive but necessary presence as Truffaut's "dark twin" – that, at least, is how I too often think of him – who helps me sharpen my response to Truffaut and to understand their milieu. Biographies by Antoine de Baecque, Colin McCabe, and Richard Brody leave me with the impression that, if they were less than friends, they were more than affectionate acquaintances. You might say they were close-ish rather than close, held in orbit around each other by film and mutual respect rather than deep personal emotion. The book is primarily about Truffaut, but it is also occasionally about my effort to come to terms with Godard, especially during the 1960s, when they were as aware of each other's work as Matisse and Picasso early in their careers. When Truffaut jokes that there will be more references in *Fahrenheit 451* than in Godard's body of work to date he's pointing to this aspect of their relationship.[18] Godard's films of that first astonishingly creative period look back more often to Truffaut's than to those of any of his other contemporaries. Is Truffaut saying hello to Godard across a decade-long silence when a secretary in his last film, *Confidentially Yours*, types with two fingers just like the character named David Goodis does in *Made in U.S.A.* (1966)? David Goodis happens to be the author of *Down There*, the novel behind *Shoot the Piano Player*, Truffaut's second major film. When I started the book I didn't anticipate that by its end I would have a higher, though still highly critical, regard for Godard. Mick Jagger reportedly dismissed him after the making of

Jean-Luc Godard and Truffaut in the mid-'60s, riding the crest of the New Wave.

Sympathy for the Devil / One + One (1968) as "such a fucking twat."[19] This made for a good sound bite but it's stupid, a distant cousin to negative judgments by Werner Herzog (he prefers kung fu films) and Pauline Kael ("when he's good, he's superb, and when he isn't good, he's nothing").[20] When I started the book, I was probably more than a step behind Kael but by the time I finished, my position had shifted toward a "Yes, but" inflected by Andrew Sarris's nuanced view of him as "a director less dramatic than dialectical – that is to say, concerned with the oppositions less of individuals than of ideas."[21] Godard offers a version of this when he says that while Truffaut's films are "instinctive" his own are "analytical."[22] Repeated viewings of Godard's occasionally brilliant polymorphic body of film convinced me that, like him or not, Jean-Luc is a genius and one has to give him, no matter how reluctantly, the benefit of the doubt. He is among those artists who give expression to the deepest urges of an age. I can't say that of Truffaut: his world is a smaller, deeper, more personal and intimate thing. The producer Pierre Braunberger, who knew them both, distinguishes between them as follows: "François Truffaut and Alain Resnais, two filmmakers of this generation whom I admire greatly, haven't penetrated the creative process like Godard. They haven't changed the language of film."[23] I can agree with that and yet, unlike the receptive Braunberger, I find Godard's post-1970 films exasperating. Being told that they changed the language of film doesn't help when they often strike me as irrelevant to everything in life that isn't film: they intrigue and provoke but they rarely move. I'm left with the paradox that Godard is more important in the history of the evolution of film than Truffaut, yet the latter's films are more emotionally engaging and more fully achieved works of art. I admire Godard's work and understand his historical importance but it is Truffaut's films that give me pleasure, consolation, understanding, and artistic satisfaction. Where Godard is willing to innovate with every aspect of the language of film to the point of experimenting as well with my patience, Truffaut's innate conservatism (and, dare I say, common sense) is evident in his comment that "with each technical advance, with each new invention, the cinema loses in poetry what it gains in intelligence, it loses in mystery what it gains in realism."[24] In a manner of speaking, Truffaut is the avant-garde of the traditionalists. He tries to renew the very tradition of film that he criticizes in his polemical early reviews and essays. Godard, by contrast, is the director who pushes the New Wave's impulses to the limit, and yet his films rarely touch me except when the irresistible Anna Karina is in them. Think of the famous closeup of her face as she cries while watching Carl Dreyer's *The Passion of Joan of Arc* in *Vivre sa vie*. I watch *Breathless* at least once a year, but with an emotional detachment Brecht would admire. Do we really care what happens to Jean Seberg and Jean-Paul Belmondo any more than we care about the fate of Quentin Tarentino's characters? The argument in *Pierrot le fou* between Karina and Belmondo about the rival claims of ideas and feelings suggests that Godard knew he had a problem with the flow of the audience's sympathy in response to his own withholding of feelings. When Belmondo tells Karina "You never have ideas, only feelings," she answers with the Truffauldian challenge of "Feelings contain ideas." Pascal and Martha Nussbaum would agree. Anna Akhmatova's response to *Doctor Zhivago* can stand for mine to most of Godard's work, "It is a failure of genius."[25]

Did I learn anything new about Truffaut while writing the book? More important than the already mentioned renewed respect for Godard was my realization that I had underestimated the narrowness of Truffaut's range of themes and concerns. If Godard's development calls to mind a man with a camera going off in several directions simultaneously, Truffaut's is more on the order of two steps forward and one step back with each new project shot through with self-reference and a dialogue with films of the past. As early as 1968 he tells an interviewer, "There is a new cinema and I am not part of it," and then perceptively adds, "I feel myself in the situation of a figurative painter who resolutely continues to be figurative while hoping that that kind of painting will not disappear entirely."[26] The only painter he seems to have noticed was the figurative master Balthus. Though I have always given an almost automatic nod of agreement to Truffaut's repeated comment that a filmmaker makes versions of the same film over and over, I hadn't really *felt* the extent to which this is true of his body of work until I watched each film several times over a decade. Seeing them again and again it became clear that Truffaut has as narrow a thematic, emotional, and formal range as any important director I can think of, including Ozu, who has actually made the same films more than once. Each could be described as narcissistic though, with both, repetition or narrowness entails, as in Carl Dreyer, an incremental intensity of interest and depth of vision. As I wrote earlier, almost all of Truffaut's films are in some way implicated in his coming to terms with an unhappy childhood and his belief that, while "there ain't no cure for love," love and passion, however potentially destructive, are central to our lives. The films carry a family resemblance in detail and theme similar to landscapes shot at different exposures, in different seasons and over several years. There is a strong sense in which Truffaut's body of work is a single film made up of twenty-one chapters. You might say that, unlike most of us, he is centripetal and focused. He is his own best subject, and the films play hide-and-seek with us, simultaneously revealing and concealing him in the different versions of the one story and one story only that obsesses him. Pauline Kael sensed the self-restraint in Truffaut in her review of *Fahrenheit 451*: "Truffaut has it in him not to create small artificial worlds around gimmicky plots, but to open up the big world, and to be loose and generous and free and easy with it."[27] Or to use terms Susan Sontag uses to describe herself, he "has a wider range as a human being than as a director."[28] Inevitably excluded from his vision are age and its depredations, or what J.M. Coetzee describes in *Diary of a Bad Year* as "the old man in the plastic chair in the corner" in whom "there was something personal going on, something to do with age and regret and the tears of things."[29] The tears of things were rarely a concern for the directors of the *nouvelle vague* – it was a young movement. Resnais's *Vous n'avez encore rien vu* (2012), a late masterpiece, makes partial amends.

Half a century after the premier of *The 400 Blows* and three decades after his death, Truffaut has a secure place among filmmakers. His photograph is on the cover of the American edition of Charles Drazin's *Faber Book of French Cinema* (2011), and Edward Baron Turk's study of Marcel Carné places Carné "alongside Gance, Vigo, Renoir and Truffaut ... within the pantheon of French film directors"[30] – a distinguished club. Truffaut lives both in the many films of the past half century that show his influence – about which more below – and, more importantly, in those of his that have entered the canon. There is a general consensus that at least three have done so: *The 400 Blows* (1959), *Shoot the Piano Player* (1960), and *Jules and Jim* (1961). *The Wild Child* (1970) has its admirers, among them Susan Sontag and Werner Herzog. Pauline Kael thought that *Shoot the Piano Player*, *Jules and Jim*, and *The Wild Child* were his best works but called *The Story of Adèle H.* a great film and had high praise for *Small Change*. David Denby has also described *The Story of Adèle H.* as among Truffaut's greatest films. David Thomson gushes over *Mississippi Mermaid* (1969), not among my favourites. My own canon is more inclusive simply because there are too many I wouldn't want to live without. To choose simply on the basis of the ones I watch most frequently, my selected Truffaut would be *The 400 Blows, Shoot the Piano Player, Jules and Jim, The Green Room, Love on the Run,* and *The Woman Next Door*. The indispensable ones are the first two and the last.[31] *Day for Night* is in its own category primarily because Truffaut making a film is in it. And *Love on the Run*, the last of the Antoine Doinel series and undervalued by Truffaut and his critics, has a special place in my heart, maybe because it's a slippery comedy about the joy, difficulty, and failure of love – something that like most of my divorce-happy generation I know something about. It usually leaves me with moist eyes, only partly motivated by the film. I'll return to film and tears below.

IN HIS OWN WORDS I

People stubbornly want everyone to change;
me, I'm for the pig-headed guys.
I like people who are faithful.[1]

I like that which reveals the vulnerability of a person.[2]

Cinema is the art of the woman, that is, of the actress.
The director's work consists in getting beautiful women to do
beautiful things. For me, the great moments of cinema are
when the director's gifts mesh with the gifts of an actress.[3]

I like to have some characters for whom life is absolute
and others for whom it is relative.[4]

I believe that by temperament I'm not modern.
I'm more interested in rediscovering past ideas … I run …
after a lost secret rather than something in the future.[5]

If I had had a happy childhood, in a happy home with
parents who smooch over each other and all like that, well,
I wouldn't be here today.[6]

ROLAND LÉVY
AND ROLAND TRUFFAUT

Where is the father?
THE ENGLISH TEACHER, *THE 400 BLOWS*
—

After the death of his mother, Janine, on 22 August 1968, Truffaut spent several weeks in the family apartment on 33 rue de Navarin sorting through family papers, including his childhood journals. Almost simultaneously, he hired Albert Duchenne, a private detective, to find his birth father. He had known since 1944, when he was twelve, that Roland Truffaut had agreed to adopt him on marrying Janine de Monferrand in 1934. Duchenne discovered that his real father was Roland Lévy, a dentist living in Belfort. He had left Janine a few months before his son's birth, when her family opposed their marriage because he was a Jew. In 1968 Lévy was fifty-eight, divorced with two grown children. His birth son, a successful film director, was thirty-six, divorced, with two young daughters. A few weeks after Duchenne's report Truffaut went to Belfort, a dreary town in northeast France famous for Frédéric Bartholdy's huge red sandstone sculpture of the Lion of Belfort; he is also responsible for the Statue of Liberty. Truffaut knew from the detective's report that his father's daily routine included an after-dinner walk. Truffaut waited near the door of his six-storey apartment house, watched Lévy come out, and then walked away. His father had not seen him. Truffaut registered in a hotel, and then went to a movie, Chaplin's *Gold Rush*. Next morning he left for Paris. He never saw his father again and never communicated with him. The closest he comes to acknowledging him publicly is in a touchingly gentle scene in *Love on the Run* in which, sometime after his mother's death, Antoine runs into Monsieur Lucien, her lover. They visit her grave, and as they part Antoine says "Goodbye, Monsieur Lucien" and the latter, obviously moved by the meeting and the boy's continuing hostility to his mother, responds "Goodbye, my son." Truffaut seems to have told only four people about Roland Lévy: Madeleine Morgenstern, Helen Scott, who worked on the Hitchcock book, and the two producers Ilya Lopert and Pierre Braunberger. The last had escaped during the war from a Jewish detention centre in France. Truffaut later told Claude de Givray that he had always felt like a Jew, an outsider. One of the several reasons for his break with Godard in 1973 was the latter's casual anti-Semitic slur against Braunberger ("you called Braunberger a filthy Jew over the telephone").[1] Godard confirmed the truth of the assertion to Colline Faure-Poirée – "It's true, it's true" – prior to the French publication of Truffaut's letters.[2] Braunberger doesn't mention it in memoirs.

The most important fathers in Truffaut's films are the attentive and sensitive teacher in *Small Change* and the surrogate fathers Truffaut plays in *The Wild Child* and *The Green Room* – all are based to some extent on André Bazin. Antoine Doinel, the father of Alphonse, is a modern divorced father on the move in *Love on the Run*, while the tragic Bernard Coudray (Gérard Depardieu) in *The Woman Next Door* seems to have been given a son primarily to remind his former lover Mathilde (Fanny Ardant) of the child she aborted when he left her. The most memorable parent in the films is the absent and, for most of *The Story of Adèle H.*, unnamed Victor Hugo. His daughter insists at one point that "I was born of a father unknown." "Where is the father?" – the inept English teacher's pedagogical question in *The 400 Blows* – could stand as an epigraph for much of Truffaut's body of work. In the childless *Day for Night*, for instance, half a dozen characters are involved in issues of paternity. The teacher's question must have also been on Truffaut's mind for most of the 1960s after he walked out on his wife and daughters.

There is no evidence in the archives or in Truffaut's published work for the autobiographical film about the father and son that I imagine. For me it exists as a single scene of recognition and reconciliation set in twilight with the long-lost son walking diagonally across the no-longer-busy cobblestoned street toward the long-unknown father. Having noticed that the younger man is looking at him the older man stops and waits for his arrival. The actors? Truffaut is the father; Léaud the son. I imagine the scene by way of Michael Ondaatje's *Running in the Family*, where a son's long-awaited reunion with a dead father is presented through Edgar's with the blind Gloucester in *King Lear*. (Can a writer live more dangerously than by quoting Shakespeare?): "I long for the moment in the play when Edgar reveals himself to Gloucester and it never happens. Look I am the son who has grown up. I am the son you have made hazardous, who still loves you. I am now part of an adult's ceremony, but I want to say I am writing this book about you at a time when I am least sure about such words [love, passion, duty] … Give me your arm. Let go my hand. Give me your arm. 'Sweet Marjoram' … a tender herb."[3] Truffaut, like Ondaatje, couldn't go back. Did he have nothing to say? Was he constrained by his own failure as a father from asking Roland Lévy why he had abandoned him? He must have known that his own reasons were much flimsier, less excusable ("I need other women"). To write or film my imagined scene he would have had to come to terms with his own departure and the children's question: "You say you love us more than the world, so why are you leaving?" The films skirt this. To see what Truffaut might have made of it we have to turn to Noah Baumbach's Truffauldian *The Squid and the Whale*, to which I will return below.

One of the last projects Truffaut worked on was a memoir. In it he quotes Mark Twain's comment that "It's a lucky Frenchman who can tell who is his real father."[4] The sentence's pedigree goes back at least as far as Telemachus and the first book of *The Odyssey*.

EARLY FILMS: FRANÇOIS AND SAM

In his last interview, recorded five months before his death in October 1984, Truffaut advised aspiring filmmakers to spend more time watching films and less on odd jobs on a movie set: "When you see a film for the tenth time or so, a film whose dialogue and music you know by heart, you can start to look at how it is made, and you learn much more that way than you could as an assistant director."[1] This advice is based on his early wartime experience with black and white films when he went to theatre two or three times a week. Because he saw so many films on the sly and then again with his parents, the habit of multiple viewings became a norm. He records seeing, among others, Henri Clouzot's still engrossing *The Crow* (*Le Corbeau*) thirteen times, Marcel Carné's *Les Enfants du Paradis* nine times, and Sacha Guitry's still charming *The Story of a Cheat* (*Le Roman d'un tricheur*) between twelve and fourteen times. He ranked Guitry's film with Renoir's *Rules of the Game*, Bresson's *Les Dames de Bois de Boulogne*, and *The Crow* among his all-time favourites. Skipping school to see movies had good and bad consequences: "I saw my first two hundred films on the sly, playing hooky and slipping into the movie house without paying ... I paid for these great pleasures with stomach aches, cramps, nervous headaches and guilt feelings, which only heightened the emotions evoked by these films ... I felt a tremendous need to enter into the films. I sat closer and closer to the source of the screen so I could shut out the theater."[2] The last two sentences describe a life-defining moment in which a boy hears a voice and is blinded by a light from above. For the unloved boy the films were forbidden fruit, the one sure pleasure in his world, and a daily revelation of what life might be like. He also learned that our pleasures have consequences.

Truffaut tells us that he was seven when he saw the first movie that stayed with him:

> My first movie memory goes back to 1939, a few months before the Armistice. The scene was the Palais-Rochechouart, a very large movie theater opposite the Square d'Anvers. The film was *Lost Paradise* (*Paradis perdu*) with Micheline Presle, whose beauty and gentleness were extraordinary, and Fernand Gravey. The theater was full of uniformed soldiers on leave accompanied by their young wives or girlfriends. The reader may perhaps remember that Abel Gance's superb melodrama takes place in the period between 1914 and 1935, and that a large part of the film is given over to the war, the trenches, the munitions factories in which women worked etc. … The coincidence between the situation of the characters in the film and that of the spectators was such that the entire audience wept, hundreds of handkerchiefs piercing the darkness with little points of light. Never again was I to feel such an emotional unanimity in response to a film.[3]

He later adds that during that period he "liked great music in film … a certain religiosity, and stories of doomed love." Italo Calvino echoes the young Truffaut when he recalls "the films I saw between, let's say, thirteen and eighteen … when the cinema engrossed me to an extent far beyond anything that came before or after."[4]

The boy sitting close to the screen, the pleasure in the music, and the fascination with religiosity struck a chord in me and took me back to my own first movies seen in a postwar Polish refugee camp in the English Midlands near a place called Doddington Park in Cheshire. The largest buildings were the school and a small hall used for meetings, dances, Christmas celebrations, plays, and, most importantly, movies on Saturday afternoons. I've never outgrown that hall, the small white screen, and the feeling of being in a crowd joined by the hum and expectancy of escaping into an exotic, colourful, and better world from our daily lives of waiting for something to happen in the middle of nowhere. Before the film the only colour in the white room came from multicoloured movie posters on the walls. These were magical windows on England and America. The effect of the posters and occasional colour films was intensified by my lack of knowledge of the outside world. The palette of my real pleasures was limited, though I realized this only from movies. Television's later magic was a spectrum of greys.

My earliest and most vivid memory is of being troubled – I was probably five or six – by the beginnings of black and white J. Arthur Rank movies. They always opened with a huge shiny, dimpled gong dominating the screen and a very muscular man on the left, shining as if freshly rubbed with oil, raising a large wooden mallet to strike it. He was Herculean. I was sure that he was the moviemaker's personal slave and was kept to perform only this function. For a couple of years I even wondered what he did when he wasn't sounding the gong to announce the beginning of the film. Randolph Scott and John Wayne were almost as memorable, but I can't remember the details of any of the westerns I saw. Clearer are slightly later television memories of Jock Mahoney as the Range Rider and Duncan Renaldo and Leo Carrillo as the Cisco Kid and Pancho. Their closing lines – "Oh Pancho!" "Oh Cisco!" – were the first filmed English words I remember. Westerns were always a revelation, just as they had been for Hitler and Stalin. To those of us who had never seen the world outside the camp the open spaces, the mountains, the woods, and the ghost towns had a visionary quality that defined America for us, a place as mythical as ancient Rome or Camelot and as unreachable as Poland and Montenegro, where my father and mother had come from. Europeans of previous generations must have felt something similar when reading the always popular James Fenimore Cooper or the bestselling German novelist Karl May – Hitler was a fan – the Zane Grey of the continent. This was also the period when I was certain that films were shot in the countries in which they were set. Medieval historical epics must have been shot in England and France because that's where the castles were; Biblical, Greek, and Roman movies took similar advantage of the Mediterranean. Had someone told me that *The Road to Morocco* was filmed in California I would probably have tried to correct them by pointing to the camel, the sand, and the Arabic palace. I was pleased to find in George F. Kennan's *Diaries* an entry (20 July 1924) indicating he was as confused by Hollywood's historical prestidigitation at the age of twenty as I was as a boy: "We walked back by way of the Cathedral of Notre Dame. I am curious to know where the movie of *The Hunchback* was made: if in California, how did they reproduce the Cathedral so well? If in Paris, how did they make all the surroundings fit the 15th century when they are so absolutely the 20th?"[5]

A different sort of revelation came with Victor Mature and Hedy Lamarr in Cecil B. DeMille's *Samson and Delilah* and Robert Taylor and the always chaste Deborah Kerr in Mervyn Le Roy's *Quo Vadis?* These were literally thrilling movies, the first of many religious and historical epics that awakened my lifelong interest in ancient history. Peter Ustinov's slinky, porcine malevolence and Rome burning have stayed with me to this day. I knew the story of Samson from Arthur Mee's *Children's Encyclopedia* with its rich blue cloth binding and bright gold lettering. It was the one expensive thing we owned other than my father's small BSA motorcycle. Seeing *Samson and Delilah* in Technicolor was almost too much; it was as if a painting were unrolling in front of me accompanied by a symphony orchestra though I had never seen or heard one. It would be a half century before I would learn Groucho Marx's reputed comment on the movie – he never went to films in which "the man's tits are bigger than the woman's." Victor and Hedy would not have been amused, nor I. The effect of orchestral music in a place almost completely silent during the week except for an occasional radio broadcast was like unexpected dessert. These film scores defined classical music for me until my late teens. The lovers in the films introduced me and my friends to sexuality, though we had little idea of what was going on. It only occurred to me much later that most the people in the hall couldn't understand English and the films were without subtitles. For many of us the dialogue was pure sound without meaning, almost a form of music. In *Samson and Delilah*, Victor Young's music played in counterpoint to the sounds of the voices of Mature, Lamarr, and George Sanders. We interpreted gestures, facial expressions, accents, tones, and inflections with an attention Umberto Eco would have admired. Sometimes someone who was fluent would venture an explanation or summary. We might have been watching silent films in the era before *The Jazz Singer* – except for those who were treating the movies as English lessons.

The religiosity Truffaut remarked on was also a strong presence in the biblical films of the 1950s. *Intolerance* went into general release just after our arrival in Canada. It was followed by *The Ten Commandments*,

King of Kings, Ben Hur, The Bible, and many others. Then they faded almost completely. Not even Martin Scorsese and Mel Gibson have been able to resurrect enthusiasm for the genre in an ironic and anticlerical age. During the second half of the 1950s I was beginning my second decade and watching films in what seemed to me the palatial luxury of the Capitol, Seneca, and Princess, the three theatres in Niagara Falls, Ontario. At the same age Truffaut had been able to choose among 450 in postwar Paris. In Niagara Falls the aura I had felt in Doddington was still there when I climbed to the balcony and sat in the first row so that there would be no heads to distract me. There was now the added excitement of understanding what the actors were saying, not to mention popcorn. On offer was a cornucopia of mysteries, westerns, pirate movies, and, best of all, science fiction, which I didn't know existed before these movies: *The Day the Earth Stood Still, Forbidden Planet, The Blob*, and, God bless you Don Siegel, *Invasion of the Body Snatchers*. Not a European movie in sight except occasionally at the Polish Hall. Contemporary releases were supplemented on Saturdays by 1930s serials or rereleased silent classics. If you couldn't afford a movie, the several television stations screened them every night after the late news: Fridays were horror night on Buffalo's WKBW; on Tuesdays CBC-Toronto showed westerns. Because the films I saw between 1955 and 1965 were part of the excitement and anxiety in almost all of my experiences as a new Canadian, even now forgotten star-vehicles by Doris Day, Frank Sinatra, Lewis and Martin, and Elvis Presley have stayed with me almost as firmly as the non-American films I would discover during the next decade. Looking back to the movies I first saw in Niagara Falls I feel about them as André Gide did about certain childhood books: "I recall certain readings in my childhood, so voluptuously penetrating that I felt the sentence almost physically enter my heart."[6]

The Capitol, the Seneca, and the cross-town Princess have been closed for decades like Truffaut's beloved Gaumont Palace, shown in *Bed and Board*. The Last Picture Shows.

THE GODFATHER:
ANDRÉ BAZIN (1918–1958)

>Bazin was Truffaut's sponsor.
>PIERRE BRAUNBERGER[1]

—

>The man I should be if I had not been the child I was.
>ALBERT CAMUS[2]

—

Bazin wasn't the only important film critic of his time, but since he was the only one that mattered to Truffaut, his and Truffaut's will be the most prominent critical voices throughout the book. There will be qualifications and dissents, but for the most part I want to see Truffaut on his own terms, that is, terms he inherited from Bazin and modified to his needs. A glance at any contemporary bibliography of film theory and criticism indicates that their critical vocabulary and approaches are no longer in favour though they have held much of their ground and not disappeared from the scene. This state of affairs would have troubled neither: both were opponents of orthodoxies, whether of assent or dissent, though Bazin was more interested in encouraging his readers to think than was Truffaut, whose early criticism was polemical and set out to convince. The following sentence from "A Certain Tendency" is representative: "I do not believe in the peaceful co-existence of 'the Tradition of Quality' and the cinema of the auteurs."[3] One can sense Bazin's antinomianism in his joke that Hitler stole Chaplin's moustache[4] and that the comedian retaliated with *The Great Dictator*. This willingness to stand up for the outsider at a time when all were afraid of the bully captures something in Bazin's sensibility that must have appealed to Truffaut: it is the origin of his own comment that on one level World War Two was contested by Chaplin and Hitler. Bazin made permanent contributions to film with his influential comments on the auteur, documentary, deep focus photography, the inescapability of realism, the need to pay attention to the basic components of filmmaking, and the ontology of the photographic image. Despite his reverent attitude to Hitchcock, Truffaut followed Bazin in preferring Renoir because, according to Bazin, Renoir "loved people" while Hitchcock "loved only film."[5] The same distinction separates Truffaut from Godard.

Without Bazin's timely interventions in his life, it is doubtful Truffaut would have had a career in journalism and film. In others words – no Bazin, no Truffaut as we know him. Trained as a teacher, Bazin must have known that a student like Truffaut comes once in a lifetime. In every sense except the legal one, Bazin and his wife adopted Truffaut during the most difficult period of his life and gave him a home. Bazin helped him find work at *Travail et Culture*, got him out of the army when he was jailed for desertion, and, crucially, took him on as editorial assistant and writer at *Cahiers du Cinéma*. Between 1953 and 1959 Truffaut wrote 170 pieces for the magazine. In his own words, "from that day in 1948 when he got me my first film job, working alongside him, I became his adopted son. Thereafter, every pleasant thing that happened in my life I owed to him."[6] Truffaut's early work with Bazin was the equivalent of a BA in film studies and journalism with the not insignificant difference that we continue to read his freshman essays. Bazin was the first in a line of several surrogate film fathers – Cocteau, Rossellini, and Renoir. Like Bazin, each had chosen a risky career in the arts that was coextensive with the creation of a nonconformist self. Bazin, a Catholic and a Sartrean, showed Truffaut both a potential career path and an ideal selfhood to aspire to. He may not have had the creativity of the filmmakers Truffaut admired, but he had an intellectual clarity and an incandescent Franciscan moral stature that set him apart. Never dogmatic or ideological, Bazin was the best sort of mentor for Truffaut in that he never tried to impose his values. He had strong views about film – especially about realism (pro) and montage (against) – but he didn't try to turn Truffaut into a disciple, though Truffaut became one anyway. I think of Bazin as a soft theorist – the parts of his criticism cohere into a whole – before theory became inseparable from jargon and ideology. After his death in 1958, Truffaut described him as "an exceptional human being [whose] goodness was almost legendary"[7] and as a man "from before original sin."[8] Truffaut's "adoption" after the filming of *The 400 Blows* of the troubled and rebellious Jean-Pierre Léaud was a Bazin-like gesture, as was his solicitude for Bazin's widow and son.

Bazin was particularly influenced by Emmanuel Mounier's Personalism, which, like Sartre's existentialism, was impatient with theory and metaphysics and emphasized the need for social action.[9] In the arts this meant the inseparability of ethics and aesthetics. Not surprisingly, he preferred realistic films over fantasy or what he called "poetic realism." This did not prevent him, however, from recognizing the originality of Carné's *Les Visiteurs du soir* (*The Night Visitors*), of which he wrote that "it would mark a date, the beginning of an influence, the origin of a style."[10] Though a leftist, he was independent of the period's uncritical tilt to the communist left as is attested by his article "Soviet Cinema and the Myth of Stalin," published in 1950, a time when the French left was still treating Stalin as if he were the second coming of Marx; when Stalin's political stock declined, it turned to Mao. Despite his strong reservations about aspects of "A Certain Tendency of French Cinema," Truffaut's 1954 attack on the French film establishment, Bazin nevertheless not only helped him rewrite the essay, he also published it in *Cahiers*. He must have noticed that its point of departure was his own article on Bresson's *Le Journal d'un curé de campagne* (*The Diary of a Country Priest*). Three years later he suggested in the same journal that Truffaut and Rohmer had turned the idea of the auteur as the central creative figure in film into a dogma that made the director nearly infallible. The disagreement shouldn't distract attention from the fact that in his iconoclastic essay Truffaut had followed in Bazin's footsteps in his emphasis on the auteur as more important than the scriptwriter, the need for formal and technical analysis, and the critic's responsibility to new work. Bazin's presence in Truffaut's career can also be seen in the following: admiration for the music of Maurice Jaubert; the view of film as a fundamentally realistic popular art; the emphasis on a core of sympathetic characters; and the canonization of Renoir and Welles as seminal directors, not least because they were involved in the writing of their own scripts. Bazin's suggestion in 1947 that the director uses the camera like a pen suggests a basis for the claim that the film director is much more an auteur than a *cinémateur*, *écraniste*, or *metteur en scène*.

In Sarris's summary, "Only the director is capable of preserving formal order in all the chaos of filmic creation. Only the director can provide a unity of style out of all the diverse ingredients at his disposal."[11]

During the quarter century between Bazin's death in 1958 and his own in 1984, Truffaut never wavered in his loyalty. He found employment for Florent Bazin and he regularly helped Janine, Bazin's widow. In the litany of sins he ascribes to Godard in the 1973 letter ending their friendship not the least is his callous treatment of Janine. Truffaut edited and wrote sympathetic introductions to the several translated collections of Bazin's critical writings that established his reputation outside France: *What Is Cinema?*, *French Cinema of the Occupation and Resistance*, *The Cinema of Cruelty*, *Orson Welles*, and *Jean Renoir*. It's no exaggeration to say that Truffaut's international reputation secured them a hearing with major American publishers. Truffaut also remembered Bazin in his films, both in the several father figures – think of Dr Itard in *The Wild Child* – but also in the characters hampered by a disability, as Bazin was with a stutter. Among these are Victor, the speechless wild child; Georges the speech-impaired boy adopted by Julien Davenne in *The Green Room*; Ferrand, the director in *Day for Night*, described by his crew as "stone deaf"; the bookseller with a cane and the lawyer with an ear trumpet in *The Story of Adèle H.*; and the man in the wheelchair in *Small Change*. All are characters not caricatures. Each is treated with the consideration Bazin extended even to the strangers to whom he always offered a lift when there was room in his small car. "Whether the world is good or evil I cannot say, but I am certain that it is men like Bazin who make it a better place. For, in believing life to be good and behaving accordingly, André had a beneficial effect on all who came in contact with him, and one could count on the fingers of one hand those who behaved badly towards him."[12] Notice in the last sentence that Truffaut can't even imagine Bazin behaving badly. In Truffaut's prose, this respectful and reverential tone and attitude are reserved for one man.

"It'll never work—you're a moviegoer and I'm a film buff."

You could say that Truffaut was a film buff who loved movies.

1 JANUARY 1954: "A CERTAIN TENDENCY IN FRENCH CINEMA"

> Truffaut was a critic in the tradition of the great critics of French art from Diderot to Malraux, people who had a style.
> JEAN-LUC GODARD[1]
> —

> I made *Wuthering Heights*. Wyler only directed it.
> SAMUEL GOLDWYN[2]
> —

"A Certain Tendency" is the kind of essay every critic dreams of writing. It's like a slap in the face or a gunshot in a church. Discussed by everyone in France interested in movies or culture, it marked a seismic shift in a field. Debate about it continued throughout Truffaut's life, and it has its place today in critical anthologies and histories of film. What more could a twenty-two-year-old, relatively unknown journalist-critic want? A contemporary equivalent would be a polemical no-holds-barred essay in a small but influential film journal dismissing the movies of Martin Scorsese, Steven Soderbergh, Clint Eastwood, and Oliver Stone as "the cinema of the fathers." The target of Truffaut's ground-clearing piece was the French film establishment, which, among its many sins, made the director, who should be involved in writing the scenario and should have control of the film, subordinate to the screenwriters. For the purposes of the essay, the latter are represented by the very successful team of Jean Aurenche and Pierre Bost. Their literary adaptations represented "the tradition of quality" with a formulaic psychological realism that only seemed anti-bourgeois or anti-establishment. Implicated with them were the producers and directors whose films depended on cultural prestige gained from literary adaptations and were shot in a conformist fashion. Truffaut attacked them for being anti-cinematic *littérateurs* whose adaptations preserved a novel's plot but ignored its style. They gave the public an acceptable simulacrum of nonconformity and culture: watching an adaptation of *The Red and the Black* audiences had the impression they were seeing high-quality cinema when what was on offer was at best high-class kitsch or what Dwight Macdonald called mid-cult. In a sentence that wouldn't surprise us in Sartre, Fredric Jameson, or Catherine Breillat, Truffaut asked "What then is the value of an anti-bourgeois cinema made by the bourgeoisie for the bourgeoisie?"[3] In other words, they made old-fashioned movies that failed to offer a new vision of life and stood in the way of what in December 1957 *L'Express* would dub *la nouvelle vague*. Though Bazin had reservations about the essay's take-no-prisoners attack, he himself had prepared the ground for it in 1948 with "In Defense of the Avant-Garde," a call for movies that help to renew cinema. Looked at historically Truffaut's essay was an act of cultural parricide in the cause of the liberation of the sons: that some of the indicted ancestors had produced outstanding work was downplayed for the moment. Truffaut would make amends later.

The Truffaut of "A Certain Tendency" isn't politically on the left but he is anti-establishment and contrarian. His anger, however, is marked by ambivalence because some of the directors attacked had made films he enjoyed in his youth. Still, there was no doubt in his mind that most of the popular French cinema of the 1940s and 1950s suffered from a formal and thematic sclerosis whose aetiology was in prewar film. The creative block became particularly noticeable after 1945 when, able to see American films for the first time in five years, the French realized that the majority of their own were old-fashioned. In retrospect, it's worth noting that controversial as Truffaut's essay may have been, some films of the kind he was championing had already been made by Bresson, Jean-Pierre Melville, Jacques Becker, and Renoir.

The following are the five major points of Truffaut's revisionism: a new attitude to adaptation and scriptwriting; filming outside the studio; more personal films and fewer narrowly literary adaptations of classics; more freedom for the director from the studio system; and "*le politique des auteurs*" (or what Andrew Sarris called "auteur theory"). The last was and continues to be the most controversial point in Truffaut's argument and has had the longest staying power: it still survives even in recent theory-inflected criticism (see Douglas Keesey's *Catherine Breillat*). More than half a century after "A Certain Tendency" a young director can still get some critical attention simply by referring to himself as an auteur and drawing on the reflected and now faded glory of the New Wave. As I wrote earlier, the term suggests that directors who are auteurs – especially if they write the script – stand in the same self-expressive relationship to the film as novelists do to their novels or painters to their paintings. Even in a studio system directors are the individuals who bring the disparate elements of the filmmaking together to express their vision of life and film. Fritz Lang and Howard Hawks may make studio mysteries or westerns using studio talent, but their films enact *their* vision of life: each frame carries their signature. To understand that vision fully we need to know their body of work. The director's vision is like a watermark imprinted in every frame. Another way of putting this is that the auteur makes films; everyone else makes movies, a distinction Pauline Kael rejected. As Bazin recognized, the term is carelessly prescriptive because it assumes that even on an off day the auteur is a better filmmaker than a non-auteur, that the worst film by Samuel Fuller (not one of my favourites) is better than the best film by Jean Delannoy. Put simply, auteur overlaps with genius, and therefore even the failures of an auteur are important: Hitchcock's *Frenzy* is perhaps as revealing as *Vertigo*. One of the more baneful consequences of the theory can be seen in the body of evasive reviews the young Truffaut – he wasn't alone – felt compelled to write in defense of the films auteurs made on bad days. Hawks's *The Land of the Pharaohs*, a ponderous spectacle, scripted partly by Faulkner, was acclaimed only because its director was a charter member of the club; by contrast, John Huston's still vibrant *The Maltese Falcon* was rejected because he wasn't. Today these reviews make embarrassing reading, even for those predisposed to value them just because they are written by an auteur. Truffaut would justify them later as having been necessary in preparing the ground for the kinds of films he, Godard, Eric Rohmer, Claude Chabrol, Jacques Rivette, and others would make – less cluttered, more personal, and more contemporary. The directors were too individual to constitute a school – Rohmer, for instance, admired adaptations because they created an interest in literature – but they were linked by a desire to make films different from those of the previous generation. Not the least of their achievement was the way they brought Paris to life on screen. Rohmer credited Truffaut with noticing that American films shot and displayed Paris far more than French ones. Paris had never been absent from French films – think of Alberto Cavalcanti or René Clair – but its appearances became more frequent, pronounced, and even celebratory as in the opening of *The 400 Blows*.

Though the article and the polemics it generated established Truffaut as the hottest film critic of his generation, it was obvious by the mid-1960s that he had tired of the debate and regretted some of the dismissive judgments he had made. Even as late as 1984 he was still trying to explain himself to undo some of the damage: "I don't know if there was actually a plan behind the New Wave, but as far as I was concerned, it never occurred to me to revolutionize the cinema or to express myself differently from previous film makers. I always thought the cinema was just fine, except for the fact that it lacked sincerity. I'd do the same thing others were doing, but better."[4] When I read Truffaut in this mood I have to remind myself that this is the voice of a successful fifty-two-year-old director looking back at a turf war he started when he was an angry young man just a few years away from the streets. He may have been doing a soft-shoe shuffle in his fifties because he knew that his most recent film, *The Last Metro*, had been made in a studio and was closer in many respects to the tradition of quality than it was to *Shoot the Piano Player* and the other early groundbreaking New Wave films whose fast camera work, editing, improvised lighting, music, and street language shouted their difference and made them revolutionary. Even the slang of his first two titles, *Les Mistons* and *Les Quatres Cents Coups*, announces the dissonant voice of a new kid on the block.

I wonder if Truffaut ever thought about the fact that, of the New Wave's *bande à part,* Godard remained the most faithful to their antinomian vision? Uneven, unpredictable, and later almost disdainful of his audience, he kept taking the aesthetic and technical side of the movement's revolution in directions that even someone like Jacques Rivette probably hadn't anticipated. Truffaut had started the quarrel with French cinema's patriarchs, but it was Godard who continued it seriously, taking it from a neighbourhood skirmish to a permanent revolution. Truffaut's attachment to film's and France's past, his partial embrace of modernity, his refusal to think of narrative as a tyranny, his thick, Balzacian sense of reality, his respect for the audience, and his reverence for the grandmasters of the tradition prevented him from becoming a more original and challenging filmmaker. In retrospect it seems clear that he was happy improving on the old masters, some of whom he had watched as a youth and then nervously belittled as a young journalist. One of his never-realized projects was a film based on Jules Renaud's *Poil de carotte* (*Carrot Top*). A classic story of an unloved boy, it had already been filmed twice by Julien Duvivier, who in old age was hoping to film a new version starring Jean Gabin. Did their paths cross while each was trying to make a film of the novel both loved? Incidentally, Duvivier was on the Cannes jury that awarded the prize to *The 400 Blows*. He must have sensed the resemblance between Truffaut's film and Renaud's novel. The two men knew each other: did they talk about Renaud?

Four months after the outbreak of the civil war in French film *Caméra* published Henri Cartier-Bresson's "The Moment of Truth," an attack on the scripted realism of Bill Brandt's photographs. Those were the days.

What would Truffaut and Bazin have made of the French Ministry of Culture's celebration in 2004 of the fiftieth anniversary of the publication of "A Certain Tendency"? Its official website enshrines – the incense is appropriate – the essay as "a unique achievement: without question the only piece of critical writing to amount to a decisive break in the history of an art-form." Caught up in its own rhetorical exuberance and its self-gratulatory pleasure in being on the side of history, it goes on to celebrate Truffaut's essay as "the death warrant" of the old and the proclamation of the birth of the New Wave.[5] Not bad for a school dropout, runaway, and army deserter.

THE MISCHIEF MAKERS (1957): SOME BOYS AND A GIRL ON A BICYCLE

> Woman are magic ... and I became a magician.
> PHILIPPE LAUDENBACH, *CONFIDENTIALLY YOURS*
> —

I don't think I saw *The Mischief Makers*, Truffaut's first notable film, until after his death. Modest in ambition and surprisingly accomplished, it follows quite closely Maurice Pons's bittersweet short story "*Les Mistons.*" The film is without dialogue and is narrated by the French actor who dubbed all of James Dean's movies. Truffaut's title refers to a group of five boys who follow for several months a young couple because, according to the voiceover, "not being old enough to love Yvette, we decided to hate her and harass her love affair." The film's action stretches from spring to autumn and ends with Gérard's (Gérard Blain) death while mountain climbing. It begins with a series of long takes of Yvette (Bernadette Lafont's debut at seventeen), barefoot and with her long white skirt trailing like a wedding train, bicycling through Nîmes and its countryside rendered in a shimmering impressionist black and white. It ends with a scene echoing the ending of *The Third Man* (1951): "on one of the first days of October, coming out of school, we ran across on the banks the colour of autumn Yvette Jouve, silent, transfigured by grief, in mourning for Gérard. Astonished, we were stuck to the sidewalk. Yvette passed through us, all in black, without seeing us." This recalls not only the sombre and darkly dressed Alida Valli walking resolutely and punishingly past Joseph Cotten and straight at the camera but also anticipates Jeanne Moreau (Julie Kohler) in *The Bride Wore Black*. In the film, though not in the story, Yvette and Gérard plan to marry on his return. Julie Kohler's marriage ends on the church steps; in a manner of speaking so does Yvette's, with people entering a church for a funeral rather than the expected wedding. The five young boys are replaced in the later film by five men whose mischief is tragic when they accidentally shoot the groom as the wedding party steps out of the church into the sunlight. Truffaut introduces a suggestion of death twice before Gérard's offscreen accident. In the opening scene he shows Yvette bicycling past a rural sunlit cemetery; a second, longer scene shows the boys in the Roman arena in Nîmes playing at gangsters and shooting each other with make-believe pistols and machine guns – a very early hommage to the noir films and novels Truffaut and his contemporaries admired. If you're a Truffaut junkie you also know that there is what might be called a retrospective foreshadowing of disaster in Yvette's last name, Jouve: Odile Jouve is the Sybil-like character in *The Woman Next Door* whose voiceover introduces and closes that tragic love story. She is one of Truffaut's walking wounded and limps as a result of a suicide attempt caused by end of a love affair. In other words, in Truffaut's later film the name Jouve is an immediate sign for disaster in love.

Though it's fair to call the boys irresponsible rather than malevolent, they are an irritating dissonance in what would otherwise be an untroubled love story similar to innocent relationships many people remember with increasing pleasure as they age. What the boys have in common with death is that they disturb and interrupt love: their presence and actions remind us that love exists under threat and that it will end. Their various acts anticipate, though in a much softer emotional tone, the shock Gérard's death introduces into the film.

Considering that the film is less than twenty minutes long, I'm always surprised how often it anticipates Truffaut's later work. His use of allusions to favourite films appears in the already mentioned nod to *The Third Man* as well as a borrowing of the famous gag with a blocked hose in the Lumière brothers' famous *L'Arroseur arrosé*. The completely convincing boys, with whom Truffaut enjoyed working, are early models for Antoine Doinel, Victor the wild child, the boys in *Small Change*, and the children in the epilogue to *Confidentially Yours*. Yvette's bicycle ride continues across films through *Jules and Jim* and *Two English Girls*, both based on

Henri-Pierre Roché's novels. Gérard's slap of one of the boys returns in *The 400 Blows*, *Jules and Jim*, and *Confidentially Yours*. More pervasively, the film anticipates the pattern of all of his films about love and its fate. In Truffaut's world love is at best transient and at worst doomed. His happiest and most exultant lovers are Fanny Ardant and Jean-Louis Trintignant in his last film, but then we see them only until their wedding ceremony. And the film *is* a comedy.

What stays with me from *The Mischief Makers* is the sheer pleasure the camera takes in filming the unconventionally beautiful Bernadette Lafont, much closer in appearance to a young Sandra Bullock than to a beautiful starlet. She is youth incarnate, and her innocent love affair with Gérard continues to give pleasure because of Truffaut's restrained artistry and because many of us can recall something equally intense and heartbreaking. What Bach wrote on the title page of his "Six Partitas" could just as aptly be the subtitle of the film: "Composed for Lovers to Refresh Their Spirits." And it does, it does.

FILMS TRUFFAUT
DIDN'T MAKE I

Truffaut's letters make it clear that he never lacked ideas for films. As early as the 1950s he was on the lookout for stories with film potential. Once established, he often had scriptwriters engaged on several projects at once. In 1950, at eighteen, he wrote a script about a young woman who is raped twice in the attic of her family home, first by her cousin and six years later by her husband's boss. He hoped it would star Liliane Litvin, an ex-girlfriend whose departure had driven him to attempt suicide and whom he would remember as Colette in *Antoine and Colette* and *Love on the Run*. Three years later, Truffaut and Eric Rohmer collaborated on *The Modern Church*. This sounds more Bressonian than Truffauldian given that he never had any interest in the Church. After shooting the short *Une Visite* in 1954, Truffaut approached the veteran Julien Duvivier with an idea for a film to be titled *The Great Lover* about the love life of an ordinary man. Generally dismissive of Duvivier's work, he was nevertheless opportunistically willing to collaborate in order to break into film. Nothing came of their discussions and not much more from two years of tossing ideas and scripts at Rossellini in 1955 and 1956. When the Italian asked for a comedy, Truffaut gave him an eighteen-page treatment about a female scriptwriter who discovers a comedian. This was followed by a script based on *Carmen* but somehow dealing with daily life in the Soviet Union. Next was an autobiographical screenplay about a young man – Antoine Doinel in all but name – who returns from the army and becomes a journalist in Paris. He has various experiences, falls in love, and, as Truffaut had done recently, flirts with suicide. Though none of the Rossellini projects went beyond discussions, an early treatment or a first script, they were as invaluable in taking Truffaut inside the world of a major filmmaker as the ten days he spent on the set of Renoir's *French Cancan* in 1955. He was only twenty-three and already two of the giants of modern film had taken him seriously enough to bring him into their circles.

Between 1956 and 1960, in addition to a flood of journalism, he wrote eight treatments or screenplays, three of which would eventually become films. After completing *The Mischief Makers*, Truffaut almost made his first feature. Working with the adventurous producer Pierre Braunberger, who was willing to risk money on new talent, Truffaut committed himself to a film based on the novel *Temps chaud* (*Hot Weather*). The producer saw the possibility of a Roger Vadim-like film about the love affairs of several women. When this didn't work out, Braunberger suggested Truffaut make a short film on a subject of his choice. (Do producers like this still exist?) Truffaut came up with the story of a couple driving through flooded fields and blocked roads south of Paris. The woman's comments on love, literature, and the weather dominate the dialogue. Godard was involved in the script and editing. They made the sixteen-minute film in 1958 but it wasn't shown until 1961. But for that, Truffaut's first full-length film would have been indebted, however indirectly, to Vadim, the soft-porn ally of the New Wave. We tend to forget that, because of Bardot, *And God Created Woman* was an international hit in 1956 and made Vadim the international face of French film for almost a decade. He had the hot young actresses – Bardot, Deneuve, Fonda – and he could raise money.

After the success of *The 400 Blows* Truffaut considered Elie Wiesel's story about the last convoy of Jews sent from France to the death camps. At one point this merged with Alexandre Chambon's novel *81.490*; he had been in the same convoy and had survived Buchenwald. Perhaps the most interesting aspect of this project is that it shows Truffaut shifting from his apolitical attitude of the 1950s when he tended to be ironic about politically committed films.

In mid-1964 Truffaut was tempted by Dino de Laurentis's offer to direct an episode of a film to be titled *Three Faces*, starring Princess Soraya, the second wife of the Shah of Iran. Despite taking the time to fly to Rome to meet the producer, Truffaut backed out almost immediately. A year later he told Helen Scott that he had five ideas for films. Two of these led to *The Wild Child* and *Small Change*. The two planned for Léaud and the one for Jean-Paul Belmondo and Romy Schneider are never heard of again. A script titled *The Little Thief* was filmed only after his death by Claude Miller. The most interesting offer of 1965 came from the United States: a script about Bonnie and Clyde. Truffaut recognized that it was first-rate and even played with casting it, but in the end he knew that it was a case of the right project for the wrong director. He must have realized even before the protracted discussions with the producer that he simply didn't know enough about America to venture on such a film. For him and for most of the New Wave America existed on celluloid and between the covers of French translations of American mysteries. The only part of the country that he ever knew intimately was the Beverly Hills Hotel. There was the added problem that his spoken English was somewhere between weak and early Peter Lorre. He backed out and offered the script to Godard who got a trip to New York and an uncomfortable meeting with Warren Beatty out of it.

Almost as tempting at the time was Ray Bradbury's suggestion in 1967, a year after *Fahrenheit 451*, that Truffaut direct his screenplay of his short story "The Picasso Summer." This is about an American who sees a small man come out of the ocean at Biarritz, draw confidently in the sand with a finger, and swim away. The tide wipes out the remarkable drawings. The man is Picasso. The painter told Bradbury that he was willing to participate – as was Truffaut until he read the screenplay. The film was made in 1969 starring Albert Finney and Yvette Mimieux but never went into general release. It ends with Picasso drawing in the sand and then walking away to join his family as the waves begin to erase his work.

Looking at the abandoned projects of this period I have the impression that with one or two exceptions they overlapped with or led to those that reached the screen. *Bonnie and Clyde* would have been a mistake, but then so was *Mississippi Mermaid*. In the 1960s Wiesel's proposal wasn't Truffaut's kind of thing, but the Jewish theme would resurface nearly two decades later in *The Last Metro*. *Temps chaud* anticipates both *Such a Gorgeous Kid like Me* and *The Man Who Loved Women*, and Claude Miller's *The Little Thief* really is what Truffaut called it, "a female *400 Blows*." The Schneider-Belmondo vehicle about lovers reunited after many years anticipates *The Woman Next Door*. You could say that by 1966 Truffaut had mapped out in rough much of his later career. Because he was faithful throughout his life to a narrow if intensely felt range of memories, themes, emotions, and obsessions, his films, however ramified, would always be recognizably autobiographical, if rarely literally so. Despite the lack of an explicit goal, he always knew where he was going. And the paths he took usually led in similar and interrelated directions.

SOME TITLES FOR
THE 400 BLOWS (1959)

> A title should not be a recipe.
> The less it reveals about the contents, the better it is.
> GOTTHOLD EPHRAIM LESSING[1]

We tend to forget that titles of works of art are often less motivated, fixed, or definitive than they seem. *War and Peace,* for instance, was once *All's Well That Ends Well, La Grande Illusion* began life as *The Notebooks of Captain X*, Jean Vigo's *L'Atalante* was retitled by the producers *Le Chaland qui passe (The Passing Barge)*, and Truffaut's *The Green Room* was once the Proustian *La Disparue (The Woman Who Disappeared).* The title *The 400 Blows* was originally just one of many possibilities: in Truffaut's papers, the first fifteen are arranged in a column on the left side of a page; the rest are in four lines to the right. If rearranged and read in a single column with each title given a line, they are almost a found poem with its theme recast in a new form in each verse:

LA FUGUE D'ANTOINE, LES QUATRES CENTS COUPS [boxed], LES QUATRES JEUDIS, LES ENFANTS DU PARADIS [crossed out], LES ENFANTS OUBLIÉS, LE VAGABONDAGE, LES VAGABONDS DU JEUDI [last two words crossed out], À BAS LA RENTRÉE, LES PETITS FEIGNANTS [crossed out], LES MAUVAIS GÉNIES, LES PETITS CRÉTINS, LES PETITS RÉVOLTÉS, LES CANARDS SAUVAGES [boxed], LES PETITS VOYOUS [erased], LES ENFANTS DU CERTIF, LES JEUX DE LA RUE [crossed out], PETITS SOLDATS [boxed].[2]

Some of these would have made as good a title as the final choice in that they fulfil Raymond Chandler's criterion that a title should have "a particular magic which impresses itself on the memory ... and makes the mind ask questions."[3] In other words, they should tease and flirt with the reader without giving too much away.

Truffaut indicates in one of his letters that he also considered *The Awkward Age*, though, to stay with the Jamesian note for a moment, *What Antoine Knew* might have done as well. The final choice may have been influenced as much by Proust as by slang. Truffaut had read Proust as early as 1951 and returned to him throughout his life. He insisted in an early letter to Lachenay that "Balzac and Proust are the 2 greatest novelists in the French language."[4] Did he notice the passage in *Sodome et Gomorrhe* in which the boring pedant Brichot tediously explains the origins of curious expressions like *faire les quatre cents coups*?[5]

Of the titles Truffaut created for his films, as opposed to those suggested by the book being adapted, my favourites are *Les Quatres Cents Coups*, *Tirez sur le pianiste*, *Baisers volés*, *La Nuit Américaine*, *L'Amour en fuite*, and *La Femme d'à côté*. None of these gives away anything about the characters or the trajectory of the plot, and the first four have not only "a particular magic" but also an elusive figurative quality that makes one wonder about the film's content and genre. Thinking about titles and their alternatives, I'm reminded of the alternatives once considered for famous books: *Les Deux Cloportes*, *The Stalactites of the Past*, *The Saddest Story*, *A Man Like Any Other*, and *The Future of the Moon*; these are the rejected titles, respectively, for *Bouvard et Pécuchet*, *À la Recherche du temps perdu*, *The Good Soldier*, *L'Étranger*, and *The Adventures of Augie March*. To echo the winner at Waterloo, "The choice of the right title is a run close thing."

MAKING FILMS TOGETHER: A LETTER TO THE CAST AND CREW OF *THE LAST METRO* (21 JANUARY 1980)

> He was very eager and anxious to give [the actors]
> pleasure in working with him.
> NATHALIE BAYE[1]
> —

I print this letter out of chronological sequence because if all the films, scripts, notes, *cahiers*, and folders in the rich Truffaut archives disappeared but we still had this letter he sent to the cast and crew of *The Last Metro* on the eve of the shoot we would have a remarkable likeness of the man. It is a reminder that film directors (even auteurs) can be thoughtful, sympathetic, and generous, that there is an alternative to the von Sternberg-Preminger-Hitchcock-Godard model. Woody Allen makes one of the kindest comments I have read about Godard's directing of his actors: "I had the impression I was being directed by Rufus T. Firefly."[2] Auteur need not always be synonymous with an authoritative and emotionally distant director. Truffaut admired Hawks, Hitchcock, and Godard but he treated his crews and actors with much greater consideration and paternal concern.

My Dear Friends,

… I think that *The Last Metro* will be an easy and pleasant movie to shoot, as is always the case when the characters are more important than the situations. In short, in my opinion, only the film should get all wound up.

In any case, we must have all had a really oppressive education to find ourselves plagued by such systematic doubts about our own ability in this, one of the rare occupations that is also a calling, one that allows the elements of pleasure to occupy a front-row seat …

We are going to work with the purpose of telling an interesting and intriguing story … The camera crew, under the direction of Nestor Almendros, will do its best to create beautiful images, to evoke the period of the Occupation with accuracy …

And now, let this filming be a party, and let the party begin.
Best,
François Truffaut[3]

I find this an unforgettable document. There are brief anticipations of it in Truffaut's praise of Bergman's family-like crew and in his acceptance speech for *Day for Night* in which he receives the Oscar on behalf of the greater film family. With the exception of Almendros the letter avoids giving star status to anyone, not even the superstars Deneuve or Depardieu. Truffaut is the writer, but the grammatical subject is "we." The tone establishes the director as first among equals, a kindly older brother or a concerned friend. Almendros was not alone in remarking that Truffaut was always willing to listen to anyone during a shoot. Even if he didn't accept their suggestions, he welcomed them. He thought of his crew as an extended family. During the filming of *Day for Night* there was a party every third day; during *The Story of Adèle H.* there were regular screenings of films to help everyone deal with the isolation of shooting on Gurnsey, an island.

Watching *French Cancan* recently, I realized that I had forgotten how in the film's closing Renoir's camera pauses on each actor or small group to give them an individual curtain call. It's as if Renoir wants to make sure that we understand, "This film is not just mine, it is also theirs." A similar gesture appears in the interview on the DVD that accompanies *The Lower Depths* (1937). Discussing the script – an adaptation of Gorky's novel – Renoir praises the book and the contributions made by his co-scenarist Charles Spaak. No excess ego. For Renoir film was a democratic calling. I thought of him recently when I ran across the comment "He was more than polite. He was courteous."[4] It wouldn't be inappropriate as a description of Truffaut.

It's worth comparing Truffaut's letter to Geoff Dyer's account of life on the set of Andrei Tarkovsky's *Stalker*: "It may be difficult with so many accusations, recriminations, counteraccusations and denials to work out exactly what was going on, but the set of *Stalker*, clearly, was a far from happy ship. As Georgi Rerberg [the cameraman], put it with characteristic vehemence: 'Tarkovsky may, ultimately, have got the film he wanted, but at the cost of a heap of corpses and triple retakes.'"[5] To be fair, Nikolai Burlyaev, the lead in the earlier *Ivan's Childhood* (1962), remembers life on that set and at the hotel on the Dnieper River as "this beautiful, harmonious intimacy."[6] *Stalker* was made seventeen years after *Ivan's Childhood*. Whatever caused the change, I can't find the explanation in Tarkovsky's journals, though he may have already known about the cancer that would kill him.

THE 400 BLOWS:
A LIFE ON FILM

> Vigo had the courage to show children as seen by themselves, and better still, grown-ups as seen by children.
>
> ALBERTO CAVALCANTI[1]

Like many writers and directors whose first work is recognizably autobiographical, Truffaut spent much time after the premiere waffling and back-pedalling about his film's relationship to his life. Having in effect orphaned himself in the film, he now had to face his family as well as reporters who wanted to know about the extent to which it was true. Interviewers wouldn't let go of the issue, and his parents understandably felt betrayed by their image on screen. It took him years to repair the damage. It says something about the inevitable complexity of the relationship that Truffaut, though convinced that his parents had failed him as a child, was deeply troubled by the grief he had caused Janine and Roland and repeatedly tried to explain.

His usual contradictory response to the media was Janus-faced: on the one hand, Antoine Doinel is "like me but not me; like Jean-Pierre Léaud but not Léaud," and, on the other, that "nothing in [the film] is invented. What didn't happen to me personally happened to people I know, to boys my age and even to people that I had read about in the papers. Nothing in *The 400 Blows* is pure fiction, then, but neither is the film a wholly autobiographical work."[2] The qualified denial – one step forward, one step back – wore thinner as viewers learned more about his early years. His fudged responses in many interviews – after the victory at Cannes, he was, after all, a media figure – didn't help the parents with their public embarrassment and humiliation, especially in the neighbourhood. It's curious that none of the media asked about Robert Lachenay – René in the film – and Truffaut's biography is silent on whether his friend's mother and father were upset by being portrayed as an alcoholic and an irresponsible gambler. Had the film been made in Hollywood, the lawyers would have been lining up at the Lachenay apartment door.

The problem arises from an imbalance of sympathy in the film. Even if a director tries to be objective about a child's relationship with its parents, it is almost inevitable that the audience's sympathy will attach itself to the youngster, especially if the child's viewpoint is dominant. A child is a libido magnet. Even in Maurice Pialat's *L'Enfance nue* (*The Naked Childhood*, 1969), which Truffaut helped produce, the audience's sympathy is with the young François despite Pialat's attempt to be detached and objective: the boy is far less attractive and sympathetic than Antoine, but I find it impossible not to be more concerned for him than for the adults even when they are trying to help. Truffaut pursues this point discussing Sartre's *The Words*, a book he admired. Despite Sartre's desire to deal objectively with the child he had been, the reader's sympathy, in the book as in the film, is with the child against the adults. The emotional imbalance leads to an ethical one: readers, influenced by their own narcissistic childhood, are inevitably unfair to anyone standing between the child and the fulfilment of its desires. That Truffaut understood this is evident from his struggle to keep the too easily charming Léaud from smiling too often in the film. He also recognized, but only after the film was finished, that Jean Constantin's upbeat score created a kinetic lyrical aura around Doinel and his misadventures. The original screenplay reinforced this effect with a voiceover by René, Antoine's accomplice from beginning to end. The parents and teachers didn't stand a chance. This is also true in Jean Vigo's *Zéro de conduite* (*Zero for Conduct*, 1933), a film Truffaut admired enough to borrow from in *The 400 Blows* and *Small Change*. In retrospect, he regretted not having made Antoine's teacher ("Little Quiz") as sympathetic as the teacher in Vigo.

Discussing the film with friends, many of whom are parents, I've noticed that few remember Antoine's long list of crimes and misdemeanors. By contrast, almost all recall the mother's general lack of affection for him, the fact that she never calls him by name, and the father slapping

Antoine Doinel (Léaud) caught trying to return the typewriter he stole from his father's office (*The 400 Blows*, 1959).

him in the school. What struck me when I watched the film recently is that until the late scene between Antoine and the psychologist in which he summarizes his life, there is little to explain the *degree* of his unhappiness. There is a gap between what we see in the scenes dealing with Antoine's unhappy family life and the extreme negativity of his reaction. This is also true of his life as a pupil. The first time we see him, for instance, he is alone in the classroom writing on the board, "Here Antoine Doinel was punished by 'Little Quiz' for a pinup that fell from the sky. It will be an eye for an eye, a tooth for a tooth." The sentence gains some emotional depth and literary authority from the ending of *Père Goriot* where Eugène de Rastignac challenges Paris with "It's between the two of us now," and from Antoine's later reading of Balzac and plagiarism from him for an assignment. As T.S. Eliot writes about Hamlet, the character is "dominated by an emotion ... in *excess* of the facts as they appear."[3] Among these facts in the film are Antoine's various misdemeanors, lack of respect, and disobedience. Keep in mind that at most he is thirteen years old. Here is a complete list of his transgressions: theft of money from his parents; probable theft of a pen; forgery of a note to explain absence from school; a lie to his father about his day at school; probable theft of his father's Michelin guide; accidental fire in his room; telling the teacher that he missed school because his mother died; plagiarism from Balzac for a school assignment; theft of a still from Bergman's *Summer with Monika*; theft and attempted sale of a typewriter from his father's office; theft of 10,000 francs from his grandmother. I wonder how many of us, even in a very liberal-minded era, would be sympathetic if our child had his record. We probably watch Antoine with ambivalence. As adults we want to be critical and judgmental, but the child in us is on the side of rebellion. Even as parents we probably find ourselves influenced by Dr Spock to sympathize with the young rebel without a case. In the civil war between the parents we are and the intractable memory of the child we were, we end up betraying ourselves to the past. Wes Anderson counts on this in *Moonrise Kingdom* (2012): we want the children to escape even as we know that their return is necessary, salutary, and inevitable. Like Bergman's Monika, they can't spend the rest of their lives on the beach. We cheer for them in bad faith: we encourage in them what we fear in our own relationships with our children.

Despite his understandable identification with Antoine, Truffaut was too Renoirian not to understand that he had been less than fair to a number of characters whose viewpoints he had ignored. He said that if he were to make the film again he would change the soundtrack, make adjustments in the editing, and show the children as more shifty and undisciplined and the parents and teachers as coping with a difficult situation. This reminds me of D.H. Lawrence's remorse over having been unfair to his father in *Sons and Lovers*, and his attempt to present a more attractive version of him in the three versions of *Lady Chatterley's Lover* that he wrote in the last years of his life. There the coal miner Walter Morel is recast as the almost homophonic Mellors the gamekeeper. What I find appealing here is the artist's ability to do in art what is impossible in life. The writer or director can change events that have already unfolded in one way. We all take a childish pleasure watching a film run backwards. We may know that at the most obvious level it is little more than a mechanical trick, but at a deeper level it also appeals to our desire to stop time, change the past, elude the ending – in a manner of speaking, resist death. A director's cut like Giuseppe Tornatore's long version of *Cinema Paradiso* is particularly appealing because it fulfils our desire for a happy ending in which the lovers will be reunited however briefly. I suspect that we all understand the character in the asylum in Henning Mankell's *The Troubled Man* "who spent forty years reading the classics and changing the endings when he thought they were too tragic."[4]

The ending of *The 400 Blows* is sad but it isn't tragic because Antoine is too sly and resilient to leave us with the impression that he won't survive. At the end of his run, his gaze at the camera – borrowed from *Monika* and imitated in several films since – is the look of a tired but literally unbowed survivor. The Russian and Spanish censors weren't so sure that the ending was positive. Both attached a reassuring voiceover to the last scene. Had they consulted Truffaut, he might have sent them the upbeat ending of the original script.

> The last image here. Antoine at the beach, becomes a still and fades slowly into another live action shot: Antoine and René walking in the streets of Paris (this is a shot of them playing hooky, which we have already seen). As we hear the last words of the commentary, this image also becomes a still, reminding us that it has been taken by a street photographer.
>
> COMMENTATOR [René]: And so I get a letter from Fourcroy sur Mer, and there I succeeded in seeing Antoine. How are

we doing? Very well, thank you. And you? We are free and far from the tortures of adolescence, but when we walk along the streets we cannot help seeing as accomplices our successors in the third grade as they begin their *400 Blows*.

Four hundred blows: to raise hell. The great ending we have now is one of the signature scenes of the *nouvelle vague*, a companion piece to Belmondo and Seberg strolling down a Paris street in *Breathless*. It has also been much imitated, most recently in Noah Baumbach's *The Squid and the Whale* (2005) and Xavier Beauvois's *Le Petit Lieutenant* (2005) where the figure on the beach is Nathalie Baye who stars in *Day for Night* and *The Green Room*. In the long continuing shot, Antoine runs from left to right on the screen until he reaches a beach on the Channel. He walks toward the water, then turns slowly back toward the land and, as he looks at the camera, is caught in a freeze shot. It's a brilliant ending to an increasingly powerful sequence in which the camera keeps pace with his run for freedom: *we run by his side*. I was surprised to learn from a comment Truffaut made in an interview that "the final freeze was an accident. I told Léaud to look into the camera. He did, but quickly turned his eyes away. Since I wanted that brief look he gave me the moment before he turned, I had no choice but to hold on it: hence the freeze."[5]

The ending may have been mildly optimistic about Antoine's future, but the film continued to cause Truffaut a great deal of sadness with his parents. Roland was perhaps more surprised than Janine by his son's portrait of the family. Having adopted François, given him his name, and treated him like his own son, he was more than justified in feeling betrayed. On 20 May 1959, a month after the film's success at Cannes, he wrote him a very bitter letter:

> Maybe you'll now find time to grant me an interview concerning articles that have appeared in the press ... I leave the day and time of this rendezvous up to you, but I think we'd better meet at 33 rue de Navarin. In fact, you'll surely be moved to see these squalid lodgings again where you were so "mistreated" by ignorant parents that they later allowed you to become a glorious and disinterested "child martyr." I'm counting on your usual frankness to accept this little conversation. See you soon ... ? Your father (merely legal).

> P.S. I wish to make it clear that you'll be physically safe when you come: the garbage will be emptied and I won't inform the police stations.⁶

As if the letter weren't sufficiently bitter, Roland included a newspaper photo of his son on the film set, smoking a cigar. On the back he wrote "Portrait of an authentic shit."

Truffaut must have remembered the caption when he rejected Godard's invitation in August 1980 to join him and other New Wave alumni for a reunion in Switzerland? They had not met or communicated since he had told Godard off after receiving his out-of-line criticism of *Day for Night* in May 1973, a letter which also tried to emotionally blackmail Truffaut into financing Godard's new film. Truffaut's counterblast ended with a sentence that echoed Roland's letter: "I'm not excessively impatient as I wait for your reply, for if you're becoming a Coppola groupie, you might be short on time and you should by no means hastily throw together the preproduction work on your next autobiographical film, whose title I think I know: *Once a Shit Always a Shit*."⁷ It was three years before Truffaut managed to establish some sort of emotional truce with either Roland or Janine. Perhaps their divorce in 1962 helped. That, at least, seems implied by a poignant, confused, and even heartbreaking letter to Roland in May 1962.

> I think I love you more separately than together, that's the explanation. On the one hand there's the father and the mother, on the other the parents, it's a different notion. I've always loved my father and my mother, but I haven't always loved my parents, that's the thing. I hope I'm not shocking you by dissecting this so bluntly. I often think of Mom and you, not as parents or in relation to me, but as a couple. I think I've inherited many of mother's traits, for example, critical judgment, quick mood changes from cheerfulness to sadness, and as a husband, I resemble you a lot; at mealtime and before leaving the house in the morning, I made Madeleine and the children laugh with jokes that I got from you."⁸

The admission that he owes something, maybe much, to Janine shows a remarkable degree of self-perception. For obvious reasons he finds it

The ending of *The 400 Blows*: Antoine alone on the beach, one of the signature moments of film.

impossible to go further and to say to Roland that he also resembles Janine in his desire for freedom, his selfishness, and his infidelity. He understood that her failure to love him was paradoxically as indispensable to his rebellion, self-invention, and creativity as Bazin's love. It must also have occurred to him that, like her, he would be the cause of the breakup of his own marriage. After Janine's divorce Truffaut lunched with her regularly at the old family apartment, and he saw Roland often. Janine died in August 1968 without ever having met her granddaughters Laura and Eva. The biographers fudge the reasons. Did the girls ever regret not having tried to see their maternal grandmother? There's a story or novel or film here but there's no record of it in Truffaut's papers.

The 400 Blows was a film Truffaut had to make. It changed his life and also the course of filmmaking not only in France but in places as different as Madrid (Carlos Saura), Moscow (Andrei Tarkovsky), Tehran (Abbas Kiarostami) and Austin, Texas (Richard Linklater). It made him rich and famous, but, as the following remarkable letter to Janine indicates, it also left him deeply troubled. The fact that he could write this openly to her says something about the depth of ambivalent feeling on his side. He came closer to understanding her feelings when he went through the apartment after her death and found scrapbooks and folders in which she had closely followed his career: "I have the profession I like, unconditionally, the only possible one for me, and yet it doesn't make me happy. I'm sad, Mom, very often so sad."[9] He was thirty-one and the whole world lay before him.

JEAN-PIERRE LÉAUD with TRUFFAUT, JEAN-LUC GODARD, and BERNARDO BERTOLUCCI

> Am I being sucked into the vortex of over-interpretation?
> Occupational disease of the critic.
> It gets so many of the best of us in the end.
> The bends, the bends!
> Our lungs fill up with insight and we drown.
> ADAM MARS-JONES[1]
> —

Had Léaud's career ended in 1973 with *Day for Night*, he would be remembered for seven films he made with Truffaut, eight with Godard, two each with Jean Eustache and Jerzy Skolimowski, and singles with Bertolucci, Cocteau, Rivette, and Pier Paolo Pasolini. It's a fifteen-year career most actors would envy. Not only had he become a star but also one of the iconic figures of the New Wave. Unfortunately, at least for his critics, he outlived the movement's historical moment. David Thomson, ignoring the faith later directors like Raul Ruiz, Catherine Breillat, Aki Kaurismäki, and Olivier Assayas have shown in him, writes of his post-New Wave career as if he were dealing with a dead man walking: "As he comes up on sixty, he works as hard, and as if he were an actor. Yet for many of us he seems like a startled being caught in the haunted house and never able to find the exit."[2] There's an unexpected sour note here missing from Thomson's accounts of Hollywood's many wounded and lost – think of Montgomery Clift, an overrated actor always given the benefit of the doubt. Considering how perceptive Thomson is on Léaud in his prime – he writes of his "manic solitariness" – this is lazy and disappointing, especially the falling back on the amorphous "for many of us he seems." For many of *us* he seems a fascinating, sensitive, dark, troubled, and lost figure struggling with early greatness and the complex heritage of the New Wave. That he and Antoine Doinel resemble Truffaut hasn't helped matters.

Doinel begins as a very close portrait of the young Truffaut in *The 400 Blows* and *Love at Twenty*. But the gap between them widens significantly with *Stolen Kisses* (1968), *Bed and Board* (1970), and *Love on the Run* (1979), in which Doinel has little of the focused energy, ambition, self-awareness, or talent Truffaut had by the age of twenty. Alphonse, the actor in *Day for Night* (1973), is Antoine's twin brother, but Claude Roc in *Two English Girls* (1971) has little in common with Antoine other than his youth, melancholy, and subdued intensity. While Truffaut looked for parts for Léaud that would free him from Doinel (and Truffaut), the actor tried to find his own path by working with Godard more often during the 1960s and '70s than with Truffaut. I wonder whether Godard didn't sometimes see Léaud as Truffaut or perhaps Truffaut as he should be according to Godard – a political radical, however romantic – a Bakunin to his Lenin? If he couldn't convince his old friend to join him on the Parisian far left, maybe he could convert his acolyte? Truffaut seems most obviously present in the figure of Paul in *Masculin-Féminin* (1966), though, as I will suggest below, *Week-end* (1967) offers a more extended political dialogue with Truffaut's films. Both Doinel and Paul are spontaneous, even manic; each is obviously in need of tenderness, attention, affection, friendship, even love; each lives on the margins of society; their eyes are anxiously alert, the expression sometimes merely sly; and finally there is that defining gesture with the hand moving slowly to caress a girl's face. In *Two English Girls*, where Léaud is often situated among works of art, the gesture seems related to sculpture as if he is shaping something slowly out of the air's transparent plasticity, some ideal beauty visible only to him.

What interests me here is the possibility that one of the subtexts of *Masculin-Féminin* is a dialogue, by means of Doinel, between Godard's political and Truffaut's apolitical attitudes to life and film. I find this in a discussion between Paul and his friend Robert (the name of Truffaut's childhood friend). Though Paul has written a detailed critique of the oppression of army life, joins Robert in defacing with paint the cars of American personnel, writes letters opposing the imprisonment of Brazilian writers, and is opposed to the war in Vietnam, he is far less politically radical than Robert and seems at best a fellow traveller. His defining comment that "We can't live without tenderness" seems more like a Truffauldian categorical imperative than any of the slogans we hear in the film, including Godard's recital of Marx's justly influential comment in "A Contribution to the Critique of Political Economy" that "Man's consciousness doesn't determine his existence. His social existence determines his consciousness." Paul admires Robert, but when asked to follow him in his political activities he responds "I'll think about it." The explicit connection to Truffaut is left late, almost as if Godard doesn't want us to make it too easily. It occurs in a scene where Paul pretends to be "General Doinel" in phoning a military base to get a staff car for himself and his girlfriend, played by Chantal Goya, a singing *étoile* of the 1960s. The first time I saw the film I thought this was just another interfilmic New Wave allusion. On second thought, I'm certain there is more to it. Paul is the only character who dies in the film. Visiting an unfinished condominium he bought recently, he falls to his death. If you know Truffaut's early films, you'll recognize the nod across two years to *The Soft Skin* (1964). In that film, the breakup between Pierre Lachenay and Nicole (we never learn her surname) happens in the unfinished condominium he has purchased in anticipation of their marriage. In a manner of speaking, Godard kills Paul "Doinel" in the same apartment that Lachenay is planning his future with Nicole. It's as if Godard is responding to the hint in Truffaut's scene that the thought of suicide flickers across Lachenay's mind as Nicole's taxi pulls away several floors below him. He will never see her again.

There's a similar engagement with Truffaut by way of Léaud in Bernardo Bertolucci's *Last Tango in Paris* (1972). Playing a New Wave director, Léaud seems to be distancing himself from Doinel and, perhaps unconsciously, through a slightly parodic version of Truffaut, helping Bertolucci do the same. If Léaud *is* Truffaut, then Bertolucci is suggesting that Léaud is making the sort of already dated Truffauldian love film Bertolucci will not make. When an interviewer suggested that "With the character played by Léaud you seem to be mocking the cinephiles who were turning their backs on you or who had ceased to trust you," Bertolucci responded incompletely with "I love Léaud's character because it represents an attempt to be ironical about myself. It was quite painful for me to do this and to recognize that it was a kind of goodbye to something that I had held very dear and that I was beginning to perceive as a little ridiculous. If I am mocking anybody it's only myself."[3] This may be true, but I suspect it's also true that Léaud's gestures, his hair, and the way he ties his scarf remind many viewers of Truffaut, who, to complete the case, was never particularly interested in Bertolucci's work.

The possibility of Truffaut's shadow presence in *Last Tango in Paris* increases if you look back two years to the equally impressive and memorable *The Conformist* (1970). I want to suggest that if *Last Tango in Paris* is in part a settling of accounts with Truffaut by way of Léaud, *The Conformist* (1970) is a farewell to Godard by way of Jean-Louis Trintignant. The actor, who resembles Truffaut and will star in his last film, plays a killer ordered to shoot an exiled Italian professor who has Godard's Paris address and telephone number – 17 rue Saint Jacques; 26-15-37. In a manner of speaking, three years before Truffaut "kills" Godard in a letter, Trintignant – who *is* Bertolucci and *will be* Truffaut – "kills" him in a film. Bertolucci's apprenticeship and friendship with Godard ended the night of the Paris première of *The Conformist*. He tells the story well and deserves to be quoted at length, since Godard's biographers, Colin McCabe, Richard Brody, and Antoine de Baecque, ignore it despite the fact that it appeared in 1987 in *Bertolucci by Bertolucci*.

> Jean-Luc had given me an appointment at the drugstore on St Germain at midnight, just after the screening [of *The Conformist*]. I was very anxious to know what he thought of the film and was shuffling about nervously. The drugstore at that time of night was inhabited by tramps and shifty looking characters – or were they just the last, beloved, unhappy bunch of *cinéphiles*? From their midst, I suddenly saw Jean-Luc hurrying towards me. He hardly took the time to stop as he thrust a piece of paper in my hand and was swallowed up by the night. I opened the piece of paper and found a portrait of Mao with a few words scribbled on it in the inimitable style we have seen so often in his movies. It said in bright red felt tip: 'We must fight against egotisms and imperialisms.' I scrunched it up and tore it into little pieces. You see, Mao had become like a religious effigy which a lay, slightly batty, friar hands to a sinner, trusting that the spiritual power of the image may help him to see the (red) light. But, hélas,

> I am completely immune to any religious imagery and this Anglo-Italian-French pro-Chinese form of mysticism baffled and irritated me a lot. Even though, I must admit that, on an aesthetic level, the extraordinary presentation of the Maoist-spectacle within a Brechtian framework seemed to me nothing short of a miracle. China had become the front projection of our confused utopias. I'd rather have young people brandish a red book than a rifle.[4]

This is a revealing passage about both Godard and, unintentionally, Bertolucci. The longest part is a necessary reminder about the ideological avian flu that distorted the judgment of European intellectuals and artists of the 1960s and 1970s who didn't simply assent to Maoism but actively chose it. Think of the drift to Maoism by Philippe Sollers, Julia Kristeva, and the journal *Tel Quel*. Godard is presented as a simple-minded friar passing around meaningless portentous sentences in support of one of the century's most murderous tyrannies. Godard's *Prénom Carmen* (1983) offers an unintended echo of this figure in the character of "Uncle Jeannot" (played by Godard), the washed up and slightly dotty director trying to raise money for a film. Bertolucci doesn't come off much better in the midnight meeting on St Germain with his almost equally simple-minded admiration for the totalitarian aesthetics of the Chinese regime. His appeal to Brecht suggests that he's less confident than he seems about his stance. He might as well be saying, "Yes, yes, we know that there were excesses in China, but not only were their parades and mass gatherings beautiful and Brechtian, did you notice that the Red Guard and the young were carrying red books, not guns." Is it possible that he hadn't noticed the mass famine and the victims of the Cultural Revolution? People died.

So far as I can tell, Léaud was as apolitical as Truffaut except when he acted in Godard's political films, including the dreadful *La Chinoise* (1967), in which he gets to hold a little red book while lecturing and hectoring the audience. Cotard, who knew the film was a dead dog, found it amusing that Godard was surprised that the Chinese hated it. Bertolucci smelled a political rat in Godard. Godard was too canny not to know who was really being murdered in *The Conformist*.

After Truffaut's death, Léaud resurrects Truffaut, so to speak, in Catherine Breillat's *36 fillette* (1987), Olivier Assayas's *Irma Vep* (1996), and Bertrand Bonnello's *The Pornographer* (2001). In the last two he morphs into a moody, aging Truffaut for whom the *nouvelle vague* and early success are distant memories and for whom new projects don't come as automatically as they once did. The films implicitly ask, what would Truffaut have done after *Confidentially Yours* – his last film – or *The Little Thief* – the last project? I watched *Irma Vep* again recently partly because Assayas's *Carlos* disappointed me and partly because my notes on it don't mention Truffaut. I should explain. Given that it's about the making of a movie (think *Day for Night*), stars Léaud as a washed-up director, and is directed by Assayas, a man with an impeccable *nouvelle vague* and *Cahiers* pedigree, I was surprised by the absence of even an unconscious echo. This time around I thought there were four hints of connections. Because the movie's lead actress, played by Maggie Cheung, doesn't speak French, the director René Vidal, played by Léaud, is forced to speak English almost exclusively. The problem, and Assayas has some fun with this, is that his English is almost incomprehensible. At one point, after giving Maggie some information about the film, René turns to his assistant and says, "I'm not sure she understands everything I'm saying." His English is so poor that neither do we. I would be surprised if Assayas didn't know that Truffaut's spoken English, despite a long wrestle with lessons, wasn't much better than René's (or that René is the name of Léaud's best friend in *The 400 Blows*). In both *Irma Vep* and *Day for Night* the director faces a major crisis. In Truffaut's film it's the death of an actor; in *Irma Vep* it's the breakdown and disappearance of the director caused by his disgust with the first rushes. In both cases the insurance adjustors are called. *Irma Vep* has an early scene that calls attention to a black revolver; *Day for Night* shows Truffaut and Léaud discussing the gun with which he will shoot his character's father. Truffaut's ghost is evoked by association in the scene in which a young journalist tells Maggie that the films of Vidal and the preceding generation (read, the New Wave) were too intellectual and elitist: "René Vidal. It's the past. The old cinema … Only for the intellectuals. But now it's over. It's finished, I hope." He calls for a more popular cinema that looks to Asian cinema and directors like John Woo for its models. Maggie suggests there is room for both. For these three contemporary directors, Truffaut represents the burden of the past in the form of a phase of French film history whose dominance they find troubling even as it gives them antithetical motifs for their films. Léaud is the connection.

Léaud bridged the two generations though none of his later work is as original or memorable – how could it be? – as the films of the first fifteen years. Though he has worked steadily, his post-Truffaut years have been difficult. He suggests something of this in an unusually balanced interview with the French magazine *Elle*. When asked how he's doing, he tells the sympathetic interviewers, "I'm very content. But I know myself. It could crash."[5] And it often has since Truffaut's death. His behaviour in public has been erratic, and he has not been an easy actor to work with. Like many of us, he has put on weight; like all of us he has aged. He rarely smiles and is often rude in interviews. Watching him in some roles of the past decade, I sensed he had buried Antoine as completely as Mickey Rooney had buried Andy Hardy by the time of *The Black Stallion* (1979).

There is an actual scene from Léaud and Truffaut's relationship I would like to have on film. It takes place sometime in the early 1960s when they are living together. They attend a screening of Renoir's *Boudu Saved from Drowning*, one of Truffaut's holy films. As they leave, Léaud tells Truffaut, "I don't like this film." Truffaut answers, "It's understandable, Boudu is you." He means, of course – "He's me too. We are the same. Boudu the homeless tramp is what we might have become just as Antoine is what we were."[6] Or am I overinterpreting? Léaud refuses to speak about Truffaut.

ROBERT LACHENAY (1930–2005): THE BEST FRIEND AND THE ANCILLARY LIFE

> Not all the candidates pass.
> W.H. AUDEN[1]

Lachenay was the closest male friend Truffaut ever had. They met in school in 1943 when he was thirteen and Truffaut eleven, and they were drawn together by unhappy home lives and the love of films. The friendship cooled somewhat after the mid-1960s though they got back together after the beginning of Truffaut's illness, when he started work on his unfinished autobiography. Truffaut's letter from the later period captures the intensity of the early years and their importance to his life: "These days my thoughts turn often to the past. Our common experience belongs to that period in life one never forgets, adolescence and the formative years. Everything related to that period is part of chemical memory, I think that's what the biologists call it. In other words, should we become more or less senile, the only memories forever fresh and lively that will always stream before our eyes, like a film edited in a 'loop,' will be those that stretch from Barbès to Clichy, Abesses to Notre-Dame-de-Lorette, the Delta Ciné-club to the Champollion theatre …"[2]

Lachenay was as committed to film as Truffaut. He knew everyone in the New Wave, made a film, *The Gold Bug*, during the early heroic years – it was produced by Truffaut – and served as assistant on several shoots. But a career in commercial film didn't happen. Truffaut last refers to him in the published correspondence in 1962 when he tells Helen Scott – from whom he had few secrets – that Lachenay wasn't having any luck. As an adult Truffaut was never as intimate with a man his own age as he had been as a child with Lachenay, which is probably true of most of us and probably one of the reasons we're nostalgic about childhood. He had nearly countless "friends" or warm acquaintances, but on the evidence of the letters and the films – think of the loneliness at the heart of some of the films – he was, in the deepest sense of the world, friendless as far as men were concerned: no one played Jim to his Jules. Perhaps one of the things that drew him to Roché's novel was the portrait of a friendship that survives love, war, and death. I'm not surprised that Truffaut, like Sartre and Hitler (his examples), preferred the company of women in the evening. More surprising is that he didn't like being touched by men, but neither did Hitler nor Cézanne.

A friendship like a marriage is a dark and secret place, and its end is a parting that tastes of death. I even feel betrayed by friends who have died; they have deprived me of someone I was certain would grow old with me. I dreamed of friendships like the one Balzac describes in *The Wrong Side of Paris*, the last installment of *The Human Comedy*: "When you have shared your youth and the follies of your adolescence with another, an almost sacred sort of bond exists between the two of you; his voice and his gaze have the power to touch certain strings in your heart that can be made to vibrate only by the effect of your shared memories. Even if you have sometimes had reason to complain of him, the rights of friendship never expire."[3] I wonder if Balzac would agree that it's easier to replace a lover than a friend. Truffaut's life suggests that *he* would.

After Truffaut's death, Lachenay made three documentaries about him that are an extended tribute and mourning: *François Truffaut: Correspondance à une voix* (1988); *François Truffaut: Portraits volés* (1993); and *François Truffaut: Une Autobiographie* (2004). Lachenay had the last word, but I doubt that offered any compensation for the Balzacian fate – see *Lost Illusions* – of being the friend left behind to watch the dizzying worldwide success of the other; in other words, of playing David Séchard to Truffaut's Lucien Chardon.

With the exception of *Jules and Jim*, there are no strong male friendships in the adult films. Truffaut's heroes tend to be loners. The model is the melancholy Bertrand Morane in *The Man Who Loved Women* walking the streets of Montpellier looking for the woman who will momentarily alleviate his aloneness and distract him from his memories of his unloving mother and Véra, the woman whose departure broke his heart. The friendship with Lachenay was the most intimate of Truffaut's life except perhaps for his relationship with Madeleine Morgenstern, which changed from a marriage to a friendship during the 1960s.

SACHA GUITRY (1885–1957): *LE ROMAN D'UN TRICHEUR* (1936) AND *THE 400 BLOWS*

Guitry was the most successful playwright of his time and a filmmaker with at least one classic to his credit, *The Story of a Cheat*. Truffaut saw it at least twelve times in 1945, and ranked it among the favourite films of his youth. Watching it at the age of thirteen he might have felt as if he were watching his own life unfolding in the story of a boy who runs away from his predatory bourgeois guardians to lead a picaresque life as a gambler. In his 1977 preface to Guitry's *Le Cinéma et moi* Truffaut summed up Guitry's existential morality while calling attention to the fact that it was "a morality which doesn't offer itself as such but which consists simply in protecting oneself from the moralities of others."[1] Truffaut is describing both the character in the film and Guitry himself, but there is nothing here that would be out of place in a description of his own life philosophy or Antoine Doinel's.

It took courage to defend Guitry in the postwar years when, in the words of Truffaut's biography, he was still out of favour "for not having offered much resistance – it's the most one can say – under the Occupation."[2] Truffaut's preface, even in 1977, was another of his provocations, though not as daring as his reaching out in the 1950s to Lucien Rebatet, the anti-Semitic collaborationist film critic who had argued for the removal of Jews from the film industry. It is as if during the 1950s, when he first defended Guitry, Truffaut was willing to overlook someone's politics so long as his ideas about film were interesting. Though there's a consensus that the collaborationist drama critic in *The Last Metro* is based on Alain Laubreaux, surely Rebatet's shadow is also present. If that's so, then Truffaut is coming to terms in the film with a problematic phase in his own past. *The Last Metro* recalls his allegiance to Guitry when an actress mentions that he is holding auditions at the Théâtre de la Madeleine. The several half-serious arrests of the director Jean-Loup at the end of the war are also an affectionate nod in Guitry's direction, a reminder of his spotted past. Guitry, just to be clear, was neither a sympathizer nor an active collaborator. At worst, he didn't show much resistance and was dedicated to living his life as he pleased, no matter who was in power. This attitude is also evident in his stylish films, which, like Truffaut's, could never be mistaken for anyone else's. Perhaps the most noticeable and unconventional aspect of his style is his use of a novelistic voiceover in the narrative present. In *The Story of a Cheat* Guitry's voice narrates the story of "the Cheat's" life as the latter writes it in a café. If Ernst Lubitsch had a distinctive touch, then so did the flamboyantly theatrical Guitry. Just imagine a French Noel Coward with the one crucial change that he would sing "Mad about the Girl." When in 1957 Truffaut challenged the negative reviews of *Assassins et voleurs* (*Assassins and Thieves*), Guitry's last film, he emphasized his originality and casual professionalism. As he recognized, Guitry, who wrote, directed, and acted in his comic romances, was as much an auteur as the Hollywood directors championed by the New Wave.

Truffaut claimed he could remember his favourite films scene by scene. Watching *The Story of a Cheat* recently I noted several scenes with echoes in his films: 1. the child who runs away from a family in which he feels unloved and unwanted; 2. the young soldier who reads Balzac while sequestered (in a hospital in Guitry, in a jail in Truffaut's *Stolen Kisses*); 3. the bar scene featuring a street song or *chanson réaliste* (*Shoot the Piano Player*); 4. the insertion of brief excerpts from a First World War documentary (*The Green Room*); 5. the extensive use of voiceover (*Les Mistons, Jules and Jim, Two English Girls, The Story of Adèle H., The Women Next Door*); 6. scenes showing an individual writing a book or a letter (at least six films). I'm not sure how many of these show Truffaut recalling Guitry, but any director who saw a film a dozen times as a child probably internalized it as part of what Truffaut called his "chemical memory" and remembered it very well indeed. A scene in *Day for Night* suggests that Truffaut also recalled the films of his youth in dreams. There is a sense in which our dreams are the "films" we make when we are most like auteurs. We know that Truffaut filmed many more dreams than appear in the films. The majority, he admitted, ended up on the cutting-room floor. Like most dreams they were more interesting to a dreamer than to anyone else.

In an *hommage* published when Guitry died in 1977, Truffaut mentions that he almost met him in 1955 during the filming of his last film. When he asked for an interview, Guitry's secretary indicated that he might have one so long as he submitted the questions ahead of time. "Stupidly I refused; I was an idiot that day."[3]

SHOOT THE PIANO PLAYER (1960): ALL YOU NEED IS LOVE

> The habitual state of my life has been that of a sad lover.
> STENDHAL[1]

—

> The best films give the impression of opening doors and also of the cinema beginning, or beginning anew, with them.
> FRANÇOIS TRUFFAUT ON *VIVRE SA VIE*[2]

—

Truffaut's second full-length film is his most experimental in genre and style, almost as if he were looking over his shoulder at Godard's radical challenge to all directors in *Breathless*. *Shoot the Piano Player* is based on David Goodis's best novel, *Down There*, and follows its narrative faithfully. It also keeps almost all of its characters and major scenes while transposing them from Philadelphia and New Jersey to an unspecified French setting referred to simply as the city. The American dimension remains in the noir atmosphere and in the use of many themes Truffaut knew well from American films and novels. The latter he read in French translations. He called the film his thank you to the American films that had to some extent formed his generation. Though he admired the novel, he discovered while writing the script that he detested gangsters. Without that realization we would have a very different, probably more conventional film, something like Melville's *Bob the Gambler* (1955) or *Le Samourai* (1967). Instead, he produced what he called "a *hommage* in the form of a pastiche ... [a film] slightly ironic, never mocking."[3] *Shoot the Piano*

Player is a comic noir that divided the critics and, more importantly, fell flat at the box office when it opened in Paris on 25 November 1960. The failure with the audience, less than a year after the triumph at Cannes, left Truffaut both defiant and anxious. From now on he would alternate in interviews between asserting the director's right to make the films he wants to make and allowing for the possibility that in the end the audience may be right when it stays away. The crisis of confidence was real and profound. As a result of the setback, his branch of the *nouvelle vague* would be less innovative and challenging (closed rather than open) than it otherwise might have been. Within his body of work, *Shoot the Piano Player* is a troubling reminder of a career road not taken.

The critics on this side of the Atlantic divided into two groups that can be labelled Pauline Kael and the others. Kael's enthusiastic response is a director's dream. She understands how the film works and what it is trying to say. She has read Goodis's novel, notices the allusions to American movies, and recognizes that Truffaut's play with genres is part of the film's vision. Equally important is her emphasis on the various pleasures the film makes available. She's crazy about it and is willing to tell anyone who will listen.

> Truffaut's film busts out all over – and that's what's wonderful about it. The film is comedy, pathos, tragedy all scrambled up – much as I think most of us really experience them (surely all our lives are filled with comic horrors) but not as we have been led to expect them in films.[4]

> *Shoot the Piano Player* is both nihilistic in attitude and, at the same time, in its wit and good spirits, totally involved in life and fun. Whatever Truffaut touches seems to leap to life – even a gangster thriller is transformed into human comedy. A *comedy* about melancholia, about the hopelessness of life can only give lie to the theme; for as long as we can joke, life is not hopeless; we can enjoy it.[5]

Along the way she efficiently disposes of the opposition.

> When I refer to Truffaut's style as anarchic and nihilistic, I am referring to a style, not an absence of it. I disagree with

the critics around the country who find the film disorganized; they seem to cling to the critical apparatus of their grammar school teachers. They want unity of theme, easy-to-follow-transitions, a good, coherent, old-fashioned plot, and heroes they can identify with ... *Time* decides that 'the moral, if any, seems to be that shooting the piano player might, at least, put the poor devil out of his misery.' Who but *Time* is looking for a moral?[6]

I can't help wondering what effect this enthusiastic and perceptive response would have had on the course of Truffaut's career had something similar appeared in Paris in 1960 instead of in New York in 1962? Would the passionate support of a perceptive critic been enough to nudge him down the road where he could develop the possibilities opened up by his film?

Truffaut's justification of the film's form a decade later echoes some of Kael's comments. "I know that the result seems ill-assorted and the film seems to contain four or five films, but that's what I wanted ... But I do think that there's a coherence in *Piano Player*: love. In the film men talk only about women and women talk only about men; in the most strenuous brawls, settling of accounts, kidnapping, pursuits, everyone talks only about love: sexual, sentimental, physical, moral, social, marital, extramarital etc."[7] He doesn't mention, however, that the coherence is the result of additions he made to the novel. He kept Goodis's characters, scenes, and storyline, and he borrowed heavily from the dialogue, but almost all his additions touch in some way on love. The long opening night scene in which the piano player's brother is being chased by gangsters in a car is a good example. The first part, shot by Coutard with a handheld Caméflex, cuts rapidly between the fleeing Chico – a nod to the Marx brothers – and the menacing Buick in pursuit – a nod to American noir. This is interrupted when Chico, slips, falls against a light pole, bruises his face, and collapses on the sidewalk. He lies in near-darkness both because it is night and because many of the cheap lights strung by Coutard had exploded when it began to rain. A stranger carrying a bouquet approaches him, slaps him several times, and helps him to his feet. They walk off in the same direction immediately discussing women, love, and marriage. The third section begins when the stranger departs and the chase resumes. The chase and the collision with the pole are in Goodis, the elderly stranger isn't. The scene with him is light-hearted, sentimental, and serious. The man has bought flowers for his wife, and they occasion his fond description of their long marriage. He admits to not loving her at the start, but "I got used to her … I think I really fell in love with her two years later." They have three children. Chico admits that he longs for a wife, children, and a home, a sentiment repeated later by one of the gangsters after the kidnapping of Charlie and Léna. The domesticity described by the stranger is desired to some degree by almost all the characters, most of whom suffer from unrequited love. Truffaut arranges the lonely men in pairs: Charlie and his brother Chico; Charlie and the bartender Plyne; Ernest and Momo, the two gangsters; and the two comic sad sacks in the bar. The gangsters are classic male chauvinists who can't stop talking about "skirts," while the men in the bar see only faults in the women they are afraid to approach. There is also something of Max Ophuls's *La Ronde* in the overall dance of love: the bar's female owner loves Plyne, he loves Léna who, in turn, loves Charlie, who loves Theresa, his late wife, whose suicide he caused. Truffaut will return to Ophuls's structural device in the script about Antoine's son Alphonse that he worked on in the years after *Love on the Run* (1979).

Truffaut threads a series of small details that echo the love theme in a minor key. Charlie, for instance, lives with his teenage brother Fido. Just in case we haven't gotten the point, one of the gangsters tells Fido that his name is also the name of a dog and means "faithful." The fidelity and affection implied are surely Charlie's for his brother, the other members of the family, and the memory of Theresa: he's the faithful one. The various songs on the car radio are about love and its failure. Léna reminds Charlie that her name comes from Helen or Helena. As Plyne chokes Charlie in a headlock, he talks about his love for Léna in lines borrowed from Jacques Audiberti's fiction: "Woman is supreme. Woman is magic. To me, woman has always been supreme." The most memorable reiteration of the theme occurs in the waiter Boby Lapointe's manic and almost cryptic street song about a woman. Its chaos and violence find an expressive counterpoint in his nearly incomprehensible patois, his Joe Cocker-like physical movements, and the brawl in the bar: all suggest the force of love. The film is a gallery of the lovelorn in a world without winners. Kael is right, however, in suggesting that though the film and its director are without illusions, the overall effect is not one of disillusionment.

The film is also a gallery of motifs that recur in Truffaut's oeuvre. The Audiberti quotation resurfaces in *Confidentially Yours*. Fido's model airplanes anticipate Bertrand Morane's in *The Man Who Loved Women*. The gangster's story of his father who was hit by a car while watching a "skirt" anticipates Bertrand's death: "Got his eye on a skirt and down he goes." The ending with the lovers in the snow is one of the several echoes in the ending of *Mississippi Mermaid*.

Despite the emphasis on affection, trust, and love, Charlie is as lonely and alienated as Goodis's Eddie. The novelist's descriptions of him as "this living example of absolute neutrality" and as a man who "when he's with someone, he's alone" make it into the script.[8] Aznavour's characterization of him in an interview as "a loser" is unkind but accurate if we think of him as someone who has lost two lovers to death and suffers from what therapists call a bad, because interminable, mourning. Truffaut plants a suggestion a few minutes before the end that Charlie didn't have a chance. Echoing the Zolaesque determinism of Renoir's *La Bête humaine*, Truffaut, borrows a crucial passage from Goodis, who has the older brother say "You hadda come back. You're one of the same, Eddie, the same as me and Richard. It's in the blood."[9] The piano player didn't have a chance, and the final shot of his haggard, tense, blank face and unseeing eyes shows that he doesn't have a future. It's an image of despair: a self capable at best of a stoic emotionless existence. As Charlie looks beyond the piano, what does he see? Léna's face in the snow? Theresa's body on the sidewalk? Both? Or nothing?

In 2005, Marie Dubois (Léna) said that at the end of his life Truffaut tended to agree with the audience's judgment that the film was a failure or, as he put it more gently, that "it wasn't his best film." Wrong, wrong, wrong. This is one of those instances where, in Kierkegaard's words, "The crowd is the untruth." *Shoot the Piano Player* is fresh every time I watch it. The only weak section is the retrospective one about Charlie's career as the classical pianist Edward Saroyan. Flashbacks are always risky. The film remains one of Truffaut's (and Pauline Kael's) finest moments.

SHOOT THE PIANO PLAYER
AND
A DEBT TO THE PAST

In a catalogue of guilty pleasures there must a category for borrowing something from someone whose work you have dismissed famously as minor. That's just what Truffaut did with Jean Delannoy when he echoed *La Symphonie pastorale* (1946) in *Shoot the Piano Player* and *The Wild Child*. Whether we call it *hommage* or plagiarism, it leaves the perpetrator in an unsettling position involving a form of bad faith accompanied with an anxiety about being discovered. Delannoy is one of the usual suspects in Truffaut's "A Certain Tendency" and a 1956 letter to Rohmer dismisses his *Marie Antoinette* as "putrid." A year later, the boys in *The Mischief Makers* tear down a poster for *Chien perdu sans collier* (*Lost Dog without a Collar*) in what must be a protest against Delannoy's depiction of children. The scene implies that *The Mischief Makers* is the way to do it. There's no indication that Truffaut ever changed his view of Delannoy's films, though in later years he refused to reprint his early negative comments on him and his contemporaries.

La Symphonie pastorale is based on André Gide's popular novella and tells the story of a Protestant pastor who takes into his care a blind and barely civilized girl – a female wild child. We first see her she as walks clumsily out of the darkness, her face concealed by a mass of uncombed matted hair, and almost feral gets down on all fours to eat from the plate he has brought to the doorstep. The film also anticipates *The Wild Child* when it shows him domesticating her, naming her Gertrude, and writing a journal about her progress. Its final scene, however, points toward *Shoot the Piano Player*. The married minister confesses his love to Gertrude and offers to leave his family for her. When he discovers she has run away, he follows her through the snow. The path leads to a river where he finds some men bringing her dead body out of the water. The closeup of Michelle Morgan as she lies on the snow looks forward to the shot of the dead Léna. Another connection of a different kind is the presence of a young Jean Desailly, playing the pastor's son who is also in love with the girl. He will play the adulterous Pierre Lachenay in *The Soft Skin* (1964).

The question of the lines of influence is complicated, however, by the ending of Frank Borzage's *The Mortal Storm* (1940), which ends with James Stewart skiing with the dead Margaret Sullavan in his arms across the border to escape a German ski patrol. Did Borzage see *La Grande Illusion*? Did Delannoy see either Renoir's or Borzage's films? Other than *La Grande Illusion*, what did Truffaut see and remember?

TRUFFAUT'S *BREATHLESS* AND JEAN-LUC GODARD'S

> Hear that? It's the new wave.
> CATHERINE DEMONGEOT, *ZAZIE DANS LE MÉTRO*
> —

I reread Truffaut's untitled original treatment of *Breathless* recently, and then watched Godard's still vibrant masterpiece with a pleasure that is probably intensified today by nostalgia and tinged with sadness because of my disappointment with his later work. Thinking about it in relationship to Truffaut's original treatment, which he gave to Godard, I wondered whether Michel Poiccard (Belmondo) is what Truffaut feared at some level he might have become if not for Bazin? Keep in mind his friendship in his late teens and early twenties with Jean Genet, the gay in-house criminal among French existentialists. Another way of putting this: what would Truffaut have become had Bazin not appeared and become his guardian angel? Is the film treatment his way of living through in imagination one of his worst nightmares: street urchin, pimp, thief, hustler – Truffaut as a Genet minus the homosexuality.

If the *Breathless* treatment is Truffaut's apotropaic gesture – if I write it, it won't happen – against what might have been, for Godard the film is as much a form of wish-fulfilment as the playing with revolution in *La Chinoise* (1967). For the pampered young man rebelling against his upper-middle-class family, the film is a fantasy about being an outsider, an *étranger*, *tricheur*, or *voleur*. In *La Chinoise* I have the impression that he wants to have it both ways – to believe and to satirize – just in case the revolution goes wrong. It's interesting that both Truffaut and Godard kill Michel. In Truffaut's version he dies of an Aspirin overdose after surrendering to the police. In Godard's he is shot on a Paris street while pursued. Both Truffaut and Godard end their first full-length films with young men on the run. One gets away, one doesn't.

A POSTHUMOUS QUESTIONNAIRE
(JANUARY 2015)

Where would you like to live?
> *Anywhere so long as it is Paris and there is a view of the Eiffel Tower and there are several cinemas within walking distance.*

What would constitute perfect happiness for you?
> *The life I have has made me very happy, and, with the exception of a handful of details, I wouldn't want to change it.*

Which mistakes do you forgive most easily?
> *I never forgive my own mistakes because I know that I won't be able to prevent them from happening again. This may also explain why I have difficulty forgiving others for their "sins." I would make a poor priest.*

What were your most obvious mistakes?
> *Other than being born?* Fahrenheit 451, The Bride Wore Black, *perhaps* Such a Gorgeous Kid like Me. *There were some personal ones, but it's best not to talk about them.*

Your favourite fictional hero?
> *Maigret. The Count of Monte Cristo. Balzac's Colonel Chabert.*

Your favourite fictional heroine?
> *Stendhal's Mathilde de la Mole.*

Your favourite real life heroine?
> *I love Arletty for standing up to the postwar court that tried her for having a German officer as a lover. When they accused her of betraying France, she answered, "My heart belongs to France, but my ass belongs to the world." I wish I had said something as fine as that. What an epitaph. What a great line for a film. What a woman!*

Your favourite painter?
> *I was once quite interested in Balthus and even thought about a film, but to be honest I pay very little attention to painting.*

Your favourite composer?
> *Georges Delerue.*

What trait do you admire most in a man?
> *Honesty.*

In a woman?
> *Women have the moral integrity that allows them to forgive almost anything.*

Your favourite virtue?
> *Tolerance.*

Your favourite activities?
> *Reading, making films, being with a woman – perhaps in that order.*

Your main character trait?
> *Stubbornness. But there's also shyness. I know that I find it very difficult to be with strangers. I also find it very difficult to open up to someone, even someone I love. I wish I could say "Je t'aime" as easily as characters do in films and novels. I remember once eating alone in a Paris bistro. I noticed that Marlene Dietrich, whom I*

had never met, was sitting nearby with a man. She sent him over to invite me to join them. Not only was I unable to respond to the invitation, I left without replying in any way. It was a simple case of a panic attack. I couldn't imagine talking to someone as legendary as Dietrich. She had known von Sternberg, Cooper, Hitchcock, Welles, Preminger, and Hemingway. Just thinking of that left me breathless. Like Guitry, she remains a missed opportunity.

What do you value most in your friends?
Loyalty, discretion, and a sense of humour.

Your greatest fault?
I wish there was only one, but it's probably either lust or perfectionism. But don't tell anyone. And I'm sure that there are more that should be put in the balance.

What would be the greatest unhappiness to you?
To hurt others. Benjamin Constant is very good about this in Adolphe *his novella about his affair with Mme de Staël – there's a good film in it. "The great question in life is the sorrow we cause, and the most ingenious metaphysics cannot justify a man who has broken the heart that loved him. And besides, I hate the vanity of a mind which thinks it excuses what it explains, I hate the conceit which is concerned only with itself while narrating the evil it has done, which tries to arouse pity by self-description and which, soaring indestructible among the ruins, analyses itself when it should be repenting." You may remember that Christine says something like this to Antoine Doinel in* Bed and Board *of his novel about his relationship with his parents.*

What sort of person would you like to be?
Much better than I am, more like André Bazin or Dr Jean Itard in The Wild Child. *Instead, I continue to resemble Roberto Rossellini, a wonderful, wonderful man but not quite an ideal moral role model.*

Your favourite colour?
Blue.

Your favourite flower?
> Though there are many flowers in the films, I don't think I could name any others than roses. In other words, I rarely notice flowers except in Jeanne Moreau's Provençal garden. I have almost no interest in nature, though I do like to drive through it.

Your favourite writers?
> In the twentieth century, Proust, Audiberti, Giraudoux, Simenon, Genet. In the nineteenth, the obvious suspects, Balzac and Stendhal.

Your favourite poet?
> I never read poetry, though I love the poetry of Jacques Prévert's and Charles Trenet's songs. For me, as for Mathilde Bauchard in *The Woman Next Door*, songs like these have the lines that stay with us forever because they tell as much about life as any works of art – or at least about love. They pass a simple test: I don't have to make any effort to remember them, and often find myself singing them unaware that I'm doing so.

Your real-life heroes?
> Bazin and anyone who helps a child. I also admire anyone who stands by you when the rest of the world is against you.

Your heroes in history?
> I think we make too much fuss over soldiers and politicians; they're no more important than a good carpenter or photographer or mechanic or cleaning woman. Is there any reason to remember Pompidou or Chirac? There should be streets dedicated to those who helped the helpless or children. People like the English teacher A.S. Neill, who founded Summerhill, a school for problem children unwanted by other schools. There was also that Polish-Jewish doctor, Janusz Korczak, who ran a Warsaw orphanage. When the 192 children in it were condemned to Auschwitz, he went with them even though he could have saved himself. Wajda's best film is about him. People like that are heroes. De Gaulle, Reagan, and the others are ambitious egotists, liars, at best charlatans and minor entertainers. To call them clowns would be to insult an ancient, honourable, and useful profession.

Which historical figures do you dislike the most?
> *There are so many that it's difficult to choose. Besides I pay little attention to politics and history. I leave that to Jean-Luc.*

Your favourite names?
> *André, Robert, Roland, Bertrand, Julien, Eva, Laura, Joséphine, Madeleine, Fanny, Catherine, Cécilia, and, yes, Janine.*

What are you particularly intolerant about?
> *Lies, bullying, intolerance.*

As a former soldier, are there any military feats you admire?
> *You should have said "failed soldier" or "deserter." I hope this doesn't sound sour but I don't admire military accomplishments. I should add that when I read memoirs and histories or watch war films I'm always moved by the depth of feeling in the friendships between soldiers. I'm thinking of films like Abel Gance's* J'Accuse, *G.W. Pabst's* Kameradschaft, *or Lewis Milestone's* All Quiet on the Western Front. *I think you can sense some of this in* The Green Room. *Julien Davenne's loneliness has two causes: he misses his dead wife Julie and he can't forget the soldiers he served with in the First World War. We don't see those men, but there is a flashback showing Davenne looking around in horror at what has happened on the battlefield. He dedicates his life to their memory.*

What reforms do you most admire?
> *All those that bring people a bit more happiness without restricting their freedom, and anything that makes a child's life easier.*

What talent would you like to have?
> *To be able to swim so that Susan Schiffman would stop making fun of my fear of water. I would also like to be able to speak English fluently.*

How would you like to die?
> *In an upright position, in a clean bed with white sheets, in a brothel looking through a window overlooking the Eiffel Tower. Having said that, I also envy Sacha Guitry's last days. He was confined to a bed,*

but he insisted that they set up an editing machine on a table next to the bed so that he could complete some work on his final film. A perfect ending to a film and a life. Don't you agree?

Your present state of mind?
Can't complain.

Are you religious?
No. I'm a man without a religion who doesn't understand people who go on about God, resurrection, etc. These words have no meaning for me; they seem to refer to nothing. My characters agree with me. And I have never missed it. I mean, I don't find myself thinking "I wish I could believe in some ideology or some religion."

Your motto?
In spite of everything, malgré tout. *I have always admired Sartre's comment to an interviewer who suggested, "So far life has been good to you?" Sartre answered, "On the whole, yes. I don't see what I could reproach it with. It has given me what I wanted and at the same time it has shown me that this wasn't much. But what can you do?"*

TRUFFAUT
IN HIS LETTERS

> It's true that in daily life I prefer to write a letter rather than to telephone. The telephone is an attack. I detest hearing it ring. With a letter, you can answer when you want or not at all. That seems to me more democratic, less authoritarian.
>
> FRANÇOIS TRUFFAUT[1]
> —

Nestor Almendros described Truffaut as "a nineteenth-century man because he read a lot and especially, in my opinion, [because] he wrote a lot of letters. Even in Paris he wrote letters … He loved pneumatic mail [and] he didn't like talking on the phone."[2] Truffaut's *Correspondence 1945–1984* is a reminder that he was a prolific letter writer, as stylish with a pen or typewriter as with a camera. He might have become a journalist or novelist had he not gone into film. In addition to the twenty-one films there are also ten books, which he wrote, edited, or introduced. The number of books would be substantially higher if we count all the screenplays, his novelizations of some of them, and the posthumous compilations. Truffaut probably spent more time writing than he did filming, something which makes surprising his comment, in an informative letter surveying his career, that for a long time he was "fearful of the blank page."[3] The letters published to date constitute an autobiography of sorts though there are inevitable and expected gaps: André Bazin didn't keep letters and the important women in Truffaut's life – his wife and daughters,

Moreau, Deneuve, Schiffman, and Ardant – haven't made theirs available. With very rare exceptions the letters available are personal but not quite intimate, yet the style is so direct and the tone so open that by the book's end there is an almost rounded portrait of Truffaut.

The more interesting letters of the 1950s and '60s often overlap in their concerns with his reviews and critical pieces. Truffaut as a critic treated his pen like a sword, and he could be as cutting and acidulous as Pierre Boulez. I wonder if he and the composer (born 1925) were at all aware of their nearly contemporaneous assaults on their respective cultural establishments. By all accounts, Boulez was even more unforgiving than Truffaut. At one point he attacked Olivier Messiaen, his mentor, who needed all the Christian charity and tolerance for which he was famous when reading his pupil's latest corrective. Truffaut tells one correspondent that "Arthur Penn ... films every scene from 12 different angles out of ignorance"[4]; he laments to another the fact that Hitchcock is forced to work "with an idiot like Rod Taylor."[5] Much of this is just the predictable muscle flexing of a young critic who thinks he is also speaking for a generation and new standards. Exaggeration and electricity make the sentences memorable, and they remain alive because Truffaut wrote them. He later regretted slagging Penn and paid him the compliment of stealing from *The Miracle Worker* for *The Wild Child*. A postcard, not included in the published letters, that he sent to Marcel Carné in December 1960, after seeing his latest film, is a revealing example of Truffaut later mending fences with the French older generation. "I went to see *Terrain vague* (*Wasteland*) here [Carcassone] last night ... The audience was at first puzzled, then attentive, more and more interested, and finally genuinely moved. I write you because I reacted exactly like the audience; there are, in this film, some moments of very sharp truth and some moments of pure fantasy. I have read some very unfair articles. I hope to please you with this card as you have pleased me with this film; I have never belonged to a gang and yet I breathed, in *Terrain vague*, whiffs of my own adolescence; thank you."[6]

The letters confirm that from early adolescence Truffaut's life was devoted to movies. Not only did he spend an inordinate time watching them, he recorded his responses in a diary. The letters likewise provide a guide, almost a calendar, to his filmgoing and filmmaking. Like the Academy Award-winning *Day for Night*, the letters also offer an inside look at the film industry, at the creative and financial problems confronting a director, and Truffaut's central role in organizing everything. The letters confirm what we guessed from the films: Truffaut loved books. There are few other bodies of film as consistently and self-consciously literary. We have here a useful record of his peripatetic reading, his strong literary judgments, and the books he bought for friends. Jeanne Moreau has written that even during his last illness he still took time to send her books. There is also a great deal of scattered detail about unrealized projects. For instance, he refused to film Proust, Camus's *L'Étranger*, *Bonnie and Clyde*, or a new version of *Casablanca* (it wasn't his favourite Bogart).

The lack of published letters from the women in Truffaut's life is "what we know that we don't know" about him. If nothing else, I would like to read his correspondence with Madeleine Morgenstern and his mother, Janine. The latter is mentioned only twice. He tells one correspondent, almost in passing, that he still hates her even though she is dead. Yet it's clear from the films that he understood that, in failing disastrously as a mother, Janine taught him what would become a central theme in many of his films – love always fails and it is interesting *only* when it fails. To paraphrase Tolstoy, all happy lovers are the same, each unhappy couple is uniquely unhappy. Letters in the films are often either melancholy anticipations of unrequited love or elegies recording an eros of loss. Both descriptions also apply to many of Truffaut's screenplays, which can be read autobiographically as resentful unsent letters – "you didn't love me enough" – to Janine. Anyone uncomfortable with such a nakedly biographical approach should recall the comment in "A Certain Tendency" that the films of tomorrow would be more personal, like autobiographical novels or journals. Since Truffaut co-wrote his screenplays, I tend to think of the letters in the films as a companion volume to the correspondence, the one in which he gives a different form – more objective, oblique, and dramatic – of expression to his feelings.

Overall the letters reveal an engaging, genial individual with a playful sense of humour who takes immense pleasure in reading, friendship, going to movies, making films, and writing to friends, fans, and critics. He seems gregarious and easy-going, but one notices that, like Ferrand, the partly deaf director of *Day for Night*, he keeps his emotions under house arrest. They come out only in a handful of letters, most explosively and uncharacteristically in the previously mentioned 1973 response to Godard's dismissal of *Day for Night* and his demand that Truffaut use the profits from it to help finance his next political film: "You're the Ursula Andress of militancy, you make a brief appearance, just enough for the cameras to flash."[7] Four decades later it's still difficult to understand Godard's assumption that Truffaut should help with Godard's budget. To be fair, Jean-Luc offers in exchange the rights to *La Chinoise*, *Le Gai Savoir*, and *Masculin-Féminin*, but by then he has burned his bridges by the offensive he launched in the main part of the letter. His comparison of *Day for Night* to a train heading from Munich to Dachau and his tarring of Truffaut with the word "fascist" probably did more damage than he realized: Godard probably didn't know that after finding his birth father, Roland Lévy, Truffaut considered himself a Jew.

Truffaut's lightning response is the longest letter in the collection and, no doubt, the one most readers will remember. Two decades later, Godard attempted to heal the breach with an unexpected foreword to Truffaut's letters. It's a moving valedictory across the years; it ends in an adagio with a paradoxical paragraph: "François is perhaps dead. I am perhaps alive. But then, is there a difference." Looking back to the time when they were changing cinema while living on cigarettes, youth, and the adrenalin of "making it," he recalls the cause of the quarrel as "something else. Something stupid. Infantile. I say fortunately, because everything else was becoming a symbol, a sign of itself, a mortal decoration: Algeria, Vietnam, Hollywood, and our friendship, and our love of reality. The sign, but also the death of that sign."[8] You can sense Godard struggling to get close to what he needs to say and then losing it in an attack of Derriditis. The best I can say for it is that it carries the authority of Socrates's farewell in the *Apology*: "We must go now, I to die, you to live, but which is better is known to god alone." We now know from de Baecque's *Godard* (still untranslated) that he had two of Truffaut's letters attacking him read to him on the phone before the correspondence was published because he had not kept the originals. De Baecque refers to this as Godard's "session of melancholy self-flagellation" and notes that he agreed to their publication with "oui, oui, c'est vrai."[9] To his credit, Godard made another gesture of reconciliation a decade later, in 1998, in *Histoire(s) du Cinéma*. Here he uses the ending of *The 400 Blows* to illustrate his point in "Égalité et fraternité entre le réel et la fiction" ("Equality and Fraternity between reality and fiction"), follows it with a photograph of Truffaut in middle age, and then places him with "Becker / Rossellini / Melville / Franju / Jacques Demy / oui, c'était mes amis [these were my friends]."

However interesting one may find Truffaut's letters, he nevertheless does not rank among the greatest letter writers. His letters, unlike those of Keats, Flaubert, Tolstoy, Van Gogh, Lawrence, and Woolf, do not detach themselves from the chronological sequence of a life to stand alone. You can imagine great letters as having an aesthetic, moral, and historical value transcending their biographical one. In them the writer seems to be in the same zone of creative grace and imaginative reach as in their creative work. The best letters aspire to the status of a work of art even if the writer is not conscious of this. I offer this as a judgment on a work in progress, since the letters to Morgenstern, Laura and Eva Truffaut, Moreau, Claude Jade, Françoise Dorléac, Catherine Deneuve, Leslie Caron, and Fanny Ardant may change our minds by providing the missing complement of emotions.

Still, I am more than grateful for what we have so far. Both in French and English Truffaut's prose is as direct, supple, witty, offhand, morally intense, energetic, personal, sympathetic, febrile, angry, mercurial, and intelligent as his camera. The handwritten collage on p. 331 of the English edition confirms that most of the handwritten letters and journals in the films are in his hand. For those of us who love the man and his films and do understandably silly things like visiting his grave and his apartments and dream of phoning him, they are a posthumous gift to treasure.

JULES AND JIM (1961): WHEN WE SPEAK OF FREEDOM AND **LOVE AND DEATH**

> A thing happened to me that usually happens to men.
> MIRIAM HOPKINS, *DESIGN FOR LIVING*

—

Ann Beattie includes *Jules and Jim* in her 1976 short story "The Lawn Party."

> "Do you remember your accident?" he says.
> "No," I say.
> "Excuse me," Banks says.
> "I remember thinking of *Jules and Jim*."
> "Where she drove off the cliff?" Banks says, very excited.
> "Umm."
> "When did you think that?"
> "As it was happening."
> "Wow," says Banks. "I wonder if anybody else flashed on that before you?"
> "I couldn't say."[1]

I'm guessing that Beattie found the film appealing for the same reasons as the rest of her generation and mine. Banks, after all, assumes that others have seen it and might have "flashed" on the same scene, though she makes him misremember the ruined bridge as a cliff. The film's open attitude to sexuality and its inattention to accepted morality was a harbinger of the sexual norms of the late 1960s, at least in the younger generation. That a strong woman set the sexual *ronde* in motion appealed to the nascent feminism of the period as did the diminishing interest in parents and nuclear families. Catherine's first and perhaps only responsibility, despite her daughter with Jules, is to herself. I also wouldn't discount the appeal of the film's view of war as a stupidly tragic waste in which people's loyalties to nations trumped their more immediate human loyalties to friends and lovers. World War Two and Korea were recent memories, France was in the process of disengagement from Algeria, and America was stumbling tragically and cynically into Vietnam. Finally, it's a romantic film and the young of the era breathed the optimism of romanticism as if it were the truth. Beattie doesn't mention *Two English Girls*, but the speaker's problem and the story's narrative owe as much to that film as to *Jules and Jim*: he married Mary but was in love with her sister Patricia. It is Patricia who drives his car off the highway, killing herself and leaving him, a painter, minus an arm.

    I watch *Jules and Jim* too often, and I've noticed that since the mid-1990s, when I was in my fifth decade and my marriage had ended and another overheated relationship flamed out like a meteor, though with more collateral damage, my view of Catherine has gradually become more ambivalent, even critical. Thinking about this shift in the flow of my sympathy, I realized that I was accepting the common-sense view that we tend to respond very differently to some aspects of films in youth, adulthood, and old age. In the 1960s there was something exhilarating, fascinating, and attractive about Catherine's impatience with convention and the barriers between her desires and their realization: of course we can have it all. There was even a Catherine avatar in university, always just out of reach when, perhaps especially when, she sat next to me. In those days I would have nodded in sympathy with James Salter's desire "to write about people who cannot modify themselves to reality, whose life looks like no one else's, people who stain your life."[2] Catherine was one of these. She has the purity of a natural force, and her suicide and murder of Jim are engraved with the stamp of authentic being, of someone who wanted, to quote Walter Pater, "to burn always with this hard, gem-like flame, to maintain this ecstasy"[3] rather than surrender to a life of habit. When you're in your early twenties it's easy to sentimentalize death and to forget that Pater, an Oxford don, was a closet homosexual who wanted to live as long as possible with his sister and mother as safe and snug as a gay nun in a convent. Oscar Wilde turned Pater's words into acts, and we know the rest of *his* story. In my sixties, I tend to be more open to Dwight Macdonald's unease with Catherine: "A central difficulty of *Jules and Jim* is the nature of Catherine. Is she a free spirit, generously giving herself to life as it corporealizes itself from time to time in men, courageously living by an ethic superior to the usual bourgeois one which demands some fidelity, or at least continuity in sexual relations? Or is she a monster of selfish whim, without affective contact with others, and therefore ready to destroy her lover, and herself, when she is about to conclusively lose him?"[4] Had Truffaut been honest, he might have answered, following Flaubert, "Catherine, c'est moi." (We know he identified with Emma Bovary when he read the novel.) But that wouldn't have answered Macdonald's question. He would still have wanted to know what kind of self and life Catherine would consider satisfactory.

Truffaut was twenty-nine when the film appeared. Married with two children, he must have realized that in temperament he was closer to Catherine and Jim than to Jules (and Madeleine). He probably read the novel through the filter of his own life, the way that we always read novels that enter us, as Lawrence says, "along the blood." Given how much of his emotional (that is, sexual) life was covert, he knew that a catastrophe of some sort was just a matter of time. Every serious adulterer does. Not necessarily a car going off a ruined bridge, but nevertheless heading straight for a fall. *Two English Girls* (1971), a thematic sequel, offers a more direct representation of Truffaut's dilemma – the story of a man in love with two women – and a softer resolution. No wonder he loved these novels. There must have been occasions when he almost believed that he had written them himself or would have written something like them had he decided to be a novelist not a filmmaker. They simultaneously addressed his life and gave voice to a central concern in his films: the destructive power of love even as it opens doors to rooms we didn't know existed. He might have said, I read and filmed these books to stave off heartbreak while trying to justify myself. The margins of his working copies of Roché's novels look like the densely overwritten page proofs of Proust's *À la Recherche du temps perdu*. His notes are a personal palimpsest in a continuing dialogue with Roché that is simultaneously an argument with himself.

Watching Catherine's catlike teasing of Jules and Jim two generations later, in the twenty-first century, I find the attraction diminished – though

Catherine (Jeanne Moreau) and Jim (Henri Serre) in a playful moment (*Jules and Jim*, 1961).

not the fascination. I'm more aware of her selfishness, thoughtlessness, and neurotic compulsion, her sisterhood with Lawrence's Gudrun Brangwen in *Women in Love* or Anthony Powell's Pamela Flitton in the *Dance to the Music of Time*. She's too close to someone I knew, another high-maintenance woman who regularly made 180-degree turns on the emotional highway. Truffaut reincarnated Catherine both in the black comedy of *Such a Gorgeous Kid like Me* as the provocatively named Camille Bliss and in *The Man Who Loved Women* as Delphine, a histrionic and sexually exciting woman who enjoys sex only if it involves some degree of danger. Bertrand is at first attracted to her but quickly becomes anxious about her unusual demands. After she shoots her husband, he begins to fear her amorality. Part of Truffaut's problem with Catherine is that she is simply a more powerful screen presence than the passive Jules and the stoic and inexpressive Jim. In retrospect, their names seem to be in the title only provisionally. She steals the film and overbalances it in the direction of her view that self-fulfilment and self-creation through love trump every virtue and value. Truffaut gambles that her radical discontinuities of feeling will not overwhelm the sense of order and decorum – the always threatened tranquillity – created by the camera's slow, fluid movement, the careful composition of the longer scenes, the men's friendship, and the generally positive effect of the upbeat lyrical score. Even her song "Le Tourbillon de la vie" ("The Whirlwind of Life") suggests a dance at the same time as its words point to disorder and dissolution. The lyrics and the guitar pull in opposite directions.

That the two men accept her unspoken high valuation of herself makes it difficult to avoid being caught up in her aura. Jim, for instance, tells Jules that "all the things Catherine does, she does fully, one by one. She is a force of nature, she expresses herself in cataclysms … guided by her conviction of her own innocence." And again: "I wonder if she is really made for having a husband and children. I am afraid she will be never he happy on this earth. She is an apparition for all to appreciate, perhaps, but not a woman for any one man." He is describing without judgment from within the eye of the hurricane. And yet there is something ominous in "her conviction of her own innocence," though we may miss it the first time we see the film. In her own way, Catherine is as lovesick as Adèle Hugo. At the end of *her* movie, Adèle passes Lieutenant Pinson, "the love of her life," without seeing him. Catherine, who in the later scenes wears glasses like Adèle, no longer sees Jules or Jim: what she sees is her reflection in their words, attitudes, and acts. In her heart she is singing with Tristan and Isolde, "I myself am the world." Like a demanding Ishtar, she stops valuing Jules's love when she finds it an insufficient sacrifice to what she considers appropriate. At that point she turns to Jim before abandoning him for a similar failure. I thought of her recently while watching William Wyler's underrated *Dodsworth* (1936), when Walter Huston says to his estranged wife "Love has to stop somewhere short of suicide." Few, except Catherine, would disagree. The problem for novelists and filmmakers is that death is a very convenient way to lend emotional depth and resonance to a character and a love affair, not to mention that it helps end a story with a sense of closure. It is a good example of a thematic and formal convention overriding our expectation of truth to life. It offers instead something that might be called truth to an emotion. There are moments, as we sense a relationship disappearing into a sinkhole, when the thought of suicide cannot be willed away. Truffaut's major relationships usually hint at its presence. Remember Antoine Doinel's answer to the question "How do you know that you're in love?" – "You feel self-destructive." Thinking about the ending of *Jules and Jim*, it is worth remembering that the woman on whom Roché based Catherine – Helen Hessel – lived into old age and wrote Truffaut an appreciative letter after seeing the film. She had outlived both men. There is a photograph of her in *Correspondence 1945–1984*.

Catherine is the first of Truffaut's heroines to raise the problem of what choice one should make between what he later calls definitive and provisional love. The most explicit expression of this comes at the unsettling ending of *Stolen Kisses* in a scene Truffaut described in 1975 as showing one of his favourite themes: the permanent and the temporary. The recently engaged Christine and Antoine are sitting on a park bench when a stranger in a tan raincoat approaches them and immediately addresses Christine.

> Mademoiselle, I know that you are aware of me. For a long time I watched you secretly. But for the past few days I stopped hiding, and now I know that the moment has come. You see, before discovering you, I'd never loved anybody. But between us, things will be different. We shall be the example. We shall never leave each other ... not even for an hour. I don't work and have no responsibilities in life. You

will be my sole preoccupation. I understand that this is too sudden for you to say yes at once ... that you would first have to break off your provisional attachments to provisional people. For I am definitive. [*The man steps back and still staring at Christine, pauses*] I am very happy.

As he walks away, Christine whispers to Antoine, "That guy is completely nuts." He replies, "I suppose he is." The man may be troubled but what he says about love is relevant to almost all of Truffaut's films. More immediately, his dismissal of "provisional attachments to provisional people" sounds a distant alarm about whether the rootless, immature, and provisional Antoine is capable of making the definitive commitment to Christine required by marriage. The answer comes quickly in *Bed and Board*: as with Madeleine and François, the wife is capable of this form of definitive love, the husband isn't. Unfortunately "definitive love" is even more problematic than it seems. The concept is attached not only to characters like Christine or Muriel in *Two English Girls*, it also takes a disturbing neurotic form in Catherine, the Stranger, Adèle Hugo, Julien Davenne, and Mathilde Bauchard, all of whom are obsessive and self-destructive. In some cases, they will choose death or madness in order to be definitive. The high-maintenance Catherine is their patron saint.

Ronald Bergan's *Jean Renoir: Projections of Paradise* describes an event from life that reminds us that scenes like the one between Christine Charbon and the Stranger aren't confined to art. As Madeleine Morgenstern and Dido Renoir were lunching in Hollywood in 1985 "a youngish man at another table came over to Dido, who was then in her late seventies [and said], 'Excuse me, but I was listening to you, and you seem to me an exceptional person.' He didn't know who she was, but made a platonic declaration of love. After he left, Dido said 'He's mad, he's mad that man.'"[5] Maybe he was just a Renoir and Truffaut fan who confused life and art. Did Dido know that she was in a scene from a Truffaut film and quoting Christine Charbon? Madeleine did.

Time to return to *Jules and Jim*. Catherine isn't the film's only connection to Truffaut's other work. *Jules and Jim* is a seedbed of future lines, images, and motifs. I will cite just a few. Its opening lines, spoken by a woman against a black screen, anticipate key lines in *The Last Metro* and *The Woman Next Door*: "You said to me I love you. I said to you: wait." Jim's visits to the graveyards of the Great War to find fallen comrades are recalled in *The Green Room*. The pregnant Catherine could be writing for her sister Adèle when she writes to Jim, "This paper is your skin, this ink is my blood. I am pressing hard so that it may enter in." Adèle, it's worth noting, fakes a pregnancy. Both women, in a manner of speaking, lose their child. The film's closing voiceover summary is paraphrased in Mme Jouve's last words in *The Woman Next Door*: "The ashes were collected in urns and put into a pigeon-hole which was then sealed. If he had been alone, Jules would have mixed them together. Catherine had always wished hers to be scattered to the winds from the top of the hill … but was not allowed." Mme Jouve would like to bury the adulterous Bernard and Mathilde together – "Neither with you nor without you" – but understands this is not possible. Noticing these sorts of details, I always have the impression that Truffaut's films end only to open up again when others in the body of work extend them by recapitulating and recasting their themes and situations and finding new characters to reincarnate the old. That Truffaut does this self-consciously is evident from his comments about how often he pairs films in order to explore the same theme antithetically. "*The Soft Skin* was a film which said to intellectuals 'You liked *Jules and Jim* too much, this will make you think that love is like that, but love is also sordid, terrible…' Similarly *Such a Gorgeous Kid like Me* is a reaction away from the solemn reflective intensities *Two English Girls*."[6]

One of the major continuities is the interest in women and the presence of strong female characters – what I call Truffaut's neglected feminist side. It's remarkable how many of the films depend on independent or rebellious females: *The 400 Blows, Shoot the Piano Player, Jules and Jim, The Bride Wore Black, Mississippi Mermaid, Two English Girls, Such a Gorgeous Kid like Me, The Last Metro,* and *Confidentially Yours*. There are also strong women in minor parts in other films. All refuse to define themselves by conventional gender expectations. Some, like Catherine or Camille Bliss, are Nietzschean in their determination. Scenes dropped from *Jules and Jim* and *The Story of Adèle H.* show that Truffaut knew precisely what he was up to. The earlier film originally contained a scene, cut during editing, showing a journalist wanting to interview Catherine because she is among the first women to drive a car. Never one to waste a good idea, Truffaut wrote a similar scene for Adèle; the journalist's motive this time is the fact that she is the first woman to cross the Atlantic alone. The scene also did not survive the final cut. He probably decided the point didn't need underlining.

Truffaut was a woman's director. Like Catherine, many of his central figures are willful, confident, high-maintenance women who, ironically, help him explore some of his own problems with sexuality and relationships by questioning and redefining the nature and limits of the relationship. *Ces femmes sont moi* would not be out of place as an epigraph to his body of work.

ERIC ROHMER'S
LA COLLECTIONNEUSE (1967)
AND *JULES AND JIM*

"Rohmer is perhaps the only person in the film world
whom I trust."

FRANÇOIS TRUFFAUT[1]

—

Sometimes I think *La Collectionneuse* (*The Collector*) is Rohmer's comic answer to *Jules and Jim*, his suggestion that the story of an independent woman who "collects" men doesn't have to end tragically. Haydée, his heroine, moves easily, sensuously, and without much erotic interest from one young man to another. The prologue shows her bikinied and walking from left to right then right to left along a beach. Each time she stops, the camera, held by Nestor Almendros, pauses on different parts of her young, firm, and attractive body. It's as if Rohmer wants the male viewer to understand what the nearly anonymous men she goes out with see in her, at least at first glance or gaze. The two she stays with at a large country house in southern France are Daniel – an artist with a slight resemblance to Jules – and the taller and more handsome Adrien, who, if he had black hair and a moustache, could pass for Jim's brother.

Rohmer indicated in an interview that he'd had the idea for the film since 1949; when he finally came to shoot it on the usual minimal early *nouvelle vague* budget, he went along with the actors' suggestion that the characters be based on them and the script on their own words. Almost all the scenes were shot in one take either inside or outside the house. The ending depends on a missed rendezvous. Haydée is distracted from her appointment with Adrien when she meets two young men on their way to Rome. When she doesn't show up, Adrien decides to drive back to the house. We are left to assume that Haydée went to Italy with the strangers. Left alone, Adrien realizes that he misses his girlfriend, who is modelling in London. Daniel, frustrated earlier with the triangle and Haydée's other involvements, has gone to visit friends.

Of the three, Haydée is the most sympathetic, partly because she is also the least assertive. Like Catherine (and Arletty) she is what she is. While the two men never tire of trying to define their way of life, she does so only reluctantly when prodded by them. There's a much darker version of this type of woman in Agnes Varda's *Vagabond* (1985), in which the hitchhiking drifter doesn't seem to be looking for anything or anywhere in particular, except perhaps unconsciously for death. She's on the road but she's not on the run. If she's interested in freedom, it is freedom from rather than freedom for. If she were Melville's Bartleby the scrivener and someone asked why she is hitchhiking, she would respond "Because I prefer to." *La Collectionneuse* opened in only one theatre in Paris, but it played for months and sold 70,000 tickets. Rohmer covered his costs. Just for comparison: *The 400 Blows* sold 450,000; *Breathless* 380,000; and *Hiroshima, mon amour* 255,000.

On 16 January 2010, there was an announcement in the morning paper of Rohmer's death at eighty-nine. In the afternoon, prodded by a friend, I went to see James Cameron's expensive spectacle *Avatar* and couldn't help thinking that a one-minute sequence in it probably cost more than all of Rohmer's films. A detail that nails the contrast between two approaches to cinema: at the end of each day's filming Rohmer made tea for the cast and crew. After they left, he swept the set. Cameron's digital generation wouldn't understand the moral integrity of that act. Truffaut's defense of Rohmer in 1974 against an intemperate and stupid attack by Jean-Louis Bory is today a finely measured elegy: "Unlike you and me, Rohmer has always refused to attend film festivals and he has never cared to appear on television: he is a man of unshakeable integrity, of a logical and rigorous intellect, yes, we have to accept this idea because it's true: the best French film-maker is both the most intelligent and the most sincere. His success is as well-deserved as that of Ingmar Bergman. I hope you agree."[2] The generosity of spirit here radiates in two directions – toward the offensive Bory, whom Truffaut refuses to counter-attack, and toward Rohmer, the senior statesman of the New Wave. It is also, of course, a self-criticism of the various compromises Truffaut initiated to gain the independence he needed to make his films. He is willing to sacrifice something of himself in order to praise Rohmer. This is not the only time he does this in his letters and articles.

Rohmer's real name, by the way, was Jean-Marie Maurice Schérer. When not making films, he read Balzac and Hugo.

JULIAN BARNES'S *TALKING IT OVER* (1991) AND *JULES AND JIM*

Barnes has written about Truffaut twice that I know of: first a typically elegant, sympathetic, and perceptive review of the letters in 1990 in *The New York Review of Books* and the following year in the novel *Talking It Over*, whose triangular love plot involves several allusions to *Jules and Jim*. For instance, Stuart says that hanging out with his wife Gillian and his friend Oliver was like the French film in which the two men and woman go bicycling together. And after Gillian leaves him for Oliver, the latter also compares their relationship to the one in the film. These references suggest that the reader should keep the film in view while following the novel's three characters, Stuart (Jules), Gillian (Catherine), and Oliver (Jim). Considering the general paucity of cultural allusions in the novel, I find it difficult not to assume that Barnes wants us alert to possible comparisons in the internal dialogue he has set up with Truffaut. The film's tragic ending lends a borrowed weight of expectation to the novel's plot: will something similar happen to Oliver and Gillian or to Stuart and Gillian when the distraught Stuart moves across the street from the couple in the south of France? His arrival is ominous, but Barnes wisely swerves away from violence.

The problem with allusions is that they always imply comparisons, and sometimes the work invoked is more substantial and interesting in every way than its host. When I finished *Talking It Over* my first and admittedly ungenerous thought was that Truffaut's film will be around in the next generation but I have my doubts about the novel. Barnes told an interviewer "I always resist the idea that *Talking It Over* is a *hommage* or a reworking of *Jules and Jim*. When it comes in, it's a sort of necessary joke, it's a passing allusion … a sort of wink."[1] This sounds like a slightly defensive and late postemptive strike at readers who quite rightly took the allusion as the novel's invitation to read it in exactly the way that Barnes claims he rejects. Most of us wink in the hope that it will have consequences. In the context it's ironic that Truffaut is one of the few major artists I can think of who is always willing to acknowledge that what he has borrowed is more than just a "wink." Like Godard, he didn't suffer from the anxiety of influence. For both it stimulated creativity and they took pleasure in it. They made reference, allusion, and quotation into a filmic art.

SALMAN RUSHDIE'S
THE GROUND BENEATH HER FEET
(1999) AND *JULES AND JIM*

"Je suis comme je suis."
ARLETTY, *CHILDREN OF PARADISE*
—

There's an interesting brief summary of Truffaut's film in *The Ground beneath Her Feet*, a novel I didn't like when it was published and left unfinished until my son and daughter insisted I go back to it. I did, and after forty pages couldn't understand why I had given up on it. Now it's among my favourite Rushdies – *Midnight's Children*, *Shame*, and *Shalimar the Clown*. Rushdie is so prodigiously inventive, in ways that recall Balzac, Dickens, and García Márquez, and offers such a bazaar of pleasures, including what he calls "the high jewellery work of the writer's language,"[1] that his novels can carry a weakness or twenty that those of most other contemporary writers like Thomas Pynchon, Martin Amis, or Roberto Bolaño can't. I can overlook much when a single page offers me "Islam, that least huggable of faiths" and the sophisticated linguistic eros of "Ava, that palindromic goddess who looked just as good from the back as she did from the front."[2] The latter brought back memories of a childhood discussion with my movie-magazine-reading mother about whether Rita or Ava was more beautiful. She couldn't make up her mind.

Jules and Jim is part of a rich background of references to songs, books, and films of the 1950s and '60s interwoven into the story of Vina Aspara and Ormus Cama, a singer and composer-musician, respectively, who become international stars: think of the Eurythmics. The novel is narrated by the third member of the love triangle, a photographer named Rai whose field of cultural and historical reference is conveniently almost coextensive with Rushdie's, though the author provides a book-long puzzle by following Joyce's *Ulysses* in letting his hero make mistakes we're intended to spot: *Catch-18*, for instance, conflates Joseph Heller's *Catch-22* and Leon Uris's once popular *Mila 18*, though it may also be a wink at the original title of Heller's novel. The following is the passage that looks to *Jules and Jim*:

> A great movie star has tragically died. She was in love with two friends, who told her that her face, her smile, put them in mind of an ancient carving. They quarrelled over her. At length, after lunch in a small café, she took one of the friends for a ride in her car and deliberately drove straight off the end of a washed-out bridge, into the water. Both of them were killed. The other man, still seated at the café table, watched his beloved and his friend vanish forever.
>
> Not long before dying, the actress made a hit record, accompanying herself on acoustic guitar. Now the record is playing constantly, the first French song to zoom up the British charts, paving the way for Françoise Hardy and others. Ormus, whose French is poor, strains to understand the lyrics.
>
> Everyone to his taste, turning, turning in the whirlpool of life?[3]

By the time we read this passage, we're ready to see Vina as an Indian Catherine, Ormus as Jim (though he doesn't die with her), and Rai as the Jules who survives them to tell their story. The "whirlpool of life" is an allusion in English to the French "Le Tourbillon," the song Catherine sings to Jules, Jim, and her lover Albert in the second part of the film. An earlier description of Vina also fits Catherine: "Dionysiac goddesses: that's closer to my personal experience. What I know about Vina. Vina, who came to us from abroad, who laid waste to all she saw, who conquered and devastated every heart. Vina as female Dionysus. Vina, the first bacchante.

That, I could buy." If Vina is a "female Dionysus," then so is Catherine. In calling her both the god and a "bacchante," Rushdie perceptively recognizes that Vina, like Catherine, worships at her own shrine.

Rushdie makes two other nods in Truffaut's direction. In the opening pages of the still controversial *The Satanic Verses* (1988) the fall of two characters from the sky is compared to the fall of the child in *Small Change* (it's just a wink, nothing more). And in his memoir *Joseph Anton* (2012) he mentions listening to Jeanne Moreau affectionately remembering Truffaut and Malle at a dinner party in London on the occasion of her seventieth birthday.[4]

TRUFFAUT
IN AND OUT OF HIS TIME

> There is no evidence that [D.W. Griffith] took the slightest
> interest in new developments in literature, painting, music.
> RICHARD SCHICKEL[1]
> —

Truffaut spent more than three decades, between 1950 and 1984, amid the social, political, and cultural ferment of Parisian life and came out untouched by most of its best-known ideologies and intellectual movements, especially those associated with the Parisian *maîtres à penser* who set in motion structuralism, deconstruction, and cultural theory. On the evidence of Truffaut's films and archives, one wouldn't guess that Roland Barthes, Jacques Lacan, Michel Foucault, Louis Althusser, Jacques Derrida, or their weaker epigones had published anything. Sartre is the only thinker on his radar but less as a philosopher than as a novelist, journalist, and political activist. Marguerite Duras and Alain Robbe-Grillet, the *nouveau roman* writers most closely associated with film, are barely noticed either as filmmakers or novelists. It's worth noting that Truffaut and Derrida are very near contemporaries; the philosopher was born in Algeria in 1930 two years before Truffaut, and yet they seem to belong to different French generations. Neither mentions the other.

Truffaut's outsider status extends to his lack of interest in contemporary film. Rainer Werner Fassbinder, Werner Herzog, Margarethe von Trotta, Wim Wenders (a fan), Andrei Tarkovsky, Martin Scorsese, and Francis Coppola leave almost no trace in his writing, films, or life. His

English, French, and foreign touchstones remain the films of his youth. Late Truffaut, like late Titian or Renoir, enters the studio in order to turn back toward essentials and away from contemporary distractions. The move confirms his description of himself as a man whose eyes are always on the past, one who loves films "which have a connection with the nineteenth century, that is to say which pursue the same goals, Stendhal, let's say."[2] Though he lived a representative modern life – what is more modern than film? – Truffaut thought of himself as a man of the past, a child of the nineteenth and early twentieth centuries – a combination of Balzac, Stendhal, Paul Léautaud, Renoir, and Bazin. He extends this judgment to Léaud, whom he describes as "a young man of the nineteenth century" and remarks on "his anachronism and romanticism."[3] Distinguishing himself from Godard, he acutely points out that in his first twelve films, "Godard never alludes to the past, even in the dialogue … not once does a Godard character speak about his parents or his childhood."[4] What this means is that Godard, not Truffaut, is the filmmaker of modern life, to use the title of Baudelaire's famous essay.

As I said, the earthquake of critical theory that shook France in the second half of the twentieth century left him untouched. If he's modern, he's not quite contemporary. In fact, his estrangement from his time and his use of eros and childhood as forms of evasion are sometimes troubling. Like a Greek or Roman Stoic he seems to have achieved a sort of *ataraxia* (equanimity, imperturbability) toward everything from faddish ideas and orthodoxies of dissent at one end to political issues at the other in order to place a wall between the world and his life and art.

CARLOS SAURA
ON *THE SOFT SKIN* (1964),
OBLIQUELY

In an interview included on the *Cria Cuervos* ("Raise Ravens") DVD, Saura comments that "[i]t's the trickiest part. If you choose the wrong actors, you'll ruin the film." Truffaut probably thought something like this every time he remembered Jean Desailly, the male lead in *The Soft Skin*, who refused to play the role with the emotional restraint his director wanted. Desailly thought of his character, contra Truffaut, as a romantic hero. As a result Truffaut tended to blame the film's failure on himself and his lead. Richard Brody's brief but very positive notice in *The New Yorker* five decades later might have brought a smile to Truffaut's face, though he would probably have placed the review in the file labelled "Where Were You When I Needed You?": "François Truffaut's wrenching 1964 drama of adultery and its repercussions is a master work of erotic frenzy, humiliation and self-loathing. Just as his own marriage was breaking up, he filmed (in his family's apartment) the story of Pierre, a married middle-aged editor and internationally celebrated author who, on a lecture tour in Lisbon, meets Nicole (Françoise Dorléac), a young blond stewardess with whom he embarks on a furious affair."[1] This is one of those times when I think that the reviewer and I have seen different films with the same title. I recognize the references to "a kind of visual music ... rapid camera moves, desperate point-of-view shots, and frozen gestures" but their cumulative effect on me is the opposite of their effect on the writer. I should add that the usually reliable Dwight Macdonald also liked the film and even praised Desailly. During the filming, Truffaut and the actor had at best a polite relationship. As I said, Truffaut wanted him to play Pierre Lachenay as an ordinary man while Desailly, a veteran star of stage and screen, carried the aura of a practiced lover. Neither could have known that in 1979, two years after Truffaut's *The Man Who Loved Women*, Desailly would star in *Le Cavaleur* (the wolf or womanizer), the original title of Bertrand Morane's memoir. Desailly died in 2008 at the age of eighty-eight. His distinguished career on stage continued to the end.

THE AUTEUR
AND THE EMPTY ROOM

> After all, film directors are like prostitutes under a bridge,
> hiding their faces and calling out to customers.
> YASUJIRO OZU[1]

At least seven of Truffaut's twenty-one films faltered with the critics and at the box office, though according to Marcel Berbert Les Films du Carrosse never actually lost money in the long run on a Truffaut film. As is the case with Woody Allen's films, foreign receipts usually compensated for a small box office at home. In the 1960s Truffaut didn't have a hit between *Jules and Jim* in 1961 and *Stolen Kisses* in 1968. Despite the semi-independent status he had achieved by forming a production company, he always knew that a series of financial setbacks would mean dependence on producers and studios. Perhaps his greatest disappointment came with the failure of *Two English Girls* in 1971. Given the critical and popular success of *Jules and Jim*, he had every reason to anticipate a similar response to a colour film, also based on a novel by Roché, about a love triangle. It didn't happen. The film's failure was probably the greatest disappointment of his career after *Shoot the Piano Player*. Given that he was just recovering from a breakdown after the end of his relationship with Catherine Deneuve, it couldn't have come at a worse time. That it was followed a year later by the failure of what I take to be his worst film, *Such a Gorgeous Kid like Me*, compounded an already precarious financial situation. The Oscar-winning *Day for Night* (1973) saved him. Without it he would have had only one hit – *Small Change* (1976) between *Bed and Board* in 1970 and *Love on the Run* in 1979, both of them minor instalments of the Doinel cycle, though I must confess that the last is a favourite. *Day for Night* also allowed him to shrug off the disaster of *The Green Room* two years later, though if that had been a success it is doubtful he would have made *Love on the Run*. When the press asked him to comment on *The Green Room*, he quipped that, given the absence of an audience, he should have titled it "The Empty Room."

Truffaut's response to what Saura, another director with his share of films without an audience, calls "a disaster" was always to get back to work as soon as possible. He was canny and desperate enough to bring Antoine Doinel out of retirement on two occasions. In his last two years, despite the popularity of *The Last Metro*, he was considering doing so again. Faced with failure, he might have consoled himself with the fact that, despite the international success of *La Grande Illusion*, Renoir had never been a popular director either in France or America. He joked that with each failure he had to sell another painting by his father to finance the next film. Truffaut, like Renoir, was a likeable man who wanted to be liked. You could say that the international success of *The 400 Blows* had spoiled him. He always had a sneaking suspicion – it indicated a fundamental self-doubt – that the audience just might be right when it stayed away from a film. Four years after *Breathless*, Godard's *Les Carabiniers* had a total box office of three thousand tickets in Paris. Despite that, I can't imagine Godard worrying about the size of the audience. If anything, failure made him more defiant. By contrast, Truffaut's concern left him vulnerable and more cautious, even conservative, when considering new projects.

Saura is particularly interesting on disasters in an interview he gave in 1996. Discussing *La Noche Oscura* (1989), his film about St John of the Cross, he describes it as "the worst disaster of my life ... a disaster I am very, very proud of. They say that disasters are useful because you learn from them. That's a lie. You don't learn anything. What happens is that you stay perplexed because you don't know what the reasons for such a disaster could have been."[2] Saura doesn't mention that the failure of a film about the poet-saint followed the failure of *El Dorado* (1988), the most expensive film he ever made. With a Rossellini-like resilience he bounced back with six films in the next six years, including one of his greatest hits, *Ay, Carmela*, in 1990. Saura and Truffaut are exact contemporaries.

Each shot his first important film in 1959. The Spaniard's black and white *Los Golfos* (delinquents or "*mistons*") represents as much a break in subject and style with Spanish films as Truffaut's *The 400 Blows* does with French. *Cria Cuervos* (1975) and *Elisa, Vida Mia* (*Elisa, My Life* 1976) are his masterpieces. His late style, from 1990 on, shows a restless artist taking on any project that in some way gives expression to an aspect of himself whether music (*Tango*) or important mentors like Jorge Luis Borges, Goya, and Buñuel, about whom he made idiosyncratic films in 1990, 1999, and 2001. He proceeds on two assumptions: if something interests him deeply, it has a good chance of interesting others. On the other hand, he also believes that "The truth is that cinema is not made for the general audience. First it can't be and then it shouldn't be."[3] Truffaut wouldn't have understood the second.

Truffaut's range of interests wasn't as wide as Saura's or even wide enough to ensure a Saura-like late turn toward a new style. Renoir fashioned such a turn in the 1950s but he moved into the future by looking into a rearview mirror filled with turn-of-the-century images and subjects. A similar temptation to turn to the past – and to expose himself to the charge of nostalgia – is already evident in Truffaut with *The Last Metro*, which shows him marking time. There is little in his papers to indicate the possibility of paths not previously taken. I will return to this below.

As usual Suzanne Schiffman gets it right when she says that "With François, the most important thing was to tell a story and to tell it clearly while arousing the pleasure and interest of the spectator."[4] It's worth recalling that she also speaks of Truffaut's films as confessions. For Truffaut, when the audience rejected a film, it also rejected him.

MEETING JEANNE MOREAU IN VENICE

In his *Lettre ouverte à François Truffaut* the novelist Eric Neuhoff describes seeing Truffaut in Paris during summer 1983.

> It was during 1983. You were two rows in front of me in one of the small halls of the Empire – Violine or Corail? – where they screened for the press an English documentary about Charles Chaplin. I examined the top of your head which struck out above the seat. I was a few metres from François Truffaut. You seemed tired. You wore a silk scarf. You whispered something to your neighbour. The lights dimmed.
>
> Walking out, I didn't dare to approach you. How could I have known that I was seeing you for the first and last time?
>
> In my address book, at the letter T, there is a telephone number that I was assured is yours. I never called it. I have never erased it.[1]

My near version of this took place on Wednesday, 17 July 1996, in Venice. I was there for two months teaching a seminar on fiction at the university. My class was at the Palazzo Zorzi, about a twenty-minute walk from my apartment, which was across the canal from the Academy. There's a photograph of Gore Vidal in a gondola – in his book on Venice – a few steps from where I was staying. The class met daily in the early afternoon. The full-time members of the English department avoided me – not unusual in Italy – but the students were lively and hospitable. We went after each class to a café, and one student, Rosa Maria Plevano, invited me to visit her home in Vicenza. Her mother had translated Northrop Frye's *Anatomy of Criticism* into Italian: for that alone there should be a statue of her on one of the smaller piazzas.

On the 17th, having arrived early for class, I decided to relax in the shaded cloister of the Greek Orthodox Church across the way, San Giorgio dei Greci. The black iron barred gate was open, I went in. There were two other people there, about forty yards across the lawn, and as I got closer I realized that the small woman with the lined though not yet harrowed face sitting down and being photographed by a much younger man with very long black hair was Moreau. Looking at her I sensed I was seeing her through the filter of some of the more memorable characters she had portrayed in Malle, Antonioni, Buñuel, and Truffaut: she was both herself and this gallery of women I had seen many times. It was like the night Elle and I found ourselves in a Toronto Cajun restaurant sitting at a table next to Christopher Plummer – and he was Plummer and all the characters I had seen him play since Macbeth at Stratford in 1962. Moreau wore a very loose white linen blouse, a long cotton skirt with a vaguely patterned floral design in Mediterranean blue and citrus yellow, and a bandana in the same pattern. Sitting on a stone bench against a faded mottled pink stone wall, she was an image out of a painting by Raoul Dufy. It didn't hurt that it was a warm sunny day or that her companion was good looking and could have passed for a Roma.

I immediately decided to speak to her, though not to ask for her autograph – that would have been *de trop* since I felt in my heart of hearts that I had known her for three decades. I walked around for five minutes rehearsing my speech in slow and uncertain high-school French learned in Niagara Falls in the early 1960s from Miss Nancy Gibbs, Mr Fred Downing, and the unforgettably flamboyant Mademoiselle Stauffer. I introduced myself as a fan of the New Wave, Truffaut in particular, and told her that I had seen many of her films and admired especially *La Notte*, *Jules and Jim*, and *Diary of a Chambermaid* ... and so on. She said working with Truffaut was one of the great pleasures of her life. I said something about the concentration of talent in European film at that time, and she agreed, adding that it was an unforgettable era. When I named some of the directors she had worked with – Malle, Truffaut, Buñuel, Ophuls, Welles – she said that they were all unforgettable and very different. I know we spoke of other things, but I was so in awe of being with her in a cloister in Venice that I remembered very little afterward. I thanked her for all the pleasure her films had given me. She held out her hand casually and yet regally and smiled again. I walked out of the cloister blushing and feeling like a teenager who had just declared his love. As I crossed the narrow street to the Palazzo Zorzi and my class, I remembered from her biography that her mother was English and that she is bilingual. *Merde, merde, merde.*

Two days later as I was stepping out of the Church of Saint Zaccarias, where I had stopped to see once again Giovanni Bellini's "Pala de San Zaccaria," she and the photographer were walking slowly toward me arms entwined. We noticed each other almost simultaneously. She inclined her head slightly, gave me a smile and a "Bonjour." I responded. We passed by. Venice in the summer sun, a Bellini painting, and Moreau saying hello to *me* left me glowing and smiling. I went to a café for an olive and anchovy sandwich and a glass of Pino Grigio.

When I met Moreau I didn't think of the scene in the early pages of Walker Percy's *The Moviegoer* in which Binx Bolling sees William Holden. Binx is strolling like a *flaneur* down Canal Street in New Orleans and, seeing Holden, suddenly has an illumination about the effect such meetings have on most of us. "Holden has turned down Toulouse shedding light as he goes. An aura of heightened reality moves with him and all who fall within it feel it. Now everyone is aware of him. He creates a regular eddy among the tourists and barkeeps and B-girls who come running to the doors of the joints. I am attracted to movie stars but not for the usual reasons. I have no desire to speak to Holden or get his autograph. It is their peculiar reality which astounds me."[2] Binx, like Percy, has a Kierkegaardian bent and worries about despair and its place in daily life. Seeing Holden in "the desert" of New Orleans is a revelation on the path of his search for something to take him beyond "the everydayness of his own life" or at least show the presence of the transcendental within secular

Catherine as Jules (Oskar Werner) probably remembered her.

temporality. He recognizes that for most of us a meeting with someone famous like Holden is a momentarily exciting distraction – "You'll never guess who I saw today" – rather than a moment of significant revelation: it is special but not quite special enough to leave us with a sense of awe or feeling "aweful" in the eighteenth-century sense of the word. It is different from the meeting in the desert with someone whose work or achievement means something to us. To talk to them is dessert in the desert, a transcendent moment of unearned secular grace. By contrast, seeing Rod Stewart a few years earlier prancing self-consciously with his camera in front of the Florence Duomo did nothing for me, though I entered the event in my journal.

Percy's epigraph from Kierkegaard's *The Sickness unto Death* is worth quoting: "the specific character of despair is precisely this: it is unaware of being despair." Does a significant meeting open a door, however briefly, beyond inevitable despair if only by taking us out of a pervasive everydayness that until that moment seemed inescapable? The meeting with Moreau, a charismatic figure, brought me closer to Truffaut and created a sense of aura within the everydayness of my life. As for real despair, to this day I have only a nodding acquaintance with it by way of its less brutal cousin despondence, with which I flirted during the dark 1990s.

TRUFFAUT LOOKS BACK TO GODARD: *FAHRENHEIT 451* (1966) AND *ALPHAVILLE* (1965)

> Now they're burning books.
> OSKAR WERNER, *JULES AND JIM*
> —

There are some echoes here that may be nothing more than mnemonic irrelevance but there's too much exchange between their films of the 1960s for me to let them pass. In Godard, the government of Alphaville is controlled by Von Braun and is gradually removing words deemed useless: love, tenderness, conscience, and so on. *Fahrenheit 451* has a society in which books are banned. In each there are places outside the city where the old words and books are remembered. The private eye Lemmy Caution (Eddie Constantine) comes from the Outlands to Alphaville with Paul Éluard's volume of poems *The City of Pain*. In *Fahrenheit 451* Montag saves a copy of *David Copperfield* while the book people save old books from one generation to the next through memorization. Each film ends with an escape from the city and the promise of a relationship. Natasha's (Anna Karina's) last words to Caution as they drive through the night are "Je vous aime." Truffaut's film ends with the reunion of Montag (Oskar Werner) and Linda (Julie Christie). Both films challenge their societies with words and love. Incidentally, Truffaut's original script has a lovely pun on "des hommes-livres" and "des hommes libres": "book-men" are "free men."

FAHRENHEIT 451
AND
TRUFFAUT'S ENGLISH

Truffaut's decision to direct a movie with an English script is one of the most surprising of his career. Despite several concerted efforts at improvement, his English never progressed beyond basics. Though he was relatively comfortable reading after the mid-1960s, he told Annette Insdorf in 1980, "I still haven't read a novel in English."[1] This raises the question, if he couldn't follow English film dialogue any better than he could everyday speech, how reliable was he as a critic of films in English? His reviews, after all, are responses to French versions, either dubbed or subtitled. The script of *Fahrenheit 451* is credited to "François Truffaut and Jean-Louis Richard, based on the novel by Ray Bradbury." Only a synopsis of the script was published after the film's release. The question that hovers about the film is on whom did Truffaut depend for advice about language – either in the script or when listening to the actors delivering their lines? In neither case could he tell whether the language was natural and idiomatic. My guess is that he fell back on the writers of "additional dialogue," David Rudkin and especially Helen Scott. The bilingual Schiffman had not yet joined the crew.

Although the *Fahrenheit 451* was filmed in England, Truffaut's comments in his letters and the *Journal* suggest that he wasn't thinking of it as set in an England of the near future. In 1970 he told one correspondent that "I made a film entitled *Fahrenheit 451* which portrayed, in a highly critical manner, an imaginary society in which the state would systematically burn every book."² Among the actors considered for Montag were the non-English Paul Newman, Jean-Paul Belmondo, and Charles Aznavour. The choice of Oskar Werner, who speaks English clearly but with a marked accent, nudges the film into a *Mitteleuropa* of the imagination. This was also the intent of the firemen's uniforms which were to suggest Eastern European countries. To me, their caps suggest those of contemporary French firemen. The final scene, in which Montag joins the book-people, shows them reciting books in various languages. Truffaut's notes in the *Journal* make it clear that he wanted to give the ending a polyglot tone: "As in the novel, the men-books would pass among each other while reciting. I hired a Chinese, a Spaniard, a German, a Greek, a Japanese, a Russian, a Norwegian, an Italian, and all had to say some phrases."³ Granted that the majority of the books burned and recited are English, there's still little doubt that Truffaut wanted the viewer to sense that the society is a European dystopia not to be found on any map. By contrast, Bradbury's novel is set in southern California and most of its references are American.

Some other changes of detail and emphasis show Truffaut putting his signature on the film. For instance, by far the longest of the scenes dealing with individuals becoming book-people shows a boy memorizing Robert Louis Stevenson's *The Weir of Hermiston* with the help of a man who is probably his grandfather. We hear the following passage three times: "I do not love my father; I wonder sometimes if I do not hate him. There's my shame; perhaps my sin; at least, and in the sight of God, not my fault." Bradbury refers neither to Stevenson's novel nor to *David Copperfield*, which Montag is shown reading with some intensity earlier in the movie. Like the references to the Brontës, Jacques Audiberti, Jacques Rivette, Jean Genet, and *Cahiers*, these show Truffaut turning Bradbury's novel into a subtly autobiographical film that looks back to the language teacher's question in *The 400 Blows*, "Where is the father?" and forward to Stevenson's photograph in *The Green Room*. Truffaut jettisons much of the historical and political thrust of the novel, which ends with an atomic war. He admits in the *Journal* that the one political gesture he wanted to make was thwarted by his inability to get a book in time. He had heard that Rivette's film of Diderot's anti-Catholic *La Religieuse* (*The Nun*) had been banned in France and wanted to include the novel among the burning books. This is a good example of how the generally apolitical Truffaut inserts politics into a film. Although Bradbury wrote Truffaut to say that he was pleased with the result, I wonder whether he had hoped for something glossier with Hollywood film values and less Truffaut.

He left England as minimally competent in English as he had arrived. He would have recognized himself in Victor Hugo when the poet, who failed to become an English speaker during a nineteen-year exile in Jersey and Guernsey, explained English pronunciation in a letter to a friend: "*Southwark* in those days was pronounced *Soudric*; today, it is pronounced *Sousouorc*, or something like that. Indeed, an excellent method for pronouncing English names is not to pronounce them at all. Thus, instead of *Southampton*, say *Stpntn*."[4] Truffaut also knew Proust's letters well enough for me to be confident that he noticed Proust's comment to Antoine Bibesco about his limited English: "if you were to ask me in English for something to drink, I would not understand you, because I learned English when I had asthma and couldn't talk, I learned with my eyes and am unable to pronounce the words or to recognize them when pronounced by others. *I don't claim to know English. I claim to know Ruskin.*"[5]

THE BRIDE WORE BLACK (1967)

> ... filmed by an inspired director, the most ordinary thriller can become the most moving fairy tale.
> FRANÇOIS TRUFFAUT[1]

Despite the presence of Moreau, Charles Denner, and the always reliable Michael Lonsdale, this is one of my least favourite Truffaut films. With the first two you pretty well know what to expect, they act from their inimitable faces: Moreau could pose for an allegory of Melancholy or contemporary ennui; and Denner, his Savonarolan face and body hollowed out by grief, for Remorse. Lonsdale is more elusive and subtle, his looks and gestures usually suggest depth or complexity beneath the sometimes fussy – see *Stolen Kisses* – but slow leonine exterior. Watch him exchanging weighted lines with De Niro in *Ronin* (1998) or Eric Bana in *Munich* (2005). His resigned death-bound monk in *Of Gods and Men* (2010) is a small gem of a performance.

The Bride Wore Black stays in my memory for a handful of almost peripheral details and a couple of scenes. Truffaut is deft in his use of Moreau's white and black dresses to make the point about her paradoxical morality (can murder be justified?) and to connect the five episodes in each of which she kills one of the five men responsible for her husband's absurd death. Of the five sections only the one with Denner is memorable, mostly because it shows Moreau going beyond her primary role of a grim avenging angel. The hint that Julie Kohler finds herself reluctantly responding to Fergus the painter gives her warmth she otherwise lacks. Fergus senses danger but only to his freedom. Julie intends to carry out her planned revenge even as she begins to find him sympathetic, interesting, and attractive. His interest in her is obvious from the paintings he does of her, especially the horizontal nude on the whitewashed wall, which shows Julie lying on her right side with her head propped on her right hand. The originals are by Charles Matton, and I sometimes wonder about their current location. A recent show of his work in New York consisted in a series of large highly finished boxes, shelves, and structures titled after Giacometti, Joyce, and Proust, among others. Truffaut might have gotten the idea for a nude Moreau from Welles's *The Immortal Story*. Discussing it in his 1972 introduction to Bazin's *Orson Welles*, he comments that "In the puritanical – or at any rate very chaste work of Orson Welles, it offers us the first female nude, Jeanne Moreau, in the service of a sort of Arabian Nights tale written by a Dane and set in China."[2] Truffaut calling someone else's work "puritanical" or "very chaste" provokes a double-take since there are very few breasts and no nudes in his work. His women are very occasionally partly undressed but, with the exception of Clarisse, the prostitute in *Shoot the Piano Player*, and Marion in *Mississippi Mermaid*, they are naked briefly and never below the waist. The full-length fresco of the nude Julie Kohler is the closest he comes.

A similar point could be made about his reluctance to film scenes involving sex. Reviewing Malle's *The Lovers* (1958), he suggests that "the act of sex cannot be shown in cinema because there would be too great a gap between the abstract and the concrete, between the filmmaker's inspiration and the visual presentation of his idea. It would be repulsive and excessive." Instead, "the film-maker must show, as honestly as possible, what happens *before* and *after* love, that is, at the moment when the two partners show themselves to us as human beings entirely apart, and then joined in a perfect harmony of bodies and souls."[3] Truffaut wrote this at twenty-six. He never changed his view. He would have agreed with John Huston, who admitted to his daughter Angelica that "It embarrasses me somewhat when a kiss goes on too long on the screen. Why, I want to turn my face away. I shouldn't be there. That's something between them."[4] Or was the old satyr just putting all of us on?

To return to the paintings, they bring us closer to Julie, but not close enough to bond. At some point during the filming Truffaut must have sensed this, and probably also sensed that Moreau was too old for the role. If Julie and her husband had been childhood sweethearts, as we see in the slightly kitschy idyllic flashback that is one of Truffaut's weakest scenes, why did they wait so long to marry? There is also the problem that the plot has two serious holes. If Julie is able to find the five men, why couldn't the police? How does Julie manage to be sent to the same prison as her husband's fifth killer? Are there co-ed prisons in France? There are occasional holes in Hitchcock's plots but we rarely notice or remember them because he distracts us from them. Truffaut's seem to me of a more important order.

He was disappointed with the film and not surprised that it failed to find an audience. He blamed himself for not understanding that a script without a sympathetic character would leave viewers without a focus for their affections. Put simply, there was no one in the film to care about. In fact, I suspect the audience feels more sympathy for Fergus, for the wrongly accused teacher, played by Alexandra Stewart, and the little boy whose father (Michael Lonsdale) is murdered than for Julie. On a more personal level, he felt that he had somehow failed Moreau. They remained close friends, but they never worked again, though he did think of her for the part of Mathilde in *The Woman Next Door*.

The Bride Wore Black is notable, however, for its exceptional black and white French poster.[5] It shows Moreau standing sideways in left profile, dressed in a long-sleeved floor-length gown, her arm extended straight in front of her and holding a gun. The chromatic tension in the image comes from the straight vertical strips of alternating shining black and white paint that seem to assault or distress her dress. The background is black-brown, the credits are in white. If this couldn't convince people to buy a ticket, then maybe posters don't matter.

JACQUES DEMY, CATHERINE DENEUVE, FRANÇOISE DORLÉAC, AND TRUFFAUT

Going through a box of old magazines I ran across a 1998 issue of *CineAction* (no. 48) with Anna Karina on the front cover (from *Vivre sa vie*) and Dorléac and Deneuve on the back in a scene cut from *Les Demoiselles de Rochefort*. We see the two dancing in front of a large mirror in very short white sleeveless dresses. The film came out in 1967; Dorléac died in a car accident in June. She had been involved with Truffaut during the filming of *The Soft Skin*. Deneuve, her sister, would live with Truffaut after the making of *Mississippi Mermaid* in 1969 and would walk out on him in December 1970. Almost as if he somehow sensed these future and past connections, Demy, the most romantic and lyrical director of the generation, wrote Truffaut into the script in a scene involving both women. They play Delphine and Solange Garnier, dancers in Rochefort who want to try their luck in Paris. At one point, the doorbell of their apartment rings; Dorléac opens it, recognizes two young men interested in them, and says, "Oh, it's Jules and Jim." It might be no more than a nod in Truffaut's direction, one New Waver waving to another and a knowing audience as was common in the period. But it could also be a hint that, although Demy's love story is more sentimental and comic than Truffaut's, it will have its own sadder moments. There are a few other points at which the two films do more than touch. Each, for instance, begins with the search for an ideal woman. Jules and Jim see her in the statue they find on a Mediterranean island and recognize her human incarnation in Catherine. In Demy's film we first see Deneuve in a small oil portrait closely resembling her hanging in a Rochefort gallery. The artist is a young sailor who announces that he is looking for a woman he has never seen but whose portrait he has painted. Almost as if intensifying the already complicated situation of *Jules and Jim*, Demy structures his plot on three love stories; the two involving the sisters echo Catherine's situation in Truffaut. Each sister is loved by three very different men. There's also an unexpected emotional and thematic echo in the endings. In contrast to Truffaut's early films, Demy closes with an intricate sequence of scenes bringing the three love affairs to a happy resolution. His deferral of the last – it involves Deneuve and the sailor – to the final moment is particularly satisfying. It neither undermines the current of melancholy running through the film nor does it offer a turn to realism.

The film has a surprisingly sombre repeated motif of the murder and dismemberment of a local elderly woman. The killer turns out to be a veteran of the First World War who has been a regular at the bar run by the sisters' mother. When caught, Monsieur Dartouz confesses that he killed her because she had spurned him for forty years. We find out about this from a newspaper report the mother reads to two of the men pursuing her daughters. The article is a reminder of other love affairs and other possible endings. But more important is another obsessive decades-long love affair linking the mother and Madame Jouve in *The Woman Next Door*, each of whom is a victim of a youthful relationship. When Jouve's lover left her to go abroad, she attempted suicide by jumping off a building. In contrast, the mother left her lover and pretended to go to Mexico because she couldn't imagine herself married to a man named Monsieur Dame. Both men eventually turn up again. The possible connection between the two films may not be as great a longshot as it seems. With two exceptions, Truffaut's films show little interest in older women. Did Demy's still attractive café owner linger in his mind for a decade before he resurrected her in *The Woman Next Door*? The final possible connection between Demy and Truffaut is provided by the café owner's father, who is shown building a model airplane. Model planes and boats appear in several of Truffaut's films. As I said, Truffaut resists reuniting the elderly lovers in *The Woman Next Door*; Demy on the other hand brings the mother (Danielle Darrieux) and Monsieur Dame (Michel Piccoli) together in a happy ending that leaves the momentary impression that time has stood still.

1967 was also the year of Buñuel's *Belle de Jour*, Godard's *La Chinoise*, Luchino Visconti's *The Stranger*, Welles's *Chimes at Midnight*, and Penn's *Bonnie and Clyde*. The year's most successful French film was Claude Lelouch's *A Man and a Woman* with Jean-Louis Trintignant and Anouk Aimée. Dorléac and Jayne Mansfield died within two days of each other.

STOLEN KISSES (1968): A DEBT TO MARCEL PROUST OR ANATOLE FRANCE

For more than forty years I thought that one of Truffaut's most charming and witty scenes, a proof of his genius as a scriptwriter, is the one in *Stolen Kisses* in which Antoine and the radiantly blond and casually sophisticated Fabienne Tabard (Delphine Seyrig) have afternoon coffee in her middle-class apartment. Because he is shy, nervous, and tongue tied, she is responsible for most of the conversation. Putting a disk on the turntable, she asks him, "Do you like music, Antoine?" He answers at once, "Yes, sir." The script goes on as follows: "A close-up of Antoine as he realizes his blunder. He is petrified. Reverse shot of Fabienne as she looks up in astonishment. A quick cut on the cup he has spilled followed by a panoramic shot showing his flight as he jumps up and rushes toward the door."[1] Reading Proust's letters recently, I came across the source of "Yes, sir." I should repeat that Truffaut knew the letters well: the first volume of the English edition, *Selected Letters 1880–1903*, carries the following blurb by him: "I particularly love to read the *Correspondence* of Proust, published in chronological order. The letters become progressively more and more beautiful, more and more profound." The letter here is written to the writer Max Daireau (19 June 1913). Describing an embarrassing moment, Proust writes, "I remained rooted to the spot like the small boy in [Anatole France's] *Le Livre de mon ami* who says: 'Good morning, Sir' to the lady he loves."[2] France's semi-autobiographical novel was published in 1885 and like Paul Léautaud's *Le Petit Ami* – which Truffaut considered filming – deals with a poor boy's life in Paris. Although Truffaut mentions France only once, and then in connection with Guitry, I would give even odds that he knew the book. The boy and Paris would have been irresistible magnets. I can imagine him introducing himself to St Peter as François Truffaut, filmmaker and Parisian. If he didn't borrow the scene from France, a future Nobel Prize winner, he certainly borrowed it from Proust.

DAVID THOMSON'S
MISSISSIPPI MERMAID (1969)

Thomson is such a good writer and strong critic – easily the most interesting since Kael – that for obvious reasons it is as dangerous to quote him as it is to quote her. Still, I'll risk it because in *"Have You Seen ... ?"*[1] he presents a strong personal case for a movie I have never liked. There are days when it runs neck and neck with *Such a Gorgeous Kid like Me* for my least favourite Truffaut, which has at least one fan – Robert Ingram – who describes it as "one of Truffaut's most satisfying films."[2] Thomson is reduced by his enthusiasm to simply telling the story. I will quote a handful of sentences just to give you a sense of a great critic in heat and unplugged. He opens with "I realized some time ago that I love this film beyond reason, and so I have had to learn not to make strenuous efforts of persuasion" and closes, "Already there is a longer version of the film. It could go on, forever, this story. I wish it would." We agree that it is "about a love beyond reason," though I'd be tempted to call it an irrational love, which is not quite the same thing: think of it as the difference between reason+ and reason–. He finds it convincing and is moved by it. I'm not. He wishes it would go on forever. I wish that Truffaut had not made it or that he had made it with actors other than Belmondo and Deneuve. For me one of its few redeeming features is the scene in which we see the young Deneuve's breasts, though they are even more impressive forty years later in Leos Carax's *Pola X* (1999). A claim you can't make on behalf of many actresses in their fifties.

I will end with a near blasphemy: *Original Sin*, Michael Christopher's 2001 remake with Antonio Banderas and Angelina Jolie, is a more enjoyable movie. Sexy, melodramatic, lurid, occasionally out of control, swept along by saturated colour and Terrence Blanchard's passionate trumpet, it has a hold on the eye, the ear, and the genitals: watch Jolie as late in the night she stumbles down the stairs, hair loose and clothes in disarray, physically ragged, after having had to "pay" a group of gamblers for helping Banderas cheat them at cards. She makes us see and feel the seamy, sweaty, and trashy world Deneuve describes but never convincingly embodies. Compared to Jolie's woman of the lower depths, Deneuve is Chanel No. 5 telling us that it had once been in a brothel.

FAHRENHEIT 451 (1966), WEEK-END (1967), THE WILD CHILD (1969): A DIALOGUE?

Toward the close of *Week-end*, there is a surprisingly idyllic scene in the anarchist camp after Paul, one of the film's main characters, has been killed. The setting is the shore of the lake at twilight. On the left side of the screen a woman sits in profile reading as a rowboat with hunters and their kill approaches slowly. Undisturbed, the woman continues to read until one of the hunters addresses her as Mademoiselle Gide. The following scenes show the group eating not only the animals killed that day but, to the audience's shock, Paul. His wife Corinne (a nod to George Sand) is among them, and knowingly and without protest joins in the cannibalism. The ending is as obviously indebted to Hobbes as that of *Fahrenheit 451* is to Rousseau: "No arts; no letters; no society; and which is worst of all, continual fear and danger of violent death; and the life of man, solitary, poor, nasty, brutish, and short" (*Leviathan*). The irony implicit in Godard's vision – though I'm not sure he sees it – is that of the three alternatives his film offers (capitalism, the French Revolution, and anarchism) capitalism is the most attractive if only by default. Raoul Coutard, who shot the film, said that "around that time [Godard] had the revelation that he was a Marxist–Leninist."[1] This doesn't show in the film or, at least, its sociopolitical vision is not Marxist-Leninist in any sense that Lenin would recognize. There is always the possibility that the anarchists and the figure of Saint-Just (played by Léaud) are revolutionary stand-ins for the Marxists who would later give way in Godard's career to his hallucination about Maoism.

I began with the image of the female reader in what is momentarily a pastoral setting. The scene would not be out of place in the book-people segment of *Fahrenheit 451*, released the previous year. The final movement of Truffaut's film has a river running through it, and there are people reading and memorizing books. It's not clear what point Godard is making by placing this solitary reader among the violent and cannibalistic anarchists whose groups are mysteriously named after famous films only one of which has anything to do with revolution: *The Searchers*, *Battleship Potemkin*, *Johnny Guitar*, and *Gösta Berling*. (Is his point that even those nurtured on high culture can revert in just a few years to barbarism?) But the girl is the second young woman in the film whom we see reading and/or resisting the reversion to primitivism. The first appears in a scene that mixes genres and eras. She is both Alice in Wonderland and more confusingly Emily Brontë. She is met by Corinne and Paul after they have abandoned their car. When she exasperates them by reading Lewis Carroll's riddles aloud, they knock her down and, in an unconvincingly motivated act, set her on fire (think of *Fahrenheit 451*). The killing is one in a sequence showing the descent into barbarism. What interests me, however, is the strong possibility of two further connections to the scene in *Fahrenheit 451* in which the firemen invade a house to destroy a woman's secret library. As the Captain sweeps the books off the shelves while casually offering a superficially convincing reason for their destruction, the camera lingers for a moment on a foregrounded oversize copy of *Alice in Wonderland and Through the Looking Glass*. It is one of the few books with a white cover in the Technicolor film. When the firemen order the woman to abandon the house and her books, she refuses. Standing surrounded by her books, she watches as gasoline is poured on them, strikes a match, drops it, and burns to death with her beloved library.

What I'm suggesting is that *Week-end* answers Truffaut's film by echoing it at several points. Granted that Truffaut frames his vision within the limits of Ray Bradbury's novel, I would suggest that the film's faith in culture, humanism, and love is consistent with the values expressed by his other films. Godard's response occurs on two levels. The first is a rejection of Truffaut's humanistic meliorism: the world of the book-people and their values and affections is as doomed as the capitalist society that makes films like *Fahrenheit 451*. The juxtaposition of the female reader in *Week-end* to the hunters and the cannibalistic feast is the visual equivalent of Walter Benjamin's questionable comment that "there is no document of civilization which is not at the same time a document of barbarism."[2] Books and the culture they represent, so runs the argument, are inseparable from class, the killing of animals, and the oppression of people. Godard is suggesting that Truffaut, whether aware or not, is complicit with the repressive society of his film: the book-people are not the answer to the problem which a civilization based on books has created. One of his other questionable alternatives appears in the long didactic scene where Corinne and Paul meet Saint-Just, already mentioned in *Made in USA*, in a temporally and thematically provocative intersection of the eighteenth century with the twentieth. While walking with them, the polemical and in real life bombastic revolutionary reads loudly and almost nonstop from a volume of his works. His diatribe – and it is precisely *that* – is a denunciation of the corrupt societies that he and they live in. If *Week-end* is a response to *Fahrenheit 451*, then the effect of Léaud playing Saint-Just is unsettling: it's as if Godard is using Truffaut's "son" to answer Truffaut. But, then, perhaps answer is misleading since Godard's films usually offer a surfeit of ideas ponging off in contradictory directions like a chaotic dance of Lucretian atoms. Perhaps the most impressive aspect of *Week-end* is the not quite apocalyptic vision of the decay and decline of the contemporary world of consumer capitalism: the brilliantly set-up and shot scene of highway chaos, fire, verbal and physical violence, and carnage is its dance of death. Vico would have understood. Compare this from his conclusion to *The New Science*: "In this way, through long centuries of barbarism, rust will consume the misbegotten subtleties of malicious wits that have turned them into beasts made more inhuman by the barbarism of reflection than the first men had been made by the barbarism of sense. For the latter displayed a generous savagery, against which one could defend oneself or take flight or be on one's guard; but the former, with a base savagery under soft words and embraces, plots against the life and fortune of friends and intimates."[3] No wonder the well-read Godard is leery of books.

The last connection I want to make between the two films is perhaps the most subtle and comes from an unlikely source, *The Soft Skin* (1964), a film I can't imagine Godard liking though it made an appearance in *Masculin-Féminin*. *The Soft Skin* has a scene in which the adulterous couple fuss over a kitten and a dish of milk. The first long scene in *Week-end* shows Corinne, shot from behind, telling her analyst-lover the story of a dish of milk left out for a cat that becomes the setting, quite literally, for sex by two women and one man. The story begins with the male telling the women, "To the kitchen, pussies." It's as if Godard is telling Truffaut, if you're going to use the cat and the dish of milk as symbols or fetishes to remind the audience about offscreen sex, why not go all the way – talk about it and show it.

Perhaps Godard's final implicit comment on books and the book-people is his substitution of FIN DE CONTE, followed by FIN DE CINÉMA, for the expected FIN. In the film's future, no more pencils, no more stories, no more cinema. The enervated bookish intellectuals will be replaced by the new Scythians. And screenplays based on novels like Bradbury's will be a thing of the past. Refusing to enter the argument strictly on Godard's terms, Truffaut answers his scenario of a "barbarism of reason" with *The Wild Child*, the story of how a feral child is saved from a barbarism of mere sense by a humanist of the Enlightenment.

MAURICE PIALAT'S WILD CHILD: *L'ENFANCE NUE* (1968)

> People get emotional over memories of their childhood, but most of the time, childhood is a nightmare that one hopes to see disappear as quickly as possible. A nightmare of lack of affection, a nightmare of loneliness.
>
> FRANÇOIS TRUFFAUT[1]

Truffaut was one of the producers of *L'Enfance nue* ("The Naked Childhood"). It stars Michael Terrazon as a ten-year-old boy who gradually becomes less emotionally responsive as he is passed on from one foster home to another. One reviewer called it "The 401st Blow." *The Wild Child*, Truffaut's own film about a naked boy premiered a year later, but he had been working on it since 1964 when he read Lucien Malson's *Les Enfants sauvages: Mythe et réalité*. Not surprisingly the mistreatment of children was the only political issue that engaged him throughout his life. He was very active during this period in the organization SOS Villages d'Enfants "that had centers for taking in battered children," and he agreed in 1968 to an all-day radio program devoted to him so long as it dealt with children.[2] It's a measure of the depth of his moral and political commitment to children that when it seemed as if United Artists wouldn't provide financing for *The Wild Child* because he insisted on black and white, Truffaut went for help for the first and last time to the Centre National de la Cinématographie. In the end he didn't need it.

He must have been pleased when Pialat's film won the Jean Vigo Award. As I have said, Vigo's *Zéro de Conduite* was one of his benchmarks and one of the essential precursors of the New Wave. *The Wild Child* was released in 1970 to enthusiastic critical notices and a modestly profitable box office.

WOODY ALLEN'S *DECONSTRUCTING HARRY* (1997) AND **ANTOINE DOINEL**

Allen is on record as a Truffaut fan. So it's not surprising that there are two scenes in *Deconstructing Harry* that invite the audience to make a connection to *Stolen Kisses* and *Bed and Board*. The first shows Toby Maguire working in a shoe store, where, like Doinel in *Stolen Kisses*, he is responsive to the sexual pollen competing with the smell of shoe leather. The second involves an apartment Maguire borrows from a friend for a rendezvous with a Japanese prostitute. Doinel, you may recall, has a love affair with the Japanese Kyoko in *Bed and Board*; it almost ends his marriage. The affair concludes with a heartbreaking scene. After Christine learns of his infidelity, purely by happenstance, she dresses in a kimono, does her hair and makeup Geisha-style and waits for her husband to come home. When he enters and looks at her, tears slowly roll down her cheeks. The geisha in Wes Anderson's *Day for Night* American Express commercial also crosses over, so to speak, from *Bed and Board*.

Truffaut reviewed *Annie Hall* enthusiastically.[1] There is little in his account of Allen as a filmmaker that couldn't be said of himself. He describes him as a writer, director, and actor whose film is imbued with personal elements. And the theme? "Love, of course. Why affairs end, how they begin, isn't it the best subject for a film and also for a thousand films since each man has lived his own life and each life is worth filming so long as this is done with intuition, craft and feeling?"[2] Truffaut is on automatic pilot here; he wrote this sort of thing on the run. Still, it's another indication of the continuity between his films and his critical writings: he often liked what most resembled his own work. It reminds me of Stephen Dedalus's well-known observation in *Ulysses* that "a man of genius makes no mistakes. His errors are volitional and the portals of discovery." The genius or auteur is always, when working, a genius or auteur, and therefore, like the Pope when speaking *ex cathedra* on matters of faith and morals, infallible. In other words, if you're still with me, Truffaut is *Truffaut* even in a minor review in a commercial magazine.

PATRICE LECONTE'S
THE GIRL ON THE BRIDGE (1999)

Elle wrote me about Leconte's film a few years after she married and left Toronto. She had seen it at Telluride, liked it and – there is always a hook – found that Daniel Auteuil's self-destructive knife thrower reminded her of me. As Miss Piggy might have said, "Self-destructive, moi?" My wife had told me the same thing when we were breaking up. I had to see the film.

I never tire of it, and whenever friends haven't seen it I arrange to have them come over to watch. One of the most beautiful black and white films of its time, it makes black and white into gelato colours and flavours, and some of the stills from it could pass as photographs by Bill Brandt or paintings by Pierre Soulages. Leconte uses black and white as if they were primary colours ignored by the Fauves. The intense emotions of various scenes are translated into a spectrum of shimmering tones. The pace at which Leconte moves from scene to scene, medium shot to closeup to longshot, the electric, manic cutting, and the integration of the music with the action are all emotionally expressive. There's an element of formal play in the febrile middle section as the knife thrower (Daniel Auteuil) and his new female apprentice (Vanessa Paradis) prepare for his return to the big time and their brief fling at the top. The weighted silver knives fly paced by Benny Goodman's "Sing, Sing, Sing (with a Swing)" with the beat set by Gene Krupa – playing the sorcerer's apprentice – whose runaway drums threaten as much violence to our ears as the knives to her firm and lucent youthful skin.

Truffaut would have liked the film because of its advocacy of black and white, because of the to-the-limit love story, and because it nods in his direction several times. The film opens with a long scene in which the emotionally troubled, even suicidal, Adèle, explains her life to a psychiatrist and a small group of observers, almost an audience (compare this both to *The 400 Blows* and Léaud's scene in Breillat's *36 fillette*). For Truffauldians her name summons – I don't have to tell you, do I – Adèle Hugo while the scene as a whole recalls Antoine's interview with the psychologist at the detention centre. The two interviews have a similar emotional colouring: each is serious but has a ripple of resistant humour running through it whose origin is the main character's ambiguous tone of voice and smile, childishly sly in Truffaut, innocent and unabashed in Leconte. Adèle's summary of her disastrous serial sexual encounters is black humour – she is always falling in love and being abandoned – and could be mistaken for the much more self-aware Camille Bliss's litany of lovers. Then there is her jump from a bridge into the Seine and her rescue by the almost equally unhappy Auteuil, thirty years after Catherine's jump into the same river in *Jules and Jim*. And, finally, there is the knife thrower's encounter in the circus with Irene, a former lover (think of *The Man Who Loved Women*). Visibly shaken by him, she confesses that "For months I'd stop men in the street like you" (*The Story of Adèle H.*?). She's an associate member of Truffaut's women who go to the limit – one of those who reject provisional love. Like Mathilde she had attempted suicide. Coincidence or *hommage*? I'm betting on the latter.

Hervé Truffaut, no relation, is the executive producer. I like some coincidences even when they are without significance.

"FRANÇOIS, MY BOY"
AND
"MR HITCHCOCK"

> No, I am certainly not an innovator, because I belong to the last squad to believe in the notions of characters, situations, progression, incidents, false leads: in a word, the whole show."
>
> FRANÇOIS TRUFFAUT[1]

I think of Truffaut's conversations with Hitchcock as his graduate degree in film. He had been thinking about Hitchcock for over a decade, had reviewed his films, had seen many often enough to remember them frame by frame and used him as one of the touchstones in his championing of the auteur theory. Hitchcock, like Rossellini, was an auteur *avant la lettre*. He knew everything there was to know about making films and he had fashioned an independent career; in other words, he was another model for Truffaut. Their week of conversations in 1962 brought together a perfectly matched couple: Truffaut fulfilled his desire to meet his hero to talk about his films; Hitchcock in turn received the adulation and serious critical attention he had long craved. Sometimes I wonder, however, whether at some level the book wasn't also Truffaut's attempt to answer Bazin's ungenerous view of Hitchcock as merely "one of the most clever directors in the world" who had "contributed nothing essential to cinematic directing."[2] What does a man feel when two respected "godfathers" disagree?

"François" watches "Mr Hitchcock" while Hitchcock looks at the camera. *Hitchcock,* their book of conversations, was published in 1967.

They first met in winter 1954, when Hitchcock, having finished *To Catch a Thief* on the Côte d'Azur, was working on postsynchronization in Joinville. Truffaut and Chabrol decided to ask for an interview for *Cahiers*. Truffaut was twenty-two, Hitchcock fifty-five. The director agreed to meet them in the studio bar. In Truffaut's version of what happened, the two "failed to notice the dark-gray frozen pond in the middle of the courtyard. With a single step forward we went over the ledge, landing on a thin layer of ice, which immediately gave way. Within seconds we were immersed in a pool of freezing water and in a state of shock." When Hitchcock saw them a few minutes later, wet and shivering, he suggested an evening meeting. A year later, at a Paris press conference, he told them, "Gentlemen, every time I see a pair of ice cubes clicking together in a glass of whiskey, I think of the two of you."[3]

Seven years later, in August 1962, Truffaut flew to Los Angeles and they recorded fifty hours of interviews over a period of six days. His spoken English was shaky and he depended heavily on his invaluable assistant Helen Scott; his English simply wasn't good enough to engage in a full dialogue with Hitchcock. Though *Hitchcock* doesn't have a translation credit, Scott is given a title-page credit as collaborator. Both in the book and the letters Truffaut acknowledges his profound debt to her, and his introduction features a photograph of the three of them at work. Put simply, and the testimony is in his letters, the book couldn't have been done without her contribution to the planning stages, the interviews, the translating, and the editing.

Truffaut could never bring himself to accept Hitchcock's invitation to call him "Hitch." Whenever Hitchcock asked him to, he would reply "Of course, Mr Hitchcock." Proust, in an identical situation, avoided onomastic and perhaps sexual intimacy with the demanding Robert de Montesquiou by responding to his "Cher Marcel" with "Cher Monsieur." In 1962 Hitchcock could look back on a decade in which he had made eleven films; most had been hits and at least four are masterpieces. Any one of *Rear Window* (1954), *Vertigo* (1958), *North by Northwest* (1959), and *Psycho* (1960) would have secured him a place in a history of Hollywood and of film. As early as 1955 the twenty-three-year-old Truffaut had placed him in a pantheon among "Renoir, Rossellini, Orson Welles and a few other filmmakers."[4] This anticipated Hitchcock's growth in critical stature over the next four decades to the point that *Vertigo*, for instance, would be regularly ranked among the greatest films of the century. "François" was thirty. Behind him he had a successful career as a film critic who had changed the course of French film and he had also made the three *nouvelle vague* films for which he is best remembered today – *The 400 Blows, Shoot the Piano Player*, and *Jules and Jim*. Despite Truffaut's record and his stature among contemporary filmmakers and critics, he and Hitchcock were far from equals and he felt it: they were more like a master and an acolyte and it shows in the conversations: Truffaut is never able to bring himself to ask any questions that might embarrass or challenge Hitchcock, nor to express any reservations. To do so would have been like interviewing the Pope and wanting to discuss the problems with Aquinas's proofs for God's existence.

The two men had little in common beyond an intimate knowledge of Hitchcock's body of work and a love of making films. If they didn't speak much about films by other directors, it was probably due to the lack of time, though it's also possible that Truffaut sensed Hitchcock's lack of interest. I suppose you could say that Hitchcock's narcissism was completed by Truffaut's admiration of him: they both admired Hitchcock. They also had something in common Hitchcock wasn't aware of: as children both had been locked in a jail cell, an experience that appears in a symbolic or displaced form, a sort of autobiographical filmic shorthand, in their films. Truffaut's first question establishes the connection: "Mr Hitchcock, you were born in London on August 13, 1899. The only thing I know about your childhood is the incident at the police station. Is that a true story?" Hitchcock acknowledges it is. "I must have been about four or five years old. My father sent me to the police station with a note. The chief of police read it and locked me in a cell for five or ten minutes, saying, 'This is what we do to naughty boys' ... I truly cannot imagine what it was I did."[5] Truffaut probably knew that there were several versions of the story. Patrick McGilligan, a biographer, even raises doubts about it by pointing out that Hitchcock's father referred to him as "my little lamb without a spot" and that one of the director's associates said, "Hitch told it so often, and it was convenient for the press ... he probably came to believe it himself."[6] Whether it was true or not was less important for Truffaut than whether Hitchcock believed it revealed something about his character that he wanted known. Even the pattern of our repeated lies or exaggerations is a polygraph of who we really are. Whatever the case, the episode of an anxious night spent in a jail cell is one of the keys to his adult life and to his films. Truffaut comes close to this point in his discussion of the auteur's presence in his films: "I believe that all the interesting filmmakers – those who were referred to as 'auteurs' by the *Cahiers du Cinéma* in 1955, before the term was distorted – concealed themselves behind various characters in their movies. Alfred Hitchcock achieved a real tour de force in inducing the public to identify with the attractive leading man, whereas Hitchcock himself almost always identified with the supporting role – the man who is cuckolded, disappointed, the killer or a monster, the man rejected by the others, the man who has no right to love, the man who looks on without being able to participate."[7] I wonder whether we couldn't press this further and see Hitchcock as *both* the fit "attractive leading man" (the fantasy) and the one not "able to participate" (the reality)? In a manner of speaking, all the characters in a film *are* to some degree the auteur just as all the characters in a dream are aspects of the dreamer.

Truffaut remained faithful to Hitchcock through the remaining twenty years of his life, though he had little more to say about the films. He published a revised and expanded version of the book in 1984, four years after Hitchcock's death. In it he was able to acknowledge what a careful reading of the first edition implied and what he couldn't bring himself to say while his hero was alive: that the films after *Psycho* show a marked decline. Each time I watch *The Green Room*, I use the pause button frequently to examine the photographs in Julien's chapel for one that might suggest Hitchcock, however obliquely. It must be there.

TRUFFAUT'S TYPEWRITERS

Typewriters in Truffaut are usually associated with work and creativity – with writing, paper, ink, scripts, journals, letters, manuscripts, books, libraries, writing on the screen, presses, and the actual labour involved in the production of discourses and texts. They are prominent in his first film, and in his last two they have a moment alone on screen. *Confidentially Yours* has a deft comic vignette in which Truffaut calls attention to what Buñuel would describe as a fetish: a blond secretary demonstrates her one-finger typing technique. In *The Last Metro* the typewriter has an almost totemic value, sitting generally unused and silent on its own pedestal, like a forgotten Roman household god, guarding the entrance to Marion Steiner's rooms at the theatre: even unused, it reminds us of the writing-typing of a script, scripts being submitted and considered, books being read, and the wartime censorship everyone is aware of and which is represented by the collaborationist drama critic Daxiat. If you remember *The 400 Blows*, you wait for it to be stolen. It carries a particular emotional charge because its theft in the first film is an act against the father; although Antoine doesn't use it to write, I can't keep the idea of creativity from drifting into the scenes. It's a significant presence in *Two English Girls*, *Day for Night*, *The Man Who Loved Women*, and *The Last Metro*. In *Two English Girls* and *The Man Who Loved Women* a female typist is shown working on an erotic manuscript brought to her by a man. In the first we see Claude (Léaud) pacing around a room while dictating the section of Muriel's journal in which she confesses to having masturbated since childhood. The typist is a woman in her twenties. She is conservatively dressed; her hair is combed up to reveal her neck. She wears glasses (like Muriel) and remains expressionless even as Claude reads the most intimate revelations. The manuscript's voice and gaze are female, but the words are being dictated by a male who looks at the manuscript as he reads them to another female – who averts her gaze because of shame – in a film written by a male from a novel by another male. The voiceover tells us that Claude wants to arrange for an anonymous publication of the journals but Muriel has refused "without saying how he has hurt her." The scene anticipates Bertrand Morane's hiring of a typist to produce a clean version of his typescript of the memoir of his nearly countless love affairs. When he visits her apartment to deliver an instalment, the noticeably disturbed woman tells him that she can't continue because the manuscript is upsetting her. Both scenes allow Truffaut to expand through verbal description scenes that we have seen only in fragments in the film. He achieves a similar effect when Adèle writes her journal and simultaneously speaks in a voiceover. I also have the impression that with the reactions of the two typists Truffaut is trying to guide the audience's response in opposite ways: in the first, the typist's cool response to Muriel's confession sets a standard we are expected to follow; in the second, the typist's slightly comic embarrassment suggests a path we shouldn't take because we're supposedly more open-minded, less prurient than she is.

The last time I saw *Two English Girls*, I watched the scene with the typist tense with expectations aroused by my memory of the flustered reaction of Betrand's copyist. Even though I knew the earlier movie well, I couldn't help thinking that if anyone should be embarrassed it *should be* the typist: not only is the content sexually explicit but it is read to her by a handsome young man who, it is obvious, knows the writer. There's even a moment near the scene's end when Claude pauses behind her, on her right, and turns to look down at her exposed – I'm tempted to write nude – neck, when I expect him to lean down and kiss it. Claude and I are excited, the typist isn't.

There are many connections between Claude and Bertrand other than strong mothers, women, manuscripts, books, typists, and typewriters. Each will publish an autobiographical narrative: Claude a novel (*Jerôme and Julien*), Bertrand a memoir whose final title is *The Man Who Loved Women*. Each is a mask for the director. The question Truffaut poses with their stories is the one that hangs over his adult life: why is it not possible for a man to love and be faithful to one woman or, put another way, why is it not possible to reconcile definitive and provisional love? In *Confidentially Yours*, the secretary (Fanny Ardant) not only saves but also marries her boss (Jean-Louis Trintignant), who types with two fingers, as do Bertrand and Truffaut. The film ends with the marriage ceremony. For the moment they live happily ever after. If Trintignant writes a book, Ardant will type it.

THE ENDING OF
TWO ENGLISH GIRLS (1971)

[I wrote *Wild Palms*] to stave off what I thought was heartbreak.
WILLIAM FAULKNER[1]
—

Truffaut had read Roché's second novel, *Les Deux Anglaises et le continent*, on publication in 1956 and, according to his biography, had "read it over and over again, to the point where he knew every single line by heart."[2] He negotiated with Gallimard for the screen rights during 1968, arguing down their original demand of 150,000 francs to half that by reminding them, in a strong letter, that the novel's continuing sales had been spurred by the popularity of his film *Jules and Jim*. He also reminded them that they had failed Roché by refusing to publish his voluminous journals, which Truffaut had arranged to have typed at his own expense. Jean Gruault gave him a 552-page script in March 1969, but he didn't decide to begin work on the film until March 1971, four months after Catherine Deneuve's catastrophic departure. I have the impression that Truffaut resurrected the project at the moment when he needed help coming to terms with what had happened. Jean-Claude Brialy suggested in a letter that Truffaut "had suddenly called forth [the film] to chase the bad clouds from your mind."[3] The biography goes further in remarking "Filming to live, shooting to heal – rarely has cinema had as vital a function."[4] This sounds as if it might be an exaggeration, but I suspect that it's truer more often than we imagine, both for those who make films and those who watch them. If I try it out on Raoul Walsh, Cukor, Ford, de Sica, Chabrol, and later Godard, it doesn't sound quite as convincing, but then I'm not as familiar with their lives. On the other hand, it makes immediate sense with Bergman, Truffaut, and Tarkovsky. Though a box office failure, *Two English Girls* may have saved his life. Shot by Almendros as if the fin-de-siècle were a series of impressionist and real tableaux, this film physical about love will never have a wide popularity. I return to it or Roché's *Les Deux Anglaises et le continent* at least every couple of years with renewed pleasure and usually find something new, especially in the characters, all mysterious in their privacy, all caught in carefully controlled intimacies, all desperate to love in their own ways, all wounded by love and remorse. There are times when they seem more capable of reflecting (Muriel), writing (Claude), or sculpting (Anne) their emotions than expressing them directly. One could even say that they talk and analyze their love to death as feeling turns away from action to reflection.

There is a sense in which the film is a thematic prequel to and a dramatic recasting of the events of *Jules and Jim*. The love triangle of the earlier film reappears as two English girls, Anne and Muriel Brown, and a French friend, Claude Roc. At the end Claude rewrites their story as *Jerôme et Julien*, a title so homophonically close to *Jules and Jim* it suggests that Roché wanted to ensure that the reader made the connection. No other Truffaut film is as pervasively and comfortably literary, in the sense of lingering over and integrating writing, books, letters, and journals into the drama. As in *Jules and Jim*, what might be called the novelistic power of the original merges with the power of film to lend the film the combined force, interest and pleasure of both. We feel the novel within the film less in the characters and story – though it is certainly there – than in the film's devotion to the written word as it is made physical in the film's attention to the various dimensions of language written, printed and spoken. The film opens with the credits appearing against a beige background of copies of Roché's novel, arranged first with their spines showing, then with the front cover, and finally with pages underlined and heavily overwritten by Truffaut. The lovers' letters in the film are also in Truffaut's handwriting, a trace suggesting that the film in all its aspects is about him. The autobiographical imprint is reinforced in the restored version's last words – "I look old this evening" – which are spoken by Truffaut though thought by Claude: I have the impression in the scene that I am looking at a quadruple exposure of the kind that is common in some of Godard's later work: Roché (novelist), Truffaut (director), Léaud (actor), and Roc (character) are superimposed one upon the other to form a single complex cinematic image. Male viewers of a certain age probably see themselves in my imagined multiple exposure as well.

Someone who knows film and films well could deliver a master class on how to adapt a scene in a novel into an effective film scene on the basis of what Truffaut does with Roché's ending. The novel closes with Anne happily married with four children, Muriel with two; both families live in Canada in the Thousand Islands area near Kingston, Ontario. Claude's mother is still alive, and, as Claude puts it, "I live with Claire and my books."[5] Anne writes Claude that Muriel's daughter, Myriam, will be in Paris at the Gardens of the Trocadéro on a particular date and encloses a photograph. Claude takes the hint and looks for Myriam but doesn't introduce himself when he sees her. The daughter's resemblance to her mother is striking and a powerful reminder to Claude of their love affair. Walking home he looks at himself in shop windows and feels weak. On his return, Claire remarks, "What's the matter? You seem old this evening?"[6]

Truffaut simplifies the details without simplifying or attenuating Roché's emotional impact. In the film Anne has no children and dies of tuberculosis. Claire dies of old age. Truffaut extends the number of years since Claude has seen Muriel from thirteen to fifteen and moves the scene in which Claude sees the daughter to the Musée Biron (the Rodin Museum). This links it to two earlier scenes in the movie – not in the novel – in which Claude discusses Rodin's "Balzac" and, in an allusion to his love affairs with the sisters, "The Kiss." I haven't examined the film's several scripts but I don't hesitate to suggest that Claude's comments were written by Truffaut not Jean Gruault. They remind us of Antoine's touching but ill-fated shrine to Balzac in *The 400 Blows*, Lachenay's book about Balzac (*The Soft Skin*), Antoine reading Balzac's *The Lily in the Valley* in military prison (*Stolen Kisses*), and Truffaut's lifelong admiration of the novelist who incidentally was also haunted by his mother's failure to love him. Balzac's presence is one of Truffaut's signatures. (Godard may be having some fun with this in *Pierrot le fou* when Belmondo dials "Paris, BALZAC 75–02" and reprimands the operator, "So you've forgotten Balzac, too.") But the most significant change Truffaut makes involves Muriel's daughter. In the novel Claude has been told she is coming, and because he has her photograph he recognizes her. In the film there is no

Claude (Léaud) and Anne (Kika Markham) visit a Paris art gallery in *Two English Girls* (1971).

letter; he knows only that Muriel has a daughter. When he notices a group of English girls in the Musée Biron he simply wonders whether one of them might be Muriel's child. His memories of the intense and troubling love affair with Muriel, who describes herself as "an amorous Puritan," have no current point of focus and no possible closure. He is still in love with and mourns a woman who said that, even if she married another, she would love him forever. If nothing else, this is one way of reconciling the definitive and the provisional though it leaves one of the partners hanging. The film replaces the novel's shop window with a taxi window that reflects Claude in the foreground and the English girls behind him. Instead of ending with Claire's words, it ends, as I said, with Truffaut's voiceover: "I look old this evening."

The autobiographical traces suggest that there is far more of Truffaut in the film than we suspected when it was released in 1971. Consider the following; (1) the Brown and Roc families are fatherless since both fathers die when the children are young; (2) the interest in Balzac; (3) mothers – Janine had died in 1968, Claude is unable to escape his mother's oedipal presence even after her death ("He had lost the most demanding of his women"); (4) Claude's description of his suicide attempt at the age of fifteen isn't in the novel, but it is in Truffaut's life; (5) at the film's end Claude is in his mid-forties; Truffaut was thirty-nine; (6) both the novel and the film explore love affairs between provisional and definitive characters.

Truffaut's marriage to Madeleine Morgenstern and his relationship with Deneuve both foundered on his provisional character. I suppose we might describe him as definitive about being provisional or faithful to infidelity. In the novel, which I sometimes think of as co-written by Truffaut, Anne thinks of Muriel and Claude as "two absolute beings."[7] The deeply Christian Muriel, who thinks that everyone has a predestined mate, dismisses Claude (while loving him) because of his love affairs. She is definitive about being definitive and yet chooses to sleep with him once. I can imagine Claude in old age summing up his life with Gertrude's comment in Dreyer's eponymous last film: "I have suffered much and often been mistaken, but I have loved." It could also be Roché and Truffaut's epitaph, though it would mean something significantly different for them than for Dreyer's determined and single-minded heroine.

TWO ENGLISH GIRLS, AGORA (2009), AND SEEING RED ON THE SCREEN

> We were in a political movie ... Walt Disney with blood.
> ANNA KARINA, *MADE IN USA*
> —

My candidate for the most shocking scene in Truffaut's films occurs in *Two English Girls*, a film described by him as "a film which would not show physical love but which would be a 'physical film about love.'"[1] The scene in question shows Muriel and Claude meeting after a difficult separation originally insisted on by their mothers. Muriel, the film's resident neurotic Puritan and at this point still a virgin, has finally decided to have sex with Claude. After their lovemaking and after they have left the bed, the camera zooms in on the red stain on the white sheets. It looks like the Japanese flag, though more immediately relevant is its recall of the bright red lettering on the white books behind the opening credits. Several reviewers treated it as a moral and artistic provocation. Even the faithful Schiffman had reservations about the scene, which doesn't occur in Roché. Truffaut's answer comes a decade later with a playful and slightly obscure allusion in *The Woman Next Door*. Mathilde Bauchard (Fanny Ardant) is an artist specializing in children's books. Her editor notices a sketch of a fallen boy lying in a pool of bright red blood. When he objects that this might disturb young readers, she reassures him that children will be less troubled by the scene and the colour than their timid parents.

Alejandro Amènabar's *Agora* doesn't look back to Truffaut, but it does have a scene with a similar concern with a woman's blood. The philosopher Hypatia (Rachel Weisz) is being courted by one of her Alexandrian students. When he takes his courting public with a declaration of love and a musical performance, she gives her answer in an equally public venue, her lyceum. In front of the gathered class of male students, she hands him a piece of white linen coloured by her menstrual blood. She explains that she wants him to see that she's not quite the ideal woman he imagines, that she has a physical side.

Neither scene is as bloody as, say, the climax of *Carrie* or the endings of *Bonnie and Clyde* or *The Wild Bunch*. Neither film is explicitly or openly sexual. You could even make the case that the sex in each is muted, and even the colour red is for the most part absent from each cameraman's palette. Yet both scenes deliver a profound frisson because the content and the colour are so surprising. I wonder whether the men or women in the audience are more shocked and repelled. My guess is the men, but at my back I hear Germaine Greer's sardonic challenge in *The Female Eunuch*, directed at her female readers, "If you think you are emancipated, you might consider the idea of tasting your menstrual blood – if it makes you sick, you've got a long way to go, baby."[2]

Buñuel must have had Spanish clergy in mind when he included a similar scene in *Viridiana* (1961). It shows Ramona, a servant, examining the sheets of Don Ramon's bed in search of evidence that he has deflowered his niece. Truffaut doesn't mention the scene anywhere, but he knew the film. The always watchable Fernando Rey played the uncle, Don Jaime. Unfortunately *Viridiana* was in black and white. Buñuel almost reshoots the scene in colour in *Tristana*, in which Rey is once again an uncle with a virginal niece, played this time by Deneuve. As if unable to let go the image, Buñuel ends his last film, *That Obscure Object of Desire* (1977), with a bloodied dress on a bed.

In 2012 Mozambique issued seven stamps celebrating Truffaut's career. He would have been pleased that one shows him with Hitchcock.

TRUFFAUT, GODARD, AND *TIMBRES*

> I'm sure Jean-Luc never sticks his stamps
> on the right corner of the envelope – I do.
> FRANÇOIS TRUFFAUT[1]
> —

There are no stamp collectors in Truffaut or Godard's films, and their biographies are silent about the hobby. So far as I can tell from the relevant French stamp catalogues, Truffaut has not appeared on a stamp, but on 20 September 1986, twenty-three months after his death, a still from *The Wild Child* appeared on a stamp in a series marking the fiftieth anniversary of the French National Film Industry. One of the others had a still from Renoir's *La Grande Illusion*. Truffaut would have been pleased and honoured by their joint appearance. For a nation so closely identified with film, France has been slow to honour its great actors and directors. Georges Méliès got his stamp in 1961; Maurice Chevalier appeared in 1990 in a year of singers that also honoured Jacques Brel and Edith Piaf. Cocteau appeared in 1993; Fernandel and Yves Montand in 1994; Romy Schneider, a surprising choice, in 1998, the same year as Simone Signoret, Jean Gabin, Luis de Funes, Bernard Blier, and Lino Ventura. I wondered for some time whether Arletty was missing because of her gloriously unapologetic attitude to her wartime love affair with a German officer, but the government seems to have forgiven her in 1995 with a 100-franc commemorative coin marking the 100th anniversary of French film. She died in 1992.

I add the following from Michael Powell's *A Life in Movies* for the sake of what might be called philatelic completion. There can't be that many stories about stamps in the international film archives.

> When I met Lillian Gish at Dartmouth College in New Hampshire, where I was teaching in the winter of 1979–80, I pulled out my card case and showed her a United States ten-cent stamp that I always carried in it. On it was the portrait of a man in a broad-brimmed hat, the face of a man who would go anywhere and be afraid of nothing. Beyond him loomed a movie camera. The stamp was superscribed "D.W. Griffith Moviemaker." She said "I lobbied for years to get that stamp issued. I guess I wrote and saw more than two hundred congressmen, senators, newspaper men. I had some of the stamps made up in a plastic medallion for key rings. I still have a few. I'll send you one." It is on my key ring now, bless her.

> D.W. Griffith Moviemaker. It's enough.[2]

TRUFFAUT'S AFTERLIFE: *THE DIVING BELL AND THE BUTTERFLY* (2007)

From David Thomson's *"Have You Seen ... ?"*: "At the end of [Jean-Dominique] Bauby's life, this film incorporates the closing music from *Les Quatre Cents Coups* – sparse, stricken, yet alive – and I should say that as I heard it, and remembered it, I was in love with the thing I can only call experience. And lost in doubts over how often the movies have sought to bury these precious sights and sounds in the ceaseless dialogue of bizarre ways in which we die. A slight touch, a stroke, can turn out the light. But before then, did you see?"[1] Yes, David, I saw. The film is on a small list of films I admire very much but find very painful to watch. The list is headed by *The Bicycle Thieves* and includes von Trotta's *Marianne and Juliane*, Billie August's *Pelle the Conqueror*, and Michael Haneke's *Amour*. There's at least one scene in each that leaves a residue of unforgettable and inconsolable anguish evoked by the meeting of film and personal memory. Julian Schnabel's use of Truffaut's music at the close of *The Diving Bell and the Butterfly* brought with it Antoine's determined and ultimately triumphant run, his walk on the cold, grey beach, and his turn away from the annihilating sea toward the camera and us. My memory of Truffaut's images made Schnabel's ending more bearable because Matthieu Amalric's image coexisted momentarily with and was even subsumed by Doinel's. The boy on the run reminds us both of everything the stricken young man has lost ("these precious sights and sounds") and of Bauby's own triumphant "run." Truffaut would have said that *The Diving Bell and the*

Butterfly is a film that helps us live by preparing us for the worst while reminding us that "The worst is not, / So long as we can say 'This is the worst'" (*King Lear*, IV, i, 27–8). I've never quite bought everything in that quotation. I can imagine many moments when I might be able to speak the last clause while at the same time wishing for an exit. I don't think I will feel secure about this until Canada legalizes assisted dying.

JOHNNY GUITAR (1954): BAD FAITH IN TRUFFAUT AND DAVID THOMSON

Ronald Bergan describes Renoir's early sound film *The Night at the Crossroads* (*La Nuit du carrefour*, 1932) as "a sadly neglected masterpiece of the early sound cinema." In support he trots out Godard's judgment that it is "the only great French thriller, the greatest French adventure film."[1] This untenable critical inflation reminded me of an interview with Bernard Tavernier that is part of the *Elena and Her Men* DVD. A longtime Renoir admirer, Tavernier nevertheless sheepishly admits that he has never found the films of the 1950s particularly interesting, even though he praised them in the 1960s during the *Cahiers* campaign to gain attention for Renoir. I suspect that many of the *Cahiers* writers and New Wave fellow travellers would echo Tavernier today not just about some of Renoir's work but about many of their other critical judgments in the era. Truffaut was the worst and probably the most influential offender because he wrote so often in so many journals and tended to categorize films dogmatically on the basis of whether they were in the progressive camp or with the opposition. He rarely saw a superlative or hyperbole he didn't like when reviewing work of someone he had decided was an auteur. His 1955 review of Nicholas Ray's *Johnny Guitar* – for me an almost risible movie – shows him at his most critically vulnerable. Fourteen years later he sends Deneuve and Belmondo to see it in *Mississippi Mermaid*. I should add that Godard (*Pierrot le fou*), Wenders, and Thomson also admire it, though the last can only save it by falling back on a rhetoric that almost matches Truffaut's – the movie is "camp" and looks "as if it had been made by the surrealist movement of the 1920s" or by a director who "may have had a fever – or been drunk."[2] This is one of the few moments in Thomson's body of work where his style betrays him by showing him fumbling for a rhetorically convincing formula or phrase he can't quite reach. Not having convinced himself, he nevertheless tries to convince his reader. Truffaut is not far behind. For him initially, the film "is not far from being its author's best." But then he offers so many qualifying judgments that if you are reading slowly you begin to smell a mouse. Ray's strengths, for instance, are "not very visible perhaps to those who have never looked through a camera's eye," and though "the editing is jerky … what interests us is something else … an extraordinarily beautiful placement of individuals in a certain setting." Furthermore, Joan Crawford "used to be one of the most beautiful women in Hollywood. Now she is beyond considerations of beauty … She is becoming more manly as she grows older."[3] And so on. So far he's telling me that, unless I have directed a film, I can't really appreciate this one; that the editing is poor; and that the no longer beautiful Joan Crawford is becoming more like a man although she has yet to don a moustache. There's not much here for the PR machine promoting the movie, and yet even in 1965 Truffaut is assuring Helen Scott that "it's a film of exceptional poetic sensibility."[4] A decade later, while working on *The Woman Next Door*, *Johnny Guitar* was still on his mind as he described the hero, played by Depardieu, as "a hard man with a soft heart" like Sterling Hayden.[5]

Unlike Thomson or Truffaut, I cringe whenever Crawford or the equally miscast Mercedes McCambridge is on the screen. The former, however well "placed," looks like a colourblind grandmother: just look at her flaming red and blindingly lemon yellow blouses not to mention the communion dress she wears waiting for the posse. There's also the problem that she looks too drawn and old for the stolid Hayden, who, although he has the guitar, is clearly the passive member in the coupling. Truffaut doesn't mention McCambridge. Dressed in black, she pounds across the set with a fevered rabid look appropriate to a woman who has just escaped a long confinement in an attic, can still feel the splinters in her soul, and is desperate for some steak tartare and a bottle of bourbon before she sinks her nails into someone, anyone. She could be auditioning for her role in *Touch of Evil*. I can't believe that Truffaut didn't sense – as I think Thomson does – that the film, though made by one of the auteur brotherhood is an embarrassment, with the same sort of grotesque halflife as a zombie. Otherwise he wouldn't intensify his pro-Ray rhetoric in the final sentence: anyone who rejects *Johnny Guitar* "will never recognize inspiration, intuition, or a framed picture, a shot, an idea, a good film, or even cinema itself."[6] Why stop there? Why not add culture, civilization, our most cherished values, Shakespeare, Proust, and mother love? What he's saying is that you're either with me, *Cahiers*, and Nicholas Ray or with the old wave and the ignorant mob. There's not a hint that this is just one man's opinion.

The title *Johnny Guitar* may be Ray's worst, though his unfinished project *Wet Dreams* might have posed a serious challenge. Truffaut missed the chance of reviewing together Ray's film and the equally reality-challenged *Johnny Concho* (Don McGuire) that came out in 1956. Sinatra's shirts in the latter almost match Crawford's blouses. Come to think of it, given Sinatra's diminutive size and physique (he hovered around 120 pounds), they could have exchanged wardrobes. If they had played anorexic twins, the plot's sexual triangle might have caught fire. But I'm getting carried away and imagining something by Robert Aldrich.

A TITLE QUIZ

The first column lists in chronological order the titles of Truffaut films. The second offers a random list of titles considered and rejected for these films. Can you match them? Answers are in the endnote.[1]

A. *Les Quatre Cents Coups*   a. Le Cavaleur

B. *Antoine et Colette*   b. La Femme inconnue

C. *La Nuit Américaine*   c. La Fiancée disparue

D. *L'Argent de poche*   d. Un Enfant sous l'occupation

E. *L'Homme qui aimait les femmes* e. Les Canardes sauvages

F. *La Chambre verte*   f. Je vous présente Lucie

G. *Le Dernier Métro*   g. Les Enfants

H. *La Femme d'à côté*   h. La Fougue d'Antoine

CREATIVITY
AND
ACCIDENTS

I believe that perfection handicaps the cinema.
JEAN RENOIR[1]
—

I'm thinking about the modest accidental gestures that sometimes go into the making of a novel, a painting, or a film. Françoise Gilot records, for instance, that, when pigeons flew into his studio and left droppings on some paintings, Picasso didn't remove them because he said "[i]t makes an interesting unpremeditated effect."[2] Another example occurs in Christopher Bray's review of Robert T. Ray's *The ABCs of Classic Hollywood*. Ray begins with an "accident" in John Ford's *How Green Was My Valley* (1941): "Nobody remembers much about the movie version of *How Green Was My Valley*, but if anything from that dull film has lodged in our brain it is likely to be the tear-tempting moment when Angharad (Maureen O'Hara) leaves the church where she has just been married and the wind catches her veil and sets it billowing in the air. The gusts and gasps of romantic love have rarely been better captured on film. As the man who wrote the script, Philip Dunne, later said, 'My God, what a shot … I tried to reproduce it when I directed *10 North Frederick*, and then I realized it was a mistake … You can't reproduce those accidents.'"[3] The last sentence recalls Welles and Rossellini, both of whom believed in lucky accidents and serendipity. Rossellini, in particular, was a well-known improviser who liked to create the conditions under which accidents happened. The best-known accident occurs in *Voyage in Italy* (1953) and was the result of circumstances ultimately beyond his control though he unknowingly set them in motion. I'm thinking of the surprise appearance in the Pompeii sequence of a Roman couple buried and preserved in lava during the eruption of 79 AD. The archaeologist discovers them as Ingrid Bergman and George Sanders are filmed touring the ruins. No one could have known that a natural lava sculpture – a happenstance formation – of a couple embracing as they face death would be discovered that day just as a fictive modern couple in a troubled marriage is watching and being filmed. Rossellini could, of course, have claimed some credit by pointing out that had he not charmed the curator with some facts that implied he had read his book – they had been provided by a friend – his crew would not have been allowed to film the scene. No permission, no accident.

Truffaut liked some accidents, like the final shot of *The 400 Blows*, which was discussed above. On the other hand, he was understandably unwilling to accept Oskar Werner's supposedly accidental haircut – he said he fell asleep in the barber's chair – during the making of *Fahrenheit 451*. Truffaut resorted to using a double as often as possible, and Oskar and he never spoke again. He attributed the actor's lack of cooperation on the set to his inflated sense of himself after being nominated for an Oscar for the now-forgotten *Ship of Fools* (1965). In a manner of speaking Truffaut paid him back by killing him off in *The Green Room*, where his photograph appears in Julien Davenne's chapel devoted to his dead. Director and actor died within two days of each other in October 1984.

The accident I can't quite forgive him for keeping in the final cut happens in the last scene of *The Women Next Door*. Truffaut leaves in an awkward splice as Mathilde and Bernard move left to right in an almost slow-motion spiralling dance into the room where they will lie down on the floor to make love for the last time in an act joining love and death. If you love *Tristan and Isolde*, you probably hear, within Georges Delerue's neo-Wagnerian music, Tristan saying "Tristan you, I Isolde, no longer Tristan" and Isolde echoing "You Isolde, Tristan I, no longer Isolde!" When Mathilde shoots Bernard, as he lies on top of her, and then herself, their names and identities merge. The fault in the film splice jars against every other aspect of the fluid presentation – the near dance of death, the mood, the intensity of feeling in Mathilde's face and Georges Delerue's unifying music. If Truffaut was gambling that the audience wouldn't notice, he was wrong. Did he remember that when Judy Barton completes her transformation into Madeleine Elster in her apartment in *Vertigo* there is a hint of the *liebestod* in Bernard Herrmann's music?

A different kind of luck was involved in shooting the final scene of *Fahrenheit 451*. Putting the final touches to his only venture into science fiction, Truffaut hoped for clear weather during the shooting of the book-people walking around the forest reciting in various languages. After several rain delays, he went to bed hoping for a sunny day. Instead he woke to a snowy landscape and decided to go ahead. The result was a more muted but more convincing ending, almost black and white in contrast to the often strong reds in the rest of the film. The final minutes now offer a more tentative and realistic optimism than would have been suggested by scenes shot in full colour on a sunny day. A small detail: if you freeze the frame, the walkers and the large soft snowflakes seem to form a white-grey crosshatching as they move in opposite directions. The moment suggests the gentleness associated with Linda and Morag in the film.

The next two examples show an acceptance of deliberate imperfections rather than luck, but their effect is similar to that produced by accidents. Donald Richie points out that there are several unintended discontinuities in Ozu's films caused by his habit of sometimes making changes in the set between shots. Sometimes he simply rearranged the objects on a table. In *Tokyo Story* he reversed the seating order of two characters. When this was pointed out to him, he responded that the audience wouldn't notice. Truffaut similarly assumed the audience wouldn't notice when during postproduction he chose to extend the length of a gaze but couldn't reshoot the scene. According to Almendros he simply froze the character's look across four or five frames. When the camera man pointed out that this produced a slightly grainy effect, Truffaut insisted that "audiences are caught up in the story. They don't notice it."[4] Which didn't mean that they wouldn't be affected it by it on some level.

The interview with Almendros also cleared up a long-running mystery for me. I call it "*Bed and Board* and the Mystery of the Disappearing Art Works." If you pay attention to the scenes set in the front hall of the Doinel apartment, you'll notice that the drawings and posters on the white walls move from place to place between shots. According to Almendros this is the result of Truffaut's insistence that there be nothing distracting behind an actor's head in a shot: if there was a distracting image, he would move it. Once again he assumed the audience wouldn't notice. That he wasn't consistent in this can be seen in *The Woman Next Door* when

Mathilde shares a frame with a small oil painting of a man and woman arguing. The distress in the proleptic painting belongs to Mathilde; the painting's theme of conjugal discord eventually becomes the film's.

Truffaut's early death prevented him from seeing what Eric Rohmer calls the accidents and changes introduced by time into a work of art. "The great works of the screen get better with age, contrary to what might have been said before. Just like paintings or a sculpture, they acquire a patina, unstated in most cases, but the discomfort of the theatre, the scratches on the film, the slip-ups in the projection – to the extent that they add substance to this patina – contribute, if need be, to fortifying the respect inspired."[5] This seems a roundabout way of saying that films, like paintings, age before our eyes. I'm surprised that the thoughtful Rohmer doesn't suggest the extent to which there is a historical and biological patina coextensive with the degeneration of our eyes. I wonder whether he was opposed to the restoration or cleaning of older films. Edvard Munch tried to hurry the creation of this patina by leaving his paintings outside his studio, sometimes even in the rain.

DAY FOR NIGHT (1973): THE FAMILY MOVIE

> For Truffaut movies were more important than life.
> He was happy when he was making films."
> JACQUELINE BISSET[1]
> —

Rainer Werner Fassbinder's *Beware of a Holy Whore* (1971) and *Day for Night* came out within two years of each other; both deal with actors and film crews on location. Beyond that they are as different as, well, night and day, Fassbinder and Truffaut. They found each other's films completely without interest. Fassbinder's film stars Eddie Constantine and is shot in a Spanish villa. Work is halted by money problems and a cast and crew best described as a nest of vipers. By contrast, Truffaut's film about the making of *Meet Pamela* seems like a Renoirian home movie about Truffaut's generally happy team. Though it is tempting to think of it as part of a trilogy with *8 1/2* and *Stardust Memories*, its extended attention to the craft and artifice involved in cinema brings it closer to Renoir's *French Cancan* (1956). Truffaut mentions several other sources, including *Singing in the Rain* (1952) and *The Bad and the Beautiful* (1952).

The film resembles Renoir's in focusing on an ensemble involved in making a work of entertainment; no one speaks of art except in the sense of craftsmanship. Each film has its share of human drama in the form of overlapping love stories, but in the end these form a panorama from life for the work in progress – Ferrand's old-fashioned movie *Meet Pamela* and the launch of Danglard's (Gabin) new cancan at the renovated

Moulin Rouge. Both directors pay attention to small backstage details and encourage young performers. Ferrand tells the lovesick Alphonse (Léaud) that only their work really matters and that "People like you and I are only happy in our work." Danglard rebukes the young Nini when she says that she will perform only if Danglard promises to be faithful to her. He declares, as Ferrand would have, his desire to be faithful to each of his mistresses in his own fashion and insists in front of the troupe that his first and only real love is theatre: "Only one thing matters to me – what I create. And what do I create? You. And her. And her. We are at the service of the public." This is both true and convenient. The two directors understand that their goal is to give the fickle public pleasure. Nini, like Julie (Jacqueline Bisset), had locked herself in her dressing room and refused to continue performing. In both films the crew gathers outside the door to persuade the young performer to come out. Each film also contains a scene in which a puritanical outsider questions the morals of the entertainers. Renoir anticipates Truffaut by having Niki's former boyfriend, a passionate but conventional young man, denounce Danglard. He tells Niki that she will end up like the destitute and homeless Prunelle, an aged former dancer, who drifts in and out of the film like a *memento mori*. When the film's comic plots bring the various lovers together, she acts as an unsettling reminder of the brief bloom, transience, and decline of previous careers, love affairs, and lives. In *Day for Night*, the boyfriend is replaced by the ironically named Madame Lajoie, the local production manager's wife. She observes everything while sitting and knitting as if she were one of the Fates. When the fallout from a brief liaison hits the fan, she rises to denounce actors and filmmaking: "What's this movie business where everyone sleeps with everyone. Everyone lies. Do you think it normal? Your movie world, I think it stinks. I despise it."

Unlike Renoir, Truffaut neither films a love scene – something that Nathalie Baye says he later regretted – nor shows the director involved with his own Nini. This is something Godard brings up in his testy, envious letter attacking the film and its success: "Liar, because the shot of you and Jacqueline Bisset the other evening at Chez Francis is not in your film, and one can't help wondering why the director is the only one who doesn't screw in *La Nuit Américaine*."[2] Since it seems to have been common knowledge on the set that Truffaut and Bisset were lovers, Godard has a point. If the film deals with the film crew's amours, why not the director's? One could suggest that Truffaut sleeps with Julie (Jacqueline

Bisset) vicariously through Alphonse (Léaud), who in previous films has, after all, played Truffaut. The fact is that Truffaut does sneak the director into the film's erotic ambience. But he does this so obliquely that some viewers, including perhaps Godard, might have missed the hint. While working on the script with Joelle one evening, Ferrand receives a phone call from the desk telling him "Dominique is here. Should she come up?" He answers that he's too busy tonight and that she should return tomorrow. The camera, having shown Dominique during the call, now cuts to Bernard and Jean-François, two crew members in the lobby, trying to guess who she might be: "curvaceous … a Riviera beauty … a local call girl … 'the warrior's rest' … right" ("Pulpeuse … Beauté regionale … Call-girl locale? … 'Le repos du guerrier!' … J'allais le dire.") The clinching clue is "the warrior's rest," the title of Vadim's 1962 movie in which Bardot provides rest and recreation for a weary soldier. Dominique, in a manner of speaking, is an essential member of the crew. Truffaut then cuts to the two men watching a television quiz show in which Jeanne Moreau, a former lover, is mentioned. Explicit about the affairs of others, Truffaut deploys his customary *pudeur* and indirection when dealing with his own. My hunch is that Truffaut was willing to hint at his relationships with relatively anonymous prostitutes, but he wanted to protect Bisset from embarrassing inquiries about her relationship with her director. Julie's one-night affair with Alphonse has no counterpart in the lives of Bisset and Léaud; an affair with Ferrand would point to real life. Somehow I don't think Godard would have been satisfied with this explanation.

Day for Night is one of those films that I originally liked and enjoyed more than I admired, though after four decades this no longer matters as much as it once did. I continue to dislike *Meet Pamela*, and the film as a whole leaves me with the impression that Truffaut is coasting, though some aspects of this bother me less than others. Any time Truffaut, Baye, and Léaud are on the screen I'm happy. And there is the undeniable pleasure of feeling that I'm on a set watching a Truffaut film being made. There's another sort of insider pleasure in spotting and following Truffaut's allusions to his own life and work. There is Ferrand's homophonic punning dream of a young boy carrying a cane ("*une canne*") and stealing the stills from *Citizen Kane*, which takes us back to the director's childhood. There is the scene in which Ferrand and the camera crew refer to Alphonse's love affairs as "*salades de l'amour*" (tall tales of love) that looks back to the title of the autobiographical novel Antoine writes in *Bed and Board.* This also reinforces our impression that Alphonse is really Antoine Doinel under another name; we can't help looking back to *Bed and Board* and forward to *Love on the Run* (1979), where Alphonse is the name of Antoine's son. Finally there is a simultaneously backward- and forward-looking intrafilmic allusion when Alphonse asks Julie "Are women magic?" The sentiment was expressed a decade earlier by Plyne in *Shoot the Piano Player*, then again in *Stolen Kisses* and will return in the penultimate scene of *Confidentially Yours.* Truffaut worries the thought at least once a decade – are women magic, are they wonderful, are they exceptional? What is it that makes them perennially interesting to his male characters, that is, to himself? The most generously inclusive answer is offered by Fabienne Tabard to Antoine in *Stolen Kisses*: "You say that I am exceptional. That's true, I am exceptional. But then, every woman is exceptional ... each in her own way ... You are unique. We are, each of us, unique ... unique and irreplaceable." As she pauses speaking, she moves to the apartment window next to a portrait of Audiberti and Antoine's Balthus reproduction. She finishes by telling Antoine that just before he died her father said, "People are wonderful." Her monologue is among the most moving and revealing in Truffaut's body of work.

To return to *Day for Night*: my attention always wanders when the movie within the film takes over. *Meet Pamela*, like *The Woman Who Disappeared*, the dull romantic play in *The Last Metro*, is the film's black hole. Like Pauline Kael, I have never understood what Ferrand means when he says regretfully that movies like *Meet Pamela* will never be made again, that it marks the end of an era. Too often I find myself thinking "Thank God" for that with the same relief that would accompany the announcement that Bruce Willis, Sylvester Stallone, and Tom Cruise had retired. Since the script of *Meet Pamela* carries the must of the studio system and the old-fashioned movies he had always criticized, why is Truffaut showing Ferrand filming it? I once thought he was tipping his hat to the films he had enjoyed in the 1940s, but that no longer convinces. They were much better than *Meet Pamela*.

DAY FOR NIGHT, WES ANDERSON, AND AMERICAN EXPRESS

My son André called to ask whether I had seen Wes Anderson's affectionate pastiche of *Day for Night* in a two-minute commercial he filmed for American Express. As almost always he's a few months ahead of me. I found it on YouTube accompanied by viewers' comments. Anderson, playing Truffaut, offers a short based on the scenes in which Ferrand advises various members of his crew on dialogue, makeup, acting, and guns. These scenes in *Day for Night* enact Ferrand's early voiceover definition of a film director as "someone who is asked questions about everything." The link with American Express comes when the production manager tells Ferrand that they need 15,000 francs immediately. In the film the problem is handled by the insurance company; in the commercial it is solved painlessly and immediately by the credit card. The allusions, like the use of Georges Delerue's theme music, are primarily to *Day for Night*, though Anderson makes a small provocative alteration when he uses a stuntman named François in the film's car accident. And, as I said, *Bed and Board* makes an appearance in Anderson's question "Is that the geisha?"

The problem with the commercial as commercial is that it makes no sense outside the Truffaut Fan Club. Without *Day for Night* it loses its meaning and interest. Anderson dances nimbly and creatively around Truffaut's flame to no obvious end except to come up with a punchline that will sell plastic. I feel as uneasy about Truffaut being used in this way as I would if Fanny Ardant started doing ads for a hair shampoo called *Nouvelle Vague* against a background of wall-size projections of key scenes from *Breathless, Jules and Jim*, and *My Night at Maud's*.

Anderson is a fan and as unashamed a borrower as Godard or Truffaut. It's not surprising therefore that he remembers Truffaut's films throughout his body of work in his use of voiceover and iris lens, and in his emphasis on writing and books, which, as in Truffaut, are often foregrounded. He borrows from *Confidentially Yours* in *Rushmore* when Herman Blume (Bill Murray), in distress over a woman, lights a second cigarette and puts it in his mouth while still smoking the first. The murdering lawyer in *Confidentially Yours* does the same when he senses the police closing in. (Are the smokers imitating the suave Victor Laszlo?) There are at least four nods in *The Royal Tenenbaums* including Ben Stiller's two mop-topped sons who could pass for the lively Deluca brothers in *Small Change*, an Anderson favourite. If you've seen Truffaut's film you probably remember when they cut a friend's hair disastrously to save him the expense of a trip to the barber. Also, given Anderson's close knowledge of *Day for Night*, the go-karting scenes in *Rushmore* and *The Royal Tenenbaums* must be nods to Alphonse's escape to a go-kart track. If you're looking for Truffaut in *The Life Aquatic* (2004), let your memory linger over the following and think of this as a quiz whose answers depend on *Day for Night*.

1. The insurance or bondsman who helps Steve Zissou refinance his film project is played by Bud Cort. Do you recall a similar character in a similar situation in Truffaut?
2. Why is the original name of Steve's submersible *Jacqueline* crossed out?
3. Why does the usually chaste Anderson show the scriptgirl walking around topless?
4. Ned, Steve's "adopted" son, dies during the completion of Steve's film. Which relationship in Truffaut is Anderson recalling?
5. Why at film's end does Steve sit on a red carpet with an unidentified gold statuette next to him?

   (The answers: 1. the insurance adjuster played by Graham Greene; 2. Jacqueline Bisset; 3. the actress Dani makes a topless appearance; 4. Alexandre (Aumont) adopts a young man; 5. *Day for Night* won an Oscar.)

Finally, Anderson describes *Moonrise Kingdom* as inspired in general by *Small Change*. I would add that that the scenes of the young runaways living on a beach also owe much to Bergman's *Monika*, a Truffaut favourite.

More than once Anderson has told interviewers, "I'm a big François Truffaut fan." Like Rushdie and Barnes, one of the good guys – despite the commercial. I saw *The Grand Budapest Hotel* four times in two months. It's that good. Or, put another way, I really liked it.

8 1/2 (1963), *DAY FOR NIGHT* (1973), *STARDUST MEMORIES* (1980), *NINE* (2009)

Since I rarely like musicals, have an almost irrational dislike of Nicole Kidman, and had read the tepid reviews, I went to Rob Marshall's *Nine* expecting to be disappointed by everything except Daniel Day-Lewis. And for the most part I was. The movie seemed as lost as Guido (Day-Lewis playing Mastroianni playing Fellini), and the musical numbers, especially the songs, were flat, though Kate Hudson's cheerleader number brought back warm memories of Karen, my favourite cheerleader in high school. The flattest and most banal number was Kidman's farewell to Guido, telling him she would no longer be his muse. I could go on, but I want to turn to the final movement for which there is no equivalent in Fellini. It is as emotionally perceptive and sensitive as anything I remember from his films. The scene takes place in the screening room where Luisa, Guido's long-suffering wife played by Marion Cotillard, watches Guido's seduction on film of a young actress as he repeats to her what, I assume, he had said to Luisa many years earlier: he touches her head, loosens her hair, and thanks her for "that look."

The real surprise, however, is the unexpected *hommage* to Madame Lajoie's brief scene of denunciation of the film industry in *Day for Night*. After his mistress has attempted suicide, Guido comes out of her room to talk to the doctor. The doctor says to him, "This is a sordid business. You movie people, I suppose you don't consider yourselves bound by morality." Madame Lajoie would have felt vindicated. That Truffaut had paid attention to Fellini's great film is obvious from the scene in *Day for Night* in which a German agent, flanked by two blond Valkyries (I think of them as the Goering twins), asks Ferrand why his films are never political. In *8 1/2* Fellini shows Guido being accosted by a man who proposes "a script that opposes nuclear arms." Not surprisingly the scene is reborn in Woody Allen's take on the depressed and blocked auteur scenario in *Stardust Memories*.

Four films in dialogue across nearly half a century: 1963, 1973, 1980, and 2009. It began in 1963 when Truffaut found himself "very disturbed, moved, impressed and influenced by *8 1/2*."[1] To claim that the allusions and repetitions in these films help to forge cinema into a tradition may strike many as an exaggeration, but I think it's an idea that we might consider.

PAULINE KAEL, WIM WENDERS, AND TRUFFAUT

Reading Kael's reviews again reminded me of how much I enjoyed reading her during her period as the most influential American film critic. There is rarely a page in her various collections without a memorable phrase, image, or sentence. Today the most famous of the reviews – *Bonnie and Clyde*, *Last Tango in Paris*, *The Deer Hunter* – have an historical aura about them. Except for David Thomson, no one writing about film today gives me as much pleasure. And it's not just because of what she says but also because of the electricity of her writing as writing. For an example from Thomson, take a look at his dazzling overview of Coppola's career in *The New Biographical Dictionary of Film*.

Kael points out in her review of Wenders's *Wings of Desire* (1987) that walkers in the Berlin library recall the book memorizers in *Fahrenheit 451*. I wish I had noticed that. Her hunch is confirmed in Wenders's "Talk about Germany": "My favorite scene in the whole of cinema is the end of Truffaut's *Fahrenheit 451*. It's a science-fiction story set in a country where books have been banned, and reading is a crime. A few outcasts live in a tented city. Every one of them is a book, has learned a book by heart and says it over and over. In a wonderful longshot at the end, you see all these talking heads going around reciting in their various languages. Their Babel turns into a kind of music, a choir of mankind."[1] I would guess that in *Wings of Desire* Truffaut's "kind of music" becomes the white noise angels hear on Earth, and the tented city may have been the inspiration for the library.

My envy of Kael's film memory and intuition about Wenders's use of *Fahrenheit 451* prodded me to watch again *Until the End of the World* (1991) and *Faraway, So Close!* (1993), and I noticed two other possible links between the filmmakers. In the first film the two off-kilter crooks, Raymond and Chicago, look back to Ernest and Momo in *Shoot the Piano Player*. In the second there's a scene in which the angel Claliel stands on a balcony of a high-rise apartment watching a young girl balancing herself on a large plastic ball while she leans precariously farther and farther over the barrier. The angel wants to prevent her from falling, but he is helpless. Entranced by the hurdy-gurdy player on the ground, she continues to lean farther out. We share her view of the musician in a long iris. As she falls, the angel's anguished scream expels him into the world of human sounds and bodies with the result that he precedes her to the ground and catches her. Truffaut's version of this is in *Small Change*, where a toddler falls from a ninth-storey balcony onto a lawn and walks away. Truffaut, like Wenders, builds suspense with a long scene that emphasizes the gap between the child's innocent playfulness and the growing concern of the watching adults.

Wenders isn't a director I previously associated with Truffaut, but they have turned out to have more in common than I thought. The following comment – except for the "ontological gaze" – could have come from Truffaut: "In my films, children are present as the film's own fantasy, the eyes the film would like to see with. A view of the world that isn't opinionated, a purely ontological gaze. And only children have that gaze ... Children have a sort of admonitory function in my films: to remind you with what curiosity and lack of prejudice it is possible to look at the world."[2] Wenders reviewed both *Mississippi Mermaid* and *The Wild Child*, and in each case he made the sort of observation available only to someone working in film. In an otherwise dull review of the first he closes with the comment that "Of the six jets that leave the island of Réunion," where the first part of the film was shot, "every week, four are Boeings, two are Douglases, and one flies in CinemaScope, although it was only shot in the normal 'academy' format."[3] He's also perceptive on Truffaut's use of the iris in *The Wild Child* and in general.

> In a tin tub [the boy] is washed for the first time, in steaming hot water. The circle of the iris closes the shot once more: a smile appears on the boy's face for the first time. The old silent films certainly didn't use these fades just because there were no zoom lenses in those days. The serious way in which circle-outs centre one's vision on the detail of the image is also a kind of affection towards its objects, in stark contrast to zooms, which grab their objects and violently pull them towards us. But that isn't the only reason why this black-and-white film about a silent person resembles a film of the silent era. As in those early films, the images are distanced, and apart from simple camera movements, fixed; like them Truffaut's film is, far from being sentimental, full of a solemn sobriety.[4]

The comment that an iris can create "affection towards its objects" is a necessary reminder that technique and form create and filter the emotions we feel as much as the script does and that much of our affection or interest is absent when we read a script.

The final point of contact between Wenders and Truffaut is in their loyalty to black and white. Both would disagree with Cocteau's early comment, made at the 1932 premiere of *The Blood of the Poet* that "eventually films we consider marvellous today will soon be forgotten because of new dimensions and colour."[5] In retrospect, Cocteau's enthusiasm seems curious when we realize that all of his subsequent films were in black and white. Wenders's response to this view, though not specifically to Cocteau, comes in his 1976 essay on *Kings of the Road*: "It's a pity that black and white has become the exception. It would be good for quite a lot of films if they'd been shot in black and white. For me, black and white is more realistic than colour. Black and white can be colourful, and colour can be very black and white."[6] I'm not sure I understand the paradoxes in the last two sentences. If colour is the colour of reality, then how can a black and white film be more realistic than one in colour? It would be simpler if Wenders just argued that sometimes he preferred black and white for certain subjects. Truffaut seems to have a natural preference for black and white perhaps because it is the "colour" of the films of his youth. His most intense film memories are inextricable from black and white and, not a small consideration, from his pantheon of the greatest filmmakers. He is closer to them in black and white than in colour. If we count *The Mischief Makers* and *Antoine and Colette*, eight of his films are black and white. When he works in colour, I rarely sense the adventurousness, almost a shedding of painterly inhibitions, that there is in Godard's *Made in America* or Tarkovsky's *Nostalghia*, in which certain shots without characters reach for pure colour and approximate nonrepresentational paintings, though the colours carry symbolic and thematic intent.

There are two groups of directors that long for black and white. There are those, like Truffaut, whose most intense experience of film took place in the pre-colour era and who suggest that "with each step, each technical advance, each new invention, film loses in poetry what it gains in intelligence, it loses in mystery what it gains in realism."[7] Truffaut also thought that colour creates the illusion of real life and therefore brings a film into the orbit of documentary. More recently, Alexander Payne has suggested that since black and white "never left the world of fine-art photography why should it leave films?"[8] Then there are those like Renoir, Ozu, and Powell who began making films in the silent era and turned with some reservations to colour. Powell is explicit about his preference in *Million-Dollar Movie*: "Sometimes I think that all colour is an illusion. Maybe that is why some of my films are different from other people's films, because I see them in the bones of black and white. How lucky I was to start with a master craftsman, a master artist like Rex Ingram, and work for three years in black and white on epic themes. Film technicians are always debating about black and white, but when the crunch comes they are afraid to fight it out with the backers who only know, or think that they know, that the public wants colour. The public knows very well the difference, but is not prepared to go to the bat about it."[9] Powell has a touching confidence in the audience's judgment, and he extends it to a hunch that it wants black and white. So far as I can tell from the reception of some outstanding black and white films of the past half century, like *Raging Bull*, the public has forgotten black and white almost completely. I wonder whether some of my visual discomfort with Powell's colour films comes from the fact that he sees "them in the bones of black and white." Or is it that I'm so accustomed to the Hollywood palette that any deviation from it catches my attention? Perhaps that will be black and white's paradoxical attraction in the future: once the norm, now the exotic exception, it will attract attention because of what it isn't, because it is a break with the expected. By adding silence to colourlessness, *The Artist* (2012) doubled the bet and won. Two years later Payne's *Nebraska* (2013) and Pawel Pawlikowski's Bressonian *Ida* (2014) are unimaginable in colour. Pawlikowski, like Bresson, leaves me with the impression that if the soul has a colour, it is an early morning winter grey.

TRUFFAUT, ADAM ZAGAJEWSKI,
AND
THE FATE OF SPIRIT

An entry in the poet Adam Zagajewski's "Dangerous Considerations: A Notebook" reminds me of a significant silence in Truffaut's vision. "As always, while reading an intelligent author who writes with passion about the *sacrum*, I'm seized by religious yearnings."[1] That last sentence implies, what is clearer in the poetry, that most of the time Zagajewski stands outside the sacred precincts of religion, watching with interest, stepping inside occasionally but usually not participating. Truffaut, by contrast, doesn't look back. In his world God and spirit are empty signifiers. His apostasy from French piety and sanctimoniousness – what Kierkegaard spent his life disparaging as Christendom – is so great that even the films' music never suggests a spiritual dimension. The few times churches appear they are simply settings for a murder, a funeral, or a wedding emptied of traditional spiritual content. His central concerns are films, women, children, friends, and himself. God isn't even an absent presence. The votive chapel in *The Green Room* is deconsecrated before it can be used as a personal secular shrine, its resident saints are all Julien's and Truffaut's. It is part of a humanistic religion grounded in love that tries to avoid making promises it can't keep.

TRUFFAUT IN
THE SQUID AND THE WHALE (2005)

Noah Baumbach's low-budget Brooklyn story of a family breaking apart borrows some ideas, situations, nuance, resonance, and energy from the New Wave. To start, when Bernard (Jeff Daniels with a Truffauldian name) moves house after Joan (Laura Linney) tells him she has a lover, he puts up a black and white poster of Jean Eustache's *The Mother and the Whore* (Léaud is in it). What the poster was doing in the family home is another question. A late scene imitates and discusses *Breathless*: the husband reminds his estranged wife that they had seen it together when newly married, and then playfully and poignantly runs his thumb along his lips, like Belmondo, and says *"dégueulasse,"* Belmondo's last word. Truffaut makes five appearances. Frank (François?), the younger, troubled and rebellious son, is shown talking to himself in a mirror in what I take to be an echo of the scene in which Antoine stands in front of a mirror in *Love on the Run* and repeats his and his girlfriend's names. When Bernard reminds Frank "You liked *The Wild Child* when we saw it," there is a hint that Baumbach's film is reversing its predecessor's narrative trajectory: Frank is falling from civilization to wilderness. When Walt, the older brother, plagiarizes a Pink Floyd song for a school assignment, he repeats Antoine's copying of Balzac's "The Search for the Absolute." Each is reprimanded by a teacher. Walt's scene with a psychologist inevitably recalls Antoine's. And when he runs from the hospital, where Bernard is recovering, Baumbach films him at length, though from right to left, in imitation of the ending of *The 400 Blows*. *Frances Ha* (2013) is less obvious in showing Baumbach's familiarity with Truffaut's work though you wouldn't know it from the reviews, which tended to see it as little more than a footnote to the New Wave rather than as an attempt at a dialogue with it. Few who worry about filmic Francophilia realize that the only viewers picking up the allusions today have one foot in the grave. To the young the Paris Frances sees looks as new as Woody Allen's vision in *Midnight in Paris*. Though Baumbach borrows here from *The 400 Blows*, *Small Change*, and *Jules and Jim*, he seems to me less self-conscious in the uses to which he puts his sources than he was in his first film. His most daring gambit seems to me his use of Georges Delerue's well-known "Thème de Camille" from Godard's *Contempt*, echoes of which also sound through several melodies the composer wrote for Truffaut.

Overall, I enjoy Baumbach's *hommage* to Truffaut even as I know that it is probably too extensive, that he will need to distance himself from his teacher, perhaps to learn to steal, assimilate, and transform rather than simply borrow. The borrower always reworks the material less thoroughly than the thief and risks pastiche. In *The Squid and the Whale*, his point-by-point appropriation of Truffaut's ending leaves less room for his own vision and originality. It's a good example of a director who doesn't understand that real influence isn't simply a matter of quotation. Think of Truffaut's use of Rita Hayworth and *Gilda* in *Confidentially Yours*. He opens with a single long take of Fanny Ardant walking down a side street in Nice. A small white terrier trots briskly behind her as she walks and flashes her irresistible smile. If you've seen her in other films, you notice immediately that the lilt, rhythm, pace, and overall form of her walk – the swing of the arms, the model-like scissoring of the legs – are intensified and sped up. The scene is long enough that the image of Hayworth strutting and belting out "Put the blame on Mame, boys, put the blame on Mame" slowly surfaces behind Ardant. The resemblance is too close to be coincidental. It's enough of a hint to make us notice a number of scenes in which Almendros lights Ardant's triangular face with its strong cheeks and vulpine jaw in a way that recalls Hayworth's. The brisk walk, by the way, establishes the pace for the film in which everything from dialogue and gestures to music and montage seems to be on fast-forward. The subject may be noirish, but the pace is close to screwball romantic comedy.

Fanny Ardant has this scene in mind as well when she does her song and dance in François Ozon's *8 Women*. It's a soft take on a striptease and ends with Fanny peeling off her long black gloves and throwing the second into the "crowd" – it lands on Danielle Darrieux. Fanny and Rita reunited after nineteen years in a nod to Truffaut by the next generation.

TRUFFAUT AND PAUL LÉAUTAUD
(1872–1956)

La Chanson du Mal-aimé: À Paul Léautaud.
GUILLAUME APOLLINAIRE
—

It isn't clear when Truffaut first encountered the writing of Paul Léautaud, a minor drama critic and journal writer with impressive connections in Paris cultural circles. Truffaut's biography suggests that Léautaud first attracted his attention through a series of radio interviews in 1950 and 1951 – Mavis Gallant heard them as well. For a long time I hoped that the connection came after *The 400 Blows*, with Truffaut noticing Léautaud's name on the spine of a book at some *bouquiniste* and picking it up simply because it echoed Léaud. No such luck. The one reference in the published letters occurs in 1979 the same year as *Love on the Run*. Writing to Nathalie Baye, Truffaut signs himself Léautaud/Léaud/Léotard – the last is a reference to her boyfriend Philippe Léotard, who was in *Jules and Jim, Bed and Board, Two English Girls*, and *Such a Gorgeous Kid like Me*. In Canada he is remembered as Geneviève Bujold's troubled husband in Claude Jutra's *Kamouraska*. In *Love on the Run*, Antoine's girlfriend, Sabine, gives him a complete edition of Léautaud's journals – all nineteen volumes. Only someone already familiar with the similarities between Léautaud's, Truffaut's, and Doinel's lives would understand the reason and the reference. Eric Neuhoff comments: "Doinel bends under the load [of books] but he's in heaven. Dorothée is a sly minx. It didn't take her long to guess Antoine's tastes. 'You see all the troubles that he had with women.'"[1] Neuhoff confuses the actress Dorothée and the character Sabine, but like her he recognizes that the journal is Doinel's novel, *Les*

Salades de l'amour, writ large and with no discretion about the writer's lusts and intimacies. I can't imagine Truffaut recording and publishing any dream as revealing as the one Léautaud had at sixty-five: "A very pleasant dream last night ... I found myself with my mother, looking just as she did when I discovered her again at Calais [in 1901]. Lunch together. After lunch we made love very passionately, on her part and mine, with the same ardour. She was completely naked, her face shining with pleasure. I've always had her – in my dreams."[2] The film enters Léautaud's world when Doinel explains to Sabine that Léautaud's problem was that "he wanted to make love to his mother. So did she, sort of, but in the end she was afraid." It's an emotionally multilayered moment: a not-yet-divorced young man, falling in love with a young woman, explains to her about a writer who wanted to make love to his mother, but he doesn't mention his own longing for the love of his own unloving mother. In a more self-reflexive film Truffaut could have complicated the scene further by having Sabine surprise Doinel (and the viewer) by telling him that she knows about his life from *Bed and Board* and from his novel.

Did Truffaut envy the other man's candour, especially since he never allowed himself to be as explicit about his private life? Other than this scene in *Love on the Run* the closest he comes to a confessional mode in the films is Fergus's frank monologue in *The Bride Wore Black* about his lust for women as he paints Julie, his latest object of desire. Almost as if he wants to remind us of what he refuses to show, Truffaut hints at it with the paintings and with the reflection of Moreau's breasts in a mottled mirror. Fergus is resurrected as Bertrand Morane in *The Man Who Loved Women*. The confidence and insouciance are gone, as if the years of conquests have left him with a sense of repetition, ennui, and disillusionment. Each man defines himself as a *cavaleur* (womanizer), but Morane knows that what he offers women cannot be named. The only love that could have changed his life's emotional current and trajectory was his mother's – and *that* was never a possibility.

Truffaut returned to Léautaud in interviews he taped with Claude Givray in the months before his death when he was still thinking about a memoir. Making a final effort to explain his failed relationship with Janine, he wondered whether he should tell the story in a novel or in a journal – or in both, as Léautaud had done. Unfortunately there was little new about the relationship that could be added to what he had already revealed unless he was willing to be more candid. The Doinel films and

The Man Who Loved Women had already dealt with Janine's failings as a mother and *Such a Gorgeous Kid like Me* had imagined her as a truly free woman. What he tells Givray about his mother is simultaneously a description of Bertrand's litany of slights: "A slightly contemptuous form of authority, a certain manner of calling me 'my little one,' or 'small imbecile,' 'little cretin,' or of giving me orders, treating me like a servant."[3] Had he lived he might have realized that there was no need for the memoir to deal with Janine for the simple reason that no matter how often he dealt with the relationship he would never be satisfied with the story because it couldn't end the way he wanted it to. On the other hand, he would never stop wanting to tell it. He must have found reading Léautaud liberating. Here was a writer who had no reservations about dealing uninhibitedly with his powerful ambivalent emotions toward his mother.

Two years after *Love on the Run*, Truffaut and Jean Gruault considered adapting *Le Petit Ami*, Léautaud's autobiographical novel about his Montmartre childhood in the 1870s and 1880s. Truffaut had acquired the rights in spring 1981 from Mercure de France together with permission to use parts of the *Journal littéraire*. He was also interested in Léautaud's equally autobiographical *Lettre à ma mère*. Taken together these would have allowed him to give a complete account of the writer's childhood in the Notre-Dame-de-Lorette neighbourhood he knew well. At one point, the young Léautaud had lived on rue des Martyrs, which intersects with rue de Navarin. The focus would be on the son and the mother who had abandoned him. Léautaud left him two possible endings for the film. In the first someone can be shown discovering a dusty box after the writer's death on which is written "Flowers my mother sent me, 13 November 1901." In the second, someone at the bedside of the dying Léautaud discovers "in the breast pocket of the jacket he slept in, the photograph of a woman standing naked in a nondescript room. The woman's long hair has been combed forward so that it covers her face. Written on the picture, in Léautaud's hand, is 'If I should depart [i.e., die] never speak about me. Let no one know or even guess how much I loved you. Keep the memory for yourself, like a secret.'"[4]

Though it is unmentioned in his work, I'm sure that Truffaut knew Léautaud's most controversial manuscript, which James Harding, Léautaud's biographer, summarizes tactfully and almost clinically as follows:

> [Léautaud and his companion Madame Cayssac] were both proud of their ardor in love at an age which is politely reckoned as mature. Madame Cayssac was insatiable and used every trick, both verbal and physical, to encourage Léautaud's desire. He kept a record of their sessions which listed all the details. The *Journal particulier*, as it is called, registers the number of times they made love, the positions adopted, the techniques preferred, the obscenities uttered and the dialogue spoken. This private diary has been described as pornography. It is, on the contrary, a far from stimulating work. As an obsessive commentary on his physical enslavement by a woman whom he never truly respected *or liked* [my italics] it is a sad human document.[5]

Harding's book came out before the publication of further instalments of the *Journal particulier*. These deal with the sixty-three-year-old Léautaud's 1935 affair with the forty-nine-year-old Marie Dormay, who was more demanding and less pliant than Madame Cayssac.

Proust, who also adored his mother, detested Léautaud, as Truffaut knew since he had read his letters. Writing in January 1907 to the minor poet and critic Léo Larguier, Proust describes his response to Léautaud's *Amours* as follows: "I won't speak of the book's moral baseness, because I should be incapable of doing so [this from the creator of Charlus]. I don't know any words that could express the pain I felt on seeing a human being feign sentiments beside which those of the cruellest murderer would be estimable. I shall read aloud to you, if you have the strength, a few pages from *Amours*. After each sentence, after each word, you will give voice to your disgust, as one still used to say when I first started to read. And afterwards we shall embrace, rejoicing that we are men and not the unspeakable creature capable of writing such things." He warns Larguier not to mention his words to anyone, in case they get back to Léautaud, "one of the few people with whom I should be afraid to fight a duel. I should feel as though I were up against the angel of darkness. And I'm not pure enough to be confident of winning."[6] The last sentence suggests that the mother-obsessed Proust knew he had more in common with Léautaud than he would admit. Both "the angel of darkness" and the not "pure enough" writer wrote about forbidden desires. Proust's almost comic suggestion – it must be tongue in cheek and camp – of an embrace as a manly response to the abominations of *Amours* – "rejoicing that we are men" – is a wink that his correspondent understood: angels of darkness desire their mothers, those slightly higher in the hierarchy – seraphs or cherubs – embrace men.

Like Truffaut, Léautaud preserved or transcribed anything that caught his eye in the press into his journals. The entry from 27 July 1935, would have appealed to Truffaut: "A short news item read in *Le Quotidien* this morning or yesterday morning. In Vigo (Spain), a young girl took her fiancé for a walk in the woods. As a joke, to which he agreed, she tied him to a tree and blindfolded him; he went along with everything. Having done that and with him tightly bound and unable to see anything, she drove a knife into his breast. She was arrested. He was dead. He had another mistress, she said. There's passion, there's real love."[7] The repeated "voilà" ("There is") is particularly fine and dramatic, almost a thump on the table to end, as if the writer is both making a closing point about humanity and dropping a curtain on a scene of "real love." For Truffaut this would have been another example of the universality of the provisional and the definitive. An unfaithful or provisional lover, he is always tormented by fidelity or the definitive as if his superego knows only one note. In bed with a lover, he dreams of his Alkestis, *toujours fidèle* and always betrayed. I would be surprised if this entry isn't underlined or at least marked in Truffaut's copy of Léautaud's journals. If nothing else, he would have paused at the name of the northwestern Spanish town, Vigo – the name of one of his favourite directors.

MONTMARTRE AND "CERTIFICATION"

Jean-Pierre Melville's *Bob le flambeur* (*Bob the Gambler*, 1955), opens with a series of long panning black and white shots from the air and then along the streets of Montmartre at daybreak: Sacré Coeur, Place Pigalle – Truffaut's turf as a child and today the site of his grave. In *Bande à part*, Godard's voiceover speaks of "Place Clichy [as] one of the loveliest squares at night." There's a direct line from Melville's Atget-like visuals and the accompanying melodies to scenes in *The 400 Blows* and beyond it *Amélie*. In Godard's *Histoire(s) du cinéma* this could be a single frame containing three images superimposed one on another, existing magically in one time and space and offering Paris as a common ground, even as a silent character in the film. In this context Woody Allen's *Midnight in Paris* and Noah Baumbach's *Frances Ha* are just the latest New Wave films, new sets of moving postcards of the most beautiful city in Europe. As I mentioned in passing, Eric Rohmer made the important point in a 1984 interview that when his generation of critics began writing "we thought that French filmmakers didn't show Paris enough, whereas American filmmakers did it really well, even if it was in the form of clichés such as the Eiffel Tower or the Arc the Triomphe. François Truffaut wrote in *Cahiers*: 'the Americans are right to do this, because these places are in Paris.'"[1]

These urban settings are a good example of what Walker Percy's *The Moviegoer* – a novel for which I would trade some decades of American fiction – calls "certification": "Nowadays when a person lives somewhere, in a neighbourhood, the place is not certified for him. More than likely he will live there sadly and the emptiness which is inside him will expand until it evacuates the entire neighbourhood. But if he sees a movie which shows his very neighbourhood, it becomes possible for him to live, for a time at least, as a person who is Somewhere if not Anywhere."[2] Percy assumes, rightly I think, that the camera can bestow an aura on a place by distinguishing it aesthetically from others. It confers fifteen minutes in the spotlight of fame before it returns the place and its people to the greyness of everyday existence though the grey may glisten in a way it never has before. I recently saw a documentary about the making of Chabrol's first film, *Le Beau Serge* (1958), in Sardent, his hometown. The townspeople who had been in the film were still talking about it decades later. One sensed that the town had been changed for them by the fact that they had seen it on screen and that they knew people elsewhere had seen it as well (in Paris!). The town had been "put on the map." Of course, some were simultaneously embarrassed by some of the film's revelations.

THE STORY OF ADELE H. (1975): TRUFFAUT'S FEMINISM

> [With this film] I don't really want to make the audience cry.
> In a way, that's too easy. Perhaps I'd prefer that
> they *tremble* – yes, that's it, tremble.
> FRANÇOIS TRUFFAUT[1]

> It's fine to write with ink ... What comes out of your pen, it's
> like blood, it's your blood spilling, the blood of your thought.
> CATHERINE BREILLAT[2]

The Story of Adèle H. is like one of those Shakespearean plays that forms part of a group on the basis of a common language and concerns. For Nestor Almendros it forms what he calls "a calligraphic trilogy" with *Two English Girls* and *The Green Room* because the screen foregrounds ink, paper, reading, and writing with a pen. The film also forms a sextet of historical films with *Jules and Jim*, *The Wild Child*, *Two English Girls*, *The Green Room*, and *The Last Metro*. To ensure that we don't miss the point Truffaut prints on the screen "*The Story of Adèle H.* is true. It presents events that happened to people who existed." Though she is in her thirties in the film, Adèle is one of Truffaut's wild children, a point he makes quietly in a late scene showing her lurking in the bushes as Lieutenant Pinson and his troop ride by. She is also, of course, one of Truffaut's absolutists in love, his most extreme image of *amour fou*, one of a sisterhood that includes Catherine and Mathilde. Each enacts the will to love as ultimately a death wish.

This is Adèle's film: in none of the others, with the possible exception of *The Green Room*, is the subjectivity of one character so dominant. The focus is on realizing as intensely as possible her way of being in the world. It begins with her arrival in Halifax, Canada, in 1863 and ends with a voiceover account of her return to France in 1872, emotionally broken and perhaps mad. Maurice Jaubert's sombre neo-Romantic "Suite française" sets the tone during the opening credits, which are run over Victor Hugo's moody sepia, blue, and black romantic watercolours of seascapes and castles. The scenes alternate between the dimly lit and claustral interiors of Adèle's rooms and exterior scenes involving Albert Pinson, the soldier she has followed from Europe in the hope of marriage. The interiors, as in *Two English Girls,* are dominated by warm dark tints of maroon, brown, and blue, and Adèle is often shown in bed, cocooned in the soft honey-sepia yellow of a discreet oil lamp, surrounded by darkness. Isabelle Adjani's tensely fragile face, increasingly pale as she realizes her fate, glows out of the rich chiaroscuro, as it might from a Georges de la Tour painting. Almendros notes that in the calligraphic films "the image is really polished" much more than in the early films because the interiors are lit with candles and lamps. This was possible because he was using film stock very sensitive to light.

Adèle's unrequited love becomes an emotional wound that festers into a self-abasement that no longer has any connection to the love in which it originated. Everything she writes about Pinson, says to him, and does can be summed up as her version of Jacques Brel's "Ne me quitte pas." She tells him "You can do with me whatever you want … Even if you don't love me, let me love you … When we are married you can have the same freedom [as you do now]. You can see all the women you want." In one instance she spies on him as he and a woman prepare to go to bed; in another she pays a prostitute to go to him. Not surprisingly she is most alive when in some way dealing with Pinson: her arms and her body become animated, sometimes almost manic, her voice is strong and assertive, and her eyes, usually unfocused, bloodshot, or faintly shining with an exhausted, bruised luminescence as dim as the oil lamp in her room, return to full light and life. There is a similar contrast in her journals, which like her letters and voiceover are a fever chart of her emotional state. The entries after her meetings with Pinson are unusually vivid. A passage early in the relationship sounds like a rehearsal for a provocatively flirtatious letter: "Englishman, you love a French woman;

Monarchist, you love a republican; blond, you love a brunette; a man of tradition, you love a woman of the future; materialist, you love a woman of ideas; I love you as a sculptor loves the clay. So why do I love you, can you tell me?" The last sentence poses the mystery at the heart of the film and perhaps at the heart of relationships other than Adèle's. Adèle, Pinson, and Truffaut are at a loss for a convincing answer.

The confident moments become rarer, and toward the end we see her walking in Barbados – where she has followed Pinson's regiment – dusty, unkempt with her dress torn. When she finally runs into Pinson, she walks past him without recognition or acknowledgment. Even his shouts elicit no response. These Barbados scenes have two particularly fine instances of Truffaut's confident control of pace and rhythm. Adèle's sudden decline, for instance, begins at the end of the Halifax section when we see her walking in a dress torn at the hem. Truffaut cuts from this to a very brief scene in Barbados in which, wearing the same dress, we see her following a soldier. When she taps him on the back, she discovers that it isn't Pinson but Truffaut; it's as if the scene is offering a Flaubertian "Adèle, c'est moi." In the longer next scene in a lighter tone, one of Pinson's soldiers walks from group to group searching for him at a party to tell him that Adèle is on the island. As in a similar delaying scene in *The Woman Next Door*, this one unfolds in stops and starts as the camera follows the man's circuitous route through a crowded party to his goal. (Watching both scenes I wondered whether Truffaut was recalling Frederick Moreau's equally meandering though much longer search for Regimbart in *A Sentimental Education*.) We then see Pinson, in turn, looking for Adèle, finding her, and discovering that she no longer recognizes him. Truffaut then cuts again to her as she walks surrounded by a group of boys – the local branch of *The Mischief Makers* – teasing her as she collapses, still in the same dress. The scene ends with her rescue by Madame Baa. All this takes only a few minutes before we shift to a voice-over announcing her return to Europe.

Graham Robb, Victor Hugo's most recent biographer, and Leslie Ann Dow, Adèle's, both suggest that her decline from a talented and attractive young woman – Balzac called her the most attractive woman he had ever seen – to the madwoman of Barbados can probably be explained by schizophrenia. Dow adds to this a feminist emphasis on the role played by patriarchy: "In some ways the story of Adèle Hugo is the story of all women past and present, whom a patriarchal culture has reduced to their base value as brides, wives or mothers. Like all frustrated and oppressed women, Adèle wanted most of all to be free."[3] This universalizing suggestion runs into a problem: if schizophrenia's cause is not social but organic or genetic, then Adèle would probably have collapsed whether her father was patriarchal or not. Truffaut avoids this limitation by showing her as emotionally troubled but avoids a diagnostic label. Diagnosed as suffering from schizophrenia or patriarchy she is reduced to a case or a patient. Unlabelled, she is a particular troubled woman obsessed with love; she keeps her mystery. As one of Saul Bellow's late novels suggests, and Truffaut would agree, more die of heartbreak than of the usual catalogue of diseases. This isn't to say that the film doesn't agree to some extent with Dow's indictment of patriarchy. Adèle is haunted and oppressed by two men, her father and her lover. Each has a negative effect on her, yet she is helpless to stop loving them and to free herself of their influence. The film dramatizes the web of patriarchal relations within which Adèle is caught, but it doesn't name them except in terms generally available to the era. It is worth adding that a century later a third man rescues her story from the anonymity of an asylum and history's storage room.

The unconditional love and self-abasement she desperately offers Pinson have always been expected by her father, described accurately in the film as the most famous writer in the world at the time. Not included in the film is one of Adèle's most memorable dreams, from 1851, which gives a vivid sense of her father's ambiguous role in her life: "I was in the bedroom that I occupied at the Place-Royale, and all of a sudden my mother entered and told me, 'Your father wants to talk to you. He has gone crazy. He is exasperated. He is smashing the windows.' I ran to the salon where my father bid me enter. 'I was furious with Eugène Delacroix, who has the temerity to ask for your hand. I have sent him back the letter in which he makes this request, and I am now writing him a letter full of insults which will offend him, so that he will renounce all his pretensions toward you.'"[4] At the time of the dream, Delacroix was one of the two greatest French painters, Ingres being the other. At fifty-two he was a stylish and handsome bachelor, though perhaps oldish for Adèle. Victor Hugo would have felt honoured by his proposal. What Adèle understands in the dream is that her father's egotistical need for the love of all of the women around him, including his lifelong mistress, was insatiable; even someone as distinguished as Delacroix, whose stature in painting matched Hugo's in literature, would be deemed unworthy: in other words no one could possibly be worthy of the love of Victor Hugo's daughter except Victor Hugo. However we interpret the dream, it offers an inescapable dilemma for her. When Adèle writes in the film, "I was born of a father unknown. I was born of a father completely unknown" she expresses a truth and a wish: she has never understood her father and she often wishes that she had never known him. Her family name has brought her little but grief. The two sentences, it is worth recalling, were chosen by Truffaut for the script; each describes accurately an aspect of his own double paternity.

If the film begins in the darkness of nighttime Halifax and a portent of tragedy, it surprises by ending in daylight and a final retrospective view of Adèle as young, healthy, confident, and speaking to us while standing on rocks by the sea in Guernsey. Truffaut leads into the scene by showing the white greenishly mottled gravestones of Adèle and her mother. But even while these are on screen ("Adèle Hugo / 1830–1915") we hear a male voiceover repeating lines from earlier in the film: "Fifty years earlier, as she was about to leave Guernsey, Adèle had written in her journal 'This incredible thing that a young girl should step over the ocean, leave the world for the new world to join her lover … This thing will I accomplish.'" As these words are spoken, Adèle's own voice gradually takes over. Her lips continue to move as the final credits roll. At the end we see her triumphant: she is beautiful and admirable as she asserts her freedom and her right to a self-created self, even if that choice involves inevitable suffering, perhaps even self-annihilation. I imagine her reading Faulkner's *Wild Palms* and underlining the desolate male's defiant last words, "*Yes,* he thought, *between grief and nothing I will take grief.*"

After saving Adèle by bringing her to the Hugo family, Madame Céline Alvarez Baa stayed in Paris long enough to be seduced by the most famous writer in the world. Afterward he wrote in his diary, "the first [N]egress of my life." She returned in August 1881 to visit Adèle, by then institutionalized. Hugo's references to his daughter after her confinement at the Maison Rivet are understandably brief: "There are some emotions of which I wish to leave no trace." "I saw Adèle. My heart is broken." "Another door closed, darker than that of the tomb."[5] I find more sincere emotion in these short sentences than in many of Hugo's poems.

TRUFFAUT AND DENEUVE IN
THE STORY OF ADÈLE H.

If this is a lesson in love, well what's it for.
JOHN HIATT, "CRY LOVE"
—

I don't recall at what point I started to think that at some level the film is also about Truffaut's sense of desolation and his eventual breakdown after Deneuve's departure in December 1970. The biography refers to his hospitalization, and we know that he did little work during the first part of the following year. He had read Frances Vernor Guille's biography of Adèle in 1969, but didn't begin work on the film until 1974. It was released at the New York Film Festival in autumn 1975 with Guille in attendance. She died a few days later.

The most obvious internal link between Truffaut and his film is the scene mentioned earlier in which Adèle mistakes him for Pinson. There's something more going on here than a simple Hitchcockian cameo since, unlike Hitchcock, Truffaut usually makes an autobiographical point when he appears in his films. In *The Man Who Loved Women,* for instance, he stands in the opening scene looking at the passing line of women going to Bertrand Morane's funeral. We don't think much about this until we notice later that Morane is wearing the same light brown leather jacket as Truffaut. I tend to interpret the scene between Adèle and the anonymous soldier – whom, as he turns, we all name "Truffaut" – as showing Truffaut behind *both* characters. The disheveled and distracted Adèle *is* Truffaut as he was in the aftermath of Deneuve's departure; but she is simultaneously what Truffaut wished for or fantasized about at the time – Deneuve returning to him chastened and needing his love. In the Grove Press edition of the complete script, the first four photographs show Truffaut and Adjani together; the second photo shows the scene I'm referring to but in reverse so that we see both their faces and Almendros on the camera. Truffaut's introduction to the script gives me hope that my hunch may have some validity.

> Curiously enough, I may discover, after the fact, through what others write about my work, *the inner motivations that guided my choice of a given subject* [my italics]. Because I work instinctively rather than intellectually, it is often some two years after a film has been released that I fully understand its meaning.
>
> This delayed insight is not necessarily a handicap. I would find it very uninspiring to go through the mechanical routine of shooting a film whose meaning has been predetermined.
>
> By now, I am obviously aware that I have a predilection for films of sentiment, dealing with the painful and frustrating aspects of certain family and love relationships. Within each picture, I run into the conflict between temporary and definitive sentiments, so that I seem to be filming the same situations.
>
> Those who have an affinity for these subjects – the low-key descriptions of strong emotions – will see them as variants on a theme. Those who are bored with them will say that we repeat ourselves.[1]

This is a good example of how Truffaut anticipates the possible reception of a film with a preemptive introduction that attempts to ensure the discussion will be on his terms. All directors in the modern era do it, but Truffaut was a master of the routine. Pauline Kael was one of those who took the film as a variation on a theme: "Don Juanism has often been dealt with on the screen, but no one before Truffaut has ever treated a woman's crippling romantic fixation with such understanding, black humour and fullness."[2] Truffaut is one of the great directors of women, but in this case I wonder whether he is able to treat "a woman's crippling romantic fixation with such understanding" because he is dealing with his own. With Deneuve, as with Lilian Litvin twenty years earlier, he was blindsided by a relationship with an emotionally stronger woman. Litvin's departure resulted in a suicide attempt; Deneuve's in a collapse. He returns to the breakdown two years later in *The Man Who Loved Women*, in the scene in which Charles Denner runs into Leslie Caron many years after she left him. Caron's role recalls both Litvin and Deneuve. Truffaut is dealing with mourning, guilt, remorse, and self-abasement by putting his pain on the screen. There is also the paradoxical pleasure of having fleshed out and dramatized his emotions into a work of art. He will return compulsively to the scenario again in 1981 with Bernard and Mathilde's story in *The Woman Next Door*. I can't be alone in thinking of Abdellatif Kechiche's *La Vie d'Adèle* (*Blue Is the Warmest Colour*, 2013) as a contemporary retelling of Truffaut's film.

A DREAM:
THE STORY OF ADÈLE H.
AND **ELLE**

Though I have kept a dream journal on and off for forty years, this is one of the few dreams whose decipherment depends on word play of the kind Freud uses in *The Interpretation of Dreams*. Truffaut, by the way, never mentions Freud, Jung, or Lacan, and psychoanalysis or psychotherapy are absent from his vocabulary. The dream occurred in the year after the end of my marriage and the subsequent end of the relationship with Elle. I was watching Truffaut at least twice a week for therapy. Finding time was easy. I had tenure and my insomnia had moved in for a long stay. Elle had made the sensible decision to marry someone else, leave town, and have babies. I was watching *Love on the Run*, *The Green Room,* and *The Woman Next Door* in the middle of the night.

In the dream I am sitting in an outdoor café with Gertrude Stein – whose writing I always described to my students as one of the ten greatest frauds of the century – and Albert Finney, an actor I have liked since *Tom Jones* (1963) and whom I had seen a few days earlier in *The Green Man* (1990). It's one of those dreams in which I'm uncertain at the start where I am and then slowly begin to recognize some signposts. In this case, I begin to sense that I'm in Paris, in a café close to the Seine, near the Louvre. I'm confused by the fact that I'm sitting with Stein and Finney though my ego is large enough in the dream that I have no doubts about belonging in their company. Later in the day I will trawl through the previous day's residue and recall that I had been reading and teaching

Anne Carson, a Stein acolyte. If there was a Gertrude Stein fan club, she and William Gass would be co-presidents. Stein, Finney, and I are talking about *The Story of Adèle H.*, and I'm surprised by how vehemently they dislike it. I try to justify my admiration, to place it among Truffaut's films, and to explain the theme of provisional and absolute love. My response isn't as coherent as it is here, but like all dreamers I think that I'm remarkably articulate. The conversation deteriorates into three voices getting progressively louder. Stein's authoritative quack drowns out Finney's strong bass and my quavering tenor. When Stein reaches for her Pernod – we are all drinking Pernod though I never drink it – I notice a scar on the inside of her right wrist. I wake just after Stein begins to turn into a duck or something amorphous making incomprehensible sounds that seem to berate me for something. Whatever she is, for some reason it reminds me of Picasso's portrait of her, though I don't recall the details on waking.

I wrote the dream down in my bedside notebook and played with it on and off for the next few days. A key appeared when I remembered that I had seen Truffaut's film in 1991 – with Elle. To put it mildly, she hadn't liked it – "That woman's crazy." It made her uncomfortable, on edge, and in the end angry. After agreeing to disagree about it, we broke off discussion. I had a hunch that it hit too close to some of her memories and wounds. Perhaps she was also anxious that, given her past, she would end up like Adèle: Stein's scar was also hers. But why Stein and Finney? I cracked the code when I remembered that Elle's nickname was Ginny: Gertrude + Finney = Ginny. At a time when I simultaneously wanted to see her (Finney) and to avoid her (Stein), the dream gave me both. Everything I liked about her I gave to Finney (I suspect I also thought of myself as "Tom Jones"), the rest to Stein. The latter's sexuality reminded me that Elle had told me she "tried it once" at university.

SMALL CHANGE (1976)
AND
RENOIR'S *THE RIVER* (1951)

> There is no profit in gaining the whole world
> if one has lost one's childhood.
> ANDRÉ BAZIN[1]

In Renoir's first colour film, a child dies and a neighbour makes a Truffauldian speech whose attitude to children and death surprises both the characters and the audience: "We should celebrate that a child has died. That one escaped. We lock them in our schools, we teach them our stupid taboos, we catch them in our wars, we massacre the innocents. The world is for children. The real world. They climb trees and roll on the grass, close to the ants." I have no doubt Truffaut remembered this when he wrote the teacher's speech about children to his class toward the end of *Small Change*. Two children escape death in Truffaut's film: an infant survives a fall from a ninth-floor apartment window, and a young boy, neglected and physically abused by his mother, is taken away from her. The teacher's speech in *Small Change* is the longest not only in the film but in Truffaut's body of work. It describes children as a marginalized and powerless class at the mercy of adults busy with their lives. The "François" in the teacher's name prepares us for the link to the director as does Truffaut's brief appearance at the film's beginning, which suggests that he is its guardian spirit. The teacher tells the children that "When we hear a story as terrible as Julien's, our first reaction is to compare it with our own. I had a hard childhood, though it was much less tragic and painful than Julien's, and I remember how impatient I was to grow up, because I felt that the grownups had all the rights and that they were able to lead their lives as they wanted."

Small Change includes life's darker possibilities – its original title was *The Tough Skin / La Peau dure* – but always returns to offer a comic affirmation of what Truffaut calls "the spirit of childhood." He describes his goal in the movie as "making the audience laugh, not at the children but with them, nor at the expense of the adults either, but with them; thus we had to look for a delicate balance between gravity and humour."[2] Just before this passage in the novelization he quotes Ernst Lubitsch's comment that "An occasion to laugh is never to be despised." Kael is right that the film risks sentimentality, but it is willing to take that risk in order to offer as positive a view of childhood as possible without undermining realism. Truffaut and Schiffman understood that they were writing a screenplay about children whose childhoods were very different from Truffaut's or Antoine Doinel's. Eric Rohmer's comment on *The River* also catches something of the dialectic at the heart of *Small Change*: "Perhaps [*The River*] attempts nothing other than to reconcile us with a world whose idyllic sweetness takes none of the edge off its cruelty."[3] The cruelty and sweetness are already present in *The Mischief Makers* and return in a muted form at the end of *Confidentially Yours*, a combination of romantic comedy and noir with no children in the main cast of characters. In an early scene, however, Fanny Ardant, the secretary, tells Jean-Louis Trintignant, her boss, who has just fired her, "Get yourself an orphan [for a secretary]. They're used to being abused." And the film's last scene, under the credits, shows a children's school choir singing and then kicking a camera lens cap along the church floor. Childhood frames the film: abused orphans and playful singing children. The last scene in the church is an extension of Ardant and Trintignant's marriage ceremony and may have been the last Truffaut filmed. If we keep in mind the resemblance between Truffaut and his lead actor, you might say that he was filming his own wedding.

I can't imagine Godard agreeing with Renoir that love "is more important than social questions. It is the way to lead people to truth. There is more truth in sentimental relations than in social relations. There is more truth in the bedroom than in the office or the boardroom."[4] Truffaut, on the other hand, would have understood not only this but also Renoir's confession that he was "only interested in sentiments, love stories that may touch me."⁵ This sets up the predictable antithesis of the rational and political Godard and the sentimental apolitical Truffaut. But it doesn't quite hold up if we keep in mind the importance of love in Godard's early films and Truffaut's political activism on behalf of groups working with abused and abandoned children. His focus was never on parties or ideologies. Like John Rawls (see *A Theory of Justice*), Truffaut judged his society by how it treated its most disadvantaged and least powerful group – children. The degree of his commitment is evident in the teacher's speech quoted earlier. The only positive thing he can say in the film about an unhappy childhood is that "By some ironic justice, those who have had a difficult childhood are often better equipped to enter adult life than those who have been very sheltered, very loved; it is a kind of law of compensation."

The speech anticipates Truffaut's essay "Année d'enfance assassinée" ("A Year of Murdered Childhood") published in the *Bulletin de la Féderation Internationale des Ciné-clubs*. Ostensibly about films about children, it begins with an attack on the French government for turning a blind eye to starving children: "If we think of children, the nineteen-seventies will mark a black period and History will not forgive us, I hope, the black humour which decreed 1979 the Year of Childhood, at a time when we count by the thousands children who died of hunger or maltreatments of various kinds in Africa, Asia and elsewhere."⁶

AN AGED MAN IS BUT A PALTRY THING

There is a scene in Robertson Davies's novel *Fifth Business* in which Padre Blazon, an old priest, reminds the hero Dunstan Ramsay that Jesus died young and that his vision is therefore inevitably that of dogmatic youth, of a young man in a hurry. No one in the New Testament walks as much as Jesus or is quite as intense, energetic, and impatient – he could pass for Jean-Pierre Léaud's Jewish cousin. With death nearby, Blazon suggests that he needs "something that takes account of the accretion of experience, the sense of paradox and ambiguity that comes with years. I think after forty we should recognize Christ politely but turn for our comfort and guidance to God the Father, who knows the good and evil of life, and to the Holy Ghost, who possesses a wisdom beyond that of the incarnated Christ."[1] This has little to do directly with Truffaut who, as I suggested earlier, was as tone deaf to religion's music as he was to heavy metal or literary theory, but it reminded me that there are very few people over fifty in his films. There is nothing in his work like the scene between the reunited lovers – the future Monsieur and Madame Dame – in Demy's *The Young Girls of Rochefort* or the mother and father in Marco Tullio Giordana's *Best of Youth* (2003). Think also of García Márquez's *Love in the Time of Cholera* or Bellow's *More Die of Heartbreak*. With the exception of the man with the flowers who picks up Chico in *Shoot the Piano Player*, the middle-aged married neighbours in *Bed and Board* and Madame Jouve in *The Woman Next Door*, there is no indication in the films that there is more to being in love than "the young in one another's arms ... / Caught in that sensual music" (Yeats, "Sailing to Byzantium"). For Truffaut old love is an oxymoron.

Would Truffaut have been able to shift registers and make a great film about love after fifty? The same question comes up when I think about D.H. Lawrence. He died in 1930 at forty-five, and his last statement came in *Lady Chatterley's Lover* (1928). For him as for Truffaut, older people are primarily the inevitable generational impediments to love (*The Virgin and the Gipsy*). Not unexpectedly there is none of the understanding found in the fiction of John Updike's last decade where in the story "Free" a widower in his seventies visits a once beautiful widow with whom he had an adulterous affair many years earlier: "When his ring [at the door] was answered, he had trouble relating the Leila of his memory and imagination to the tiny woman, her nut-colored face crisscrossed by wrinkles, who opened the door to him. Her face had seen a lot of sun in these past thirty years ... From the way she held her face up and motionless he gathered he was supposed to kiss it; he abruptly realized he had brought her no present. It had been the nature of their old relationship for him simply to bring his body, and she hers. Her cheek had a dry pebbled texture beneath his lips, but warm like a dog's paw pads."[2] Updike, who died at seventy-seven, inevitably dealt with a topic Truffaut never faced, love in old age. Milan Kundera, now in his eighties and living in Paris, has written little about geriatric desire, a phonically unattractive term suggesting willful paradox. His one exception is the relatively recent *Ignorance* (2002), in which a middle-aged man finds unexpected satisfaction and humour in the arms of his wife's mother, closer in age to him than is her daughter. The result is an emotion, both lust and love, not on Truffaut's or Lawrence's love meters: "A feeling of peace envelops him: for the first time in his life, sex is located away from persecution, away from any accusation, away from worries; he has nothing to take care of, love is taking care of him, love as he's always wanted it and never had it: love-repose; love-oblivion; love-desertion; love-carelessness; love-meaninglessness."[3]

This is not quite the carnality of the aged that García Márquez offers in *Love in the Time of Cholera*, but it is still beyond scenarios dealing with love among the young, younger, and youngest featured in most contemporary movies. To the question, "Can an old body be an object of desire?"

the Colombian master offers a qualified, yes, but only if it has been loved since youth – my words not his. A similar affirmation is made in *The Best of Youth* and Arnaud Desplechin's *A Christmas Tale* (2008), where the parents' reciprocal affection and love connect the other more volatile provisional relationships and offer a lasting standard against which they can be gauged and seen to fail.

INGMAR BERGMAN,
CAVALEUR

> I believe that every word a writing man writes is put down
> with the ultimate intention of impressing some woman that
> probably dont [sic] care anything at all for literature,
> as is the nature of women.
> WILLIAM FAULKNER[1]
> —

In "Bergman's Opus," an admiring 1973 essay, Truffaut distinguishes among Ophuls, who "adopts the viewpoint of his female characters," Renoir, who "beckons us to view his heroines through the eyes of their male partners," and Bergman, who tends "to show us men through women's eyes." He then quotes without comment Bergman's exuberant tongue-partly-in-cheek response to a Swedish journal's assertion that "Bergman is much wiser about women [than men]."

> All women move me – old, young, all, short, fat, thin, thick, heavy, light, beautiful, charming, living, dead. I also love cows, she-monkeys, sows, bitches, mares, hens, geese, turkey hens, lady hippos, and mice. But the categories of female that I prefer are wild beasts and dangerous reptiles. There are women I loathe. I'd like to murder one or two, or have myself killed by one of them. The world of women is my universe. It's the world I have developed in, perhaps not for the

Le cavaleur :

* Quand l'histoire commence son manuscrit est accepté : on part à sa recherche, il est mort.
[On lit son manuscrit :
* quand l'histoire est interrompue c'est :
  — : dactylographié par la dactylo (ou lui)
  — : composition à l'imprimerie .....
  — : correction des épreuves par une femme...
  — : couverture du livre (on vient lui faire choisir chez lui ou au bureau ?)
  — : sortie du livre : .... vite à signer pour la critique..
      il ne viendra pas ... il est mort

  ※

  — "tout de même il n'a pas fait grand chose de sa vie, quel gâchis !"
  — il a quand même fait quelque chose : un livre.

  ※

(peut-être meurt-il en voulant attraper les jambes de l'infirmière .....
Il avait traversé la rue pour rejoindre une femme ... celle qu'il avait laissé tomber)

Truffaut's notes about *Le Cavaleur*, Bertrand Morane's memoir of the women he has known.

best, but no man can really feel he knows himself if he manages to detach himself from it.[2]

No public figure today would get away with a letter or website comment as playful and irreverent as this. But though Bergman is being deliberately over the top, he's also serious. It's as if he were saying, "You want to discuss my sex life, well here is my contribution to the discussion." By exaggerating he is also able to tell at least part of the truth about his attitude to women without seeming to: I've been involved with many women and their world is my universe. Did Truffaut quote the passage as a way of saying something about his own equally complicated relationship to the "the world of women" without having to reveal anything? Truffaut had several masks both in life and on screen. Here he uses Bergman to speak for him.

FAME: DAPHNE MOON, NILES CRANE, AND A TRUFFAUT FILM

> What is the number in the title of François Truffaut's first movie?
> JEOPARDY, 27 MAY 2015
> —

An episode of *Frasier* (9 April 2002) has a scene in which Daphne tells Niles "That Truffaut film you like is playing down at the La Salle." Is there another French director either of Truffaut's generation or today – Assayas? Besson? Breillat? Ozon? – whose name would have made it past the script team's and network's worries about audience recognition? The scene is in a different category from the one in *Seinfeld* in which Elaine rants against Anthony Minghella and Michael Ondaatje's *The English Patient*. That film had started life as a bestselling novel and was a recent Oscar winner for best picture. Only someone living in a shack without electricity in Montana or northern Alberta wouldn't understand the reference and the fuss.

What would Niles's favourite Truffaut have been? Given his problems with Maris, his domineering high-maintenance wife, it might have been *Jules and Jim*. On the other hand, if he went to the cinema to escape life, *Stolen Kisses* would have offered an appealing alternative; its star, Claude Jade, is Daphne's twin in gentleness, sympathy, and unthreatening beauty. Real and imagined kisses stolen with Daphne are what Miles lives on for the better part of a decade.

THE MAN WHO LOVED WOMEN (1977): TRUFFAUT AND DON JUAN

> My memory betrays me, perhaps, when it brings back only
> negative images of my mother. Mean or not,
> she taught me one thing in any case – only love matters.
> ANTOINE DOINEL[1]

Truffaut had many things in common with Albert Camus, including a very active sex life and an interest in Don Juan. Camus wrote about the fabled lover in *The Myth of Sisyphus* and often considered returning to the topic. Truffaut approached it in *Jules and Jim* and *The Man Who Loved Women*. Prompted by Roché, he wrote a scene in the script's second draft in which Jules reads to Jim from his novel *Don Juan* – eventually titled *Jacques and Julie* – but the words are really from Roché's *Two English Girls and the Continent*. As Truffaut must have realized, the Don Juan in *Jules and Jim* is Catherine, an effective disguise for what is in part Truffaut's concealed self-portrait. In this context, *The Man Who Loved Women* is a later slightly airbrushed and exculpatory version of the same story. Bertrand Morane (Charles Denner) is one of the saddest Dons in the canon – his women remark on it – even though Truffaut thought of the film as a comedy when writing it. Like the "Don Juanism" section of *The Myth of Sisyphus*, Truffaut's two films are on some level attempts to justify desire and infidelity and a man's desire to sleep with any woman he finds attractive. Camus writes in defense of male desire, of men who simply enjoy women's bodies and reject the reduction of this aspect of their desire to morality, pathology, or power. His Don "is an ordinary seducer" who recognizes that seduction is his condition of life and that

"Loving and possessing, conquering and consuming – that is his way of knowing." He is a Nietzschean "healthy man provoking a non-existent God." Unlike his contemporaries, he understands that there are no eternal values and that we live in a pure present "without hope or remorse."[2] Like Truffaut, though with a different emphasis, Camus links the Don to love and death: "The mad thing about love is that one wants to hurry and *lose* the interim. In this way one wants to get closer to the end. In this way love in one of its aspects coincides with death."[3] There is much here that wouldn't be out of place in Bertrand Morane's autobiography, whose final title is identical with the film's, or in several of Truffaut's other films in which love and death (or mourning) are co-extensive. Had Truffaut read Camus, he would have recognized a fellow *cavaleur* or Don Juan equally tempted and troubled by sex and equally secretive about it. What Camus would have immediately noticed in *The Man Who Loved Women* is that Truffaut's Don Juan repeats the pattern of his mother's life. Like her he walks the streets in search of a temporary lover, and both have a record of their affairs in stored letters and photographs. Yet neither is able to love. Camus treats Don Juan's sexuality philosophically as an example of pure erotic desire and presentness without memory. He is what he seems, and his fate is as determined as the future of an erection: each arousal occurs in the shadow of Freud's death instinct.

In Milan Kundera's *Immortality*, the Don Juan figure believes in his prime that "erotic adventures would lead him straight to the heart of life" but later realizes that "women had meant nothing to him except as erotic experiences."[4] Truffaut, in a significant contrast, gives Morane (and himself) the benefit of the moral doubt by having Geneviève, his editor, offer an exculpatory if slightly ambiguous judgment that would gladden the heart of any *cavaleur*: "Bertrand pursued an impossible happiness in quantity, in the multitude ... But of all these women who passed through his life, there remains all the same a trace, a testimony, a rectangular object, three hundred and twenty bound pages, it is called a book." She doesn't mention what we know from the earlier part of the film: Bertrand sought with literally countless women the love he had been denied by his mother and later by Véra, who seems to have been the only woman with whom he had a serious extended relationship. Psychology doesn't enter into Camus's and Kundera's narratives: Don Juan and Rubens are what they are simply because that's what they are. The film's final tragicomic scene suggests that Morane's book hasn't resolved the fundamental wound and lack in Bertrand's life: injured when struck by a car as he pursues a woman, he dies in a fall from a hospital bed as he reaches out to touch the night nurse. In Kierkegaard's version of Don Juan – based on Mozart and Da Ponte's *Don Giovanni* – Bertrand would have been "an aesthetic man … governed by sense, impulse and emotion" who suffers the bad infinity "caused by the absence of all limitations."[5] In other words, he would have been doomed to a life of endless desire that could only end in repetition, despair, or death. His book would have had nothing to do with it. As Beckett said in a letter, "Still do not understand in what way art can help us to wait patiently."[6]

JOÃO CÉSAR MONTEIRO'S
A COMÉDIA DE DEUS (1995):
THE MAN WHO LOVED GIRLS

Think of *God's Comedy* as a combination of Vladimir Nabokov's *Lolita*, Balthus's erotic paintings of girls, and Truffaut's *The Man Who Loved Women*. The story's focus is João de Deus, a thin, balding, aging manager of an ice-cream parlour in Lisbon who is as obsessed with beautiful teenage girls as Bertrand Morane is with young women. His scruffy resemblance to Murnau's Nosferatu lends his pursuit of them a simultaneously creepy and comic tinge, as if eros has been leached from what is usually to some degree erotic and in the process has become reduced to the pathetic. Not quite a seducer, he is interested only in a girl's pubic hair. He examines each as carefully as Nabokov studied his Lepidoptera before attaching his trophy with a handwritten description to a page in his "Book of Thoughts." I wouldn't compare this to Morane's haphazard collection of photographs and his book about his love affairs except for two moments in the film that glance at Truffaut. In the first, the owner of the parlour inexplicably insists on hiring a Frenchman named Antoine Doinel to help with the production of ice cream. The second is in the credits – where the other shoe falls – in Monteiro's unexpected thank you note to Jean-Pierre Léaud. Since the latter isn't in the film – except in the reference to Doinel – his contribution is unclear. But the two references seem to me Monteiro's way of paying homage to Truffaut and suggesting that his ostensibly very different and very strange film is a palimpsest on *The Man Who Loved Women*. He leaves it to us to clinch the connection.

Unlike Morane, de Deus doesn't die. He makes the mistake of involving himself with the heavyweight butcher's nubile daughter. When the father finds out, he beats the ice-cream maker severely enough to hospitalize him. The last scene shows him returning to his now empty almost dark apartment and finding his "Book of Thoughts" in the fireplace, partly burned. He picks it up, looks at a few sooty pages, and returns it to the ashes. The camera remains fixed on the fireplace as he walks out of the shadowy frame. The effect is to suggest that his only reason for living is gone and that in the end only ashes will remain of our loves, our lovers' pubic hair, and our books. I take this to be Monteiro's realistic response to Morane's editor's optimistic comment that our books survive us. Truffaut, like Shakespeare, wants it both ways: "golden lads and girls all must, / As chimney sweepers come to dust" (*Cymbeline*, IV, ii, 262–3) and "Not marble nor the gilded monuments / Of Princes shall outlive this powerful rhyme" (Sonnet 55).

LESLIE CARON

Though Caron only worked once with Truffaut, on *The Man Who Loved Women*, the biography suggests she knew both him and Madeleine quite well and that there was more to the relationship than is apparent in the public record. I have never been impressed by her as an actress, in part because she seems a one-trick pony and partly because her dancer's walk and predictable gestures call attention to themselves and away from the character. Her response on screen to almost anything happening around her is a kind of attention verging on surprise, almost as if she is pent with anticipation of her next line or move. There's something of this in Gene Kelly as well. Neither moves naturally even when they make an effort to move with ease: it's as if the athletic, fit dancer's body has to move to a metronomic kind of muscle memory uncomfortable with natural movement. (Do I dare to extend this to Fred Astaire?) Too often I also have the impression of watching a model who has wandered from a fashion runway or from the set of *Gigi*. I suspect that she's at her best when she's part of the background and primarily ornamental. Part of the problem may be her ability to wear her clothes well and to depend on them, like Deneuve, to do some of her acting for her; both rely on their beauty and wardrobe. The editors of *Le Dictionnaire Truffaut* seem impressed by this as they describe her character in *The Man Who Loved Women*: "Véra est … la plus mûre, la plus glamour, accentuée, pomponée, élégante des femmes que l'on voit" [Véra is … the most mature, the most glamorous, intense, dolled up, elegant woman that we see].[1] You can't fight "la plus glamour" and "pomponée." The possibility that beauty might not be enough in acting is raised indirectly by Truffaut's praise of Deneuve's beauty in the 1969 essay "Working with Catherine Deneuve," which unintentionally suggests a limit on what can be expected of her on screen: "Indeed Catherine Deneuve is so beautiful that any film she stars in could almost dispense with telling a story. I am convinced that the spectator will find happiness in just looking at Catherine and that this contemplation is worth the price of admission."[2] This sort of fluff reminds me simultaneously of his comments about Joan Crawford's mature beauty and of the fact that that Truffaut could have been a very successful agent and PR man. Had this been a book review, however, he would have had to make a personal disclosure about his involvement with Deneuve and her sister. He might also have had to indicate that he's speaking for only half the audience. By the criterion he introduces here, perhaps the most successful French film of the modern era is Rivette's magnificent La Belle Noiseuse (The Beautiful Troublemaker, 1991), in which the spectacularly beautiful Emmanuelle Béart is naked and nude for extended periods of time as the model being painted by Michel Piccoli. Lucky Piccoli. I wonder what happened to the dozens of sketches and paintings.

"Véra" is a small but pivotal role in The Man Who Loved Women. The great love of Bertrand's life, she broke his heart. The role requires no movement and only a narrow emotional range that combines sadness, regret, and concern. After many years, Véra and Bertrand meet accidentally in a restaurant coat room and almost immediately talk about her departure and his subsequent breakdown. (It's a scene Truffaut will rewrite for Mathilde and Bernard in The Woman Next Door.) In the film's narrative and emotional trajectory this is part of Bertrand's turn to a reconsideration of his past that includes the memoir already in progress.

In an interview on the Turner Movie Channel (11 September 2008), Caron spoke of Truffaut as to some extent a difficult director because he wouldn't elaborate on what he expected of her or about the personal inflections in the script. The second seems a curious expectation for an experienced actress to have, unless she thinks that she has a special understanding with the director. Given that her scene is straightforward, I don't quite understand what guidance she needed, though she seemed confused as to whether Véra was really Catherine Deneuve or Madeleine Morgenstern. I tend to think Véra is closer to Deneuve, but it's also possible that the scene borrows from both relationships: Véra is Deneuve at the moment when Bertrand is Truffaut; she is Truffaut when Bertrand is Madeleine, if you know what I mean. Truffaut kept Denner (and Moreau) in mind when he wrote *The Woman Next Door*. Its original title was *Sur des Rails* (*On Track*). Both films could have an epigraph based on Woody Allen's comment that it is always better to leave than to be left.

Caron visited Truffaut in September 1984. He was reading George Painter's biography of Proust and de Beauvoir's *La Cérémonie des adieux*, the story of Sartre's dismal and broken last years. She says that "It was by reading Sartre and de Beauvoir that he tried to prepare for death, to find a meaning for the end of his life." He also reread Proust's letters and noted a passage about the dead being "so much more numerous than the living."[3] The words could have come from *The Green Room*.

SUZANNE SCHIFFMAN
(1929–2001)

Sometime in the mid-1990s while spending a couple of weeks in Paris, I made a half-hearted attempt to contact Schiffman. I wanted to ask if she would be willing to do an interview about her career in film, which was also a way of asking her to talk about Truffaut, Godard, and Rivette. Truffaut had been dead for over a decade, and she had known him as well as anybody. In the end, this came to nothing more than a message on a machine, but I was reminded of it a few years later when I read her revealing short essay "Au Coeur de la méthode," about working with Truffaut. At different times she had been scriptgirl, assistant to the director, actress (*The Man Who Loved Women*), scriptwriter, and even a stand-in for Truffaut in the films in which he acted because they were the same height and size. She was as essential to his films as Jeanie Macpherson had been to Cecil B. DeMille's. She received an Oscar nomination for the script of *Day for Night* and won a César for that of *The Last Metro*.

One scene in the essay brings Truffaut to life and leaves me wishing that she had written a memoir. She describes how Truffaut could be both very open to suggestions and still unwilling to change his mind – "if he refused, he refused." "When we discussed a problem of construction or of a scene and when I proposed something that didn't suit him at all, he said: 'Suzanne, let's be logical.' His 'let's be logical' was a way of saying 'That's what I want.'"[1] He preferred working with male actors his own height: Léaud, Aznavour, Werner, Denner, and Trintignant. She recalls his pleasure when the last told him that he had always felt he should have done the roles Truffaut played in *The Wild Child*, *Day for Night*, and *The Green Room*.

As an insider Schiffman knew the degree to which some of the films based on books rather than original scenarios were autobiographical: "Being protected by a book allowed him to say more personal, even indecent things."[2] I wish she had said something about *Day for Night*, where Nathalie Baye plays Joelle (Schiffman) to Truffaut's Ferrand. In the interview included in the *Shoot the Piano Player* DVD she occupies a stool on the right of the screen while the left shows a shot of Truffaut and Baye in *Day for Night*. (By the way, David Thomson is wrong in seeing Joelle as a portrait of Helen Scott; Truffaut had already thanked Scott for her work on the Hitchcock book by giving her a five second cameo in *Bed and Board*.) Having introduced the autobiographical side of Truffaut's films, Schiffman goes on to distinguish between him and narcissistic directors who let their personal concerns or their self-importance interfere with what finally comes on the screen. For Truffaut, "the most important thing was to tell a story and to tell it clearly while arousing the pleasure and the interest of the viewer."[3] The sentence summarizes a key aspect of Truffaut's Renoirian aesthetics.

She also confirms what we sensed from some of the films of the 1970s: Truffaut had begun preferring the studio to the street. Working on location offered too many distractions and elements he couldn't control. This was his Hitchcock side. He also didn't like "the unavoidable exhibitionistic aspect of filming in public."[4] She points out the humour in the situation: while he worried that the members of the crew would call inevitable attention to themselves, the person most of the public wanted to see was the famous director.

Le Dictionnaire Truffaut, though stingy with details about her artist husband and her two children (they appear in *Two English Girls* with Truffaut's daughters), mentions that she was affectionately known as La Schife or Suzanna la Perverse (a nod to Buñuel). I prefer St Suzanne, the patron saint of craftsmanship, fidelity, friendship, and the New Wave. She was born in 1929, a year before Godard and three before Truffaut. She was old enough to span the entire era of the *nouvelle vague*, from the postwar film clubs to the major films of Truffaut, Godard, and Rivette. I'm fascinated by the fact that she was able to work with Truffaut, among the most conservative of the group, and Rivette and Godard, the most radical. In 1971, the same year that she was assistant director on *Two English Girls* she also wrote the screenplay and co-directed Rivette's *Out 1*, a twelve-hour-plus opus rarely screened even in France. She was on location with Rivette for his *Hurlevant* (*Wuthering Heights*) during the final weeks of Truffaut's life. All in all, she had a remarkable career. I suspect that had Truffaut written his projected autobiography, he might have used the word "indispensable" to describe her. Given their long relationship, he must have known that she was Jewish and had been hidden by nuns during the war. Did she know about his father? It seems likely. Her essay mentions that he had never learned how to swim and was afraid of water.

She makes a small revealing grammatical gesture in the filmed interview. Describing Truffaut, who had been dead two years, she uses the present tense: "It takes him a long time to get to know people ... He's very shy, very reserved."⁵ On the other hand, she speaks about the making of the films in the past tense. I never think of her without recalling that she was his stand-in during the filming of *The Wild Child* and *The Green Room*. François/Suzanne/François/Suzanne/Franzanne. These were moments when she wasn't simply close to him: *she became him.*

TRUFARD AND GODFAUT: RESEMBLANCES

1. Both are outsiders, though in very different ways. The almost-illegitimate Truffaut grows up poor, leaves home at fourteen, and eventually discovers that his birth father is a Jew. Godard is the almost rebellious child of a rich and well-connected Protestant family in a Catholic country.
2. Despite Godard's more conventional early education and Truffaut's early departure from school, both are autodidacts and lifelong omnivorous readers.
3. Each has a troubled relationship with his family.
4. Theft plays an important role in their lives. Truffaut steals a typewriter from his father's office and sells his best friend's books. Godard steals from his grandfather, friends, the *Cahiers* office, and finally from a company he works for in Switzerland. The last lands him in jail, where Truffaut had also spent time twice.
5. Both write for *Cahiers*, though Truffaut is the more productive.
6. For both the New Wave is inseparable from the history of the cinema.
7. Both work for significant periods of time with Léaud, Schiffman, and Coutard.
8. Each sleeps with his leading actresses and each proposes to an actress half his age: Truffaut to Claude Jade; Godard to Anna Waziemsky, who makes the mistake of accepting.

9. Each seems happiest when making a film, though Godard tends to be far harder on the "film family" than Truffaut.
10. Each attempts suicide when rejected by a woman.
11. Their work is autobiographical.
12. Each often writes the next day's scenes the night before.
13. Their voices can be heard in their films; their writing can be seen on the screen.
14. Truffaut wants to seduce and entertain an audience, Godard to challenge and educate it. Godard handles rejection much better.
15. Their films allude and refer to other films frequently and self-consciously to an unprecedented degree. Godard refers to Truffaut's films more often than Truffaut does to his.
16. Both are on the left, though Truffaut is "leftish" or "gauchisant" while Godard at his most radical is Marxist-Leninist-Maoist. Neither is religious. Each has what Truffaut describes as "a completely pessimistic view of society."[1]
17. Each has a history with prostitutes both in life and on film.
18. Film, for each, is synonymous with life.
19. Like most of their generation, both are fascinated by Sartre.
20. Each comes very close to shooting a first film different from the one that made him famous. What would the history of the New Wave have looked like without its two signature films?

BALTHUS (1908–2001)

The index of de Baecque's very long *Godard* lists twenty-four artists; Piero della Francesca is the earliest and Fritz Hundertwasser the most recent. Picasso, with fourteen references, is by far the most prominent. His *Truffaut*, by contrast, lists six: Georges Braque (twice), Picasso (three times), and Henri Cartier-Bresson, Max Ernst, André Derain, and Henri Matisse once. Truffaut's letters refer only to Van Gogh and Balthus. The latter appears four times and has the only lengthy entry on any painter. The relevant letter is to Helen Scott on 20 June 1962: "Thank you for the documents on Balthus; he's my favourite contemporary painter, and my idea is to make an extremely simple and respectful short on his work, showing the paintings without any pyrotechnical camera movements or pretentious commentary … Just as the short on Balthus is little more than a pretext to enable me to take a long, calm look at the paintings without wasting my time as a filmmaker, so this book on Hitchcock will only be a pretext for me to educate myself."[1] Though paintings and photographs play important roles throughout his films, no other artist receives the attention Balthus gets in *Stolen Kisses* and *Bread and Board*. Reproductions of his work appear in both. In the first there is a small poster of *Le Passage du commerce Saint-André des Arts* (1952–54) on the wall of Antoine's sparsely furnished room. We see it first on the morning of Mme Tabard's visit. But when examined closely, it's obvious that the reproduction shows only the right half of the painting. The five figures on the left are missing with the result that the emphasis is on the anonymous tall male figure carrying a baguette and walking away from the viewer toward rue Saint-André des Arts. A young girl stands in the foreground with her chin resting on her hand while an elfin-like balding and wizened man – he could be in Richard Dadd's *The Fairy Feller's Master-Stroke* (1864) – sits on the sidewalk behind her in profile watching the absent scene no longer available to the film's audience. It's not impossible to see the image as anticipating Antoine's eventual departure from Christine. The central male figure, dressed in brown trousers and a grey sweater is an image of self-containment, isolation, and rejection – a loner like Antoine.

The painting reappears in *Bed and Board*, where it replaces a poster of Rudolf Nureyev that the recently married Christine had hung over the marriage bed. We assume that Antoine has hung Balthus out of unease with having to compete with Chistine's obvious attraction to the Russian dancer who died of AIDS in 1993. Simply put, he's jealous: in addition to the Nureyev poster, Christine is reading Nureyev's autobiography and, when Antoine leaves, she replaces his framed bedside photograph with one of Nureyev hidden beneath it. In contrast to *Stolen Kisses*, *Le Passage du commerce Saint-André des Arts* is reproduced here in its entirety. I can't be alone in thinking it an ominous image to hang over the bed of a recently married young couple. It's as inappropriate as Masaccio's *Expulsion from the Garden of Eden* or Picasso's *Les Demoiselles d'Avignon* would be. Christine transfers it to the hallway when they separate. Did Truffaut know that Nureyev was gay? As well, did he know that the house in the rear of the painting with the sign *Registre* was the scene of Charlotte Corday's murder of Marat on 14 July 1793? Or that it was also once a library frequented by Lucien Chardon, the hero of Balzac's *Lost Illusions*, a Truffaut favourite?

Late in *Bed and Board* we also see Balthus's *Jeune Fille à la fenêtre* (1957) in the same hallway. When Christine tries to give it to the departing Antoine on the grounds that it was a gift from him, he insists that she keep it. One of Balthus's more appealing paintings, it offers the idyllic rear image of a long-haired young girl dressed in a blue sweater and grey skirt standing at a tall open window looking at a garden. A tree leans toward the centre from the left, the ground is carpeted with lemon yellow flowers, and the scene is suffused by a wash of thin nearly translucent blue light. It could be an image of a young Christine looking back at what she left behind and lost when she married Antoine.

FILM NAMES:
WHO REMEMBERS MICHEL POICCARD
AND **PATRICIA FRANCHINI?**

David Thomson suggests that "Everyone loves *Out of the Past* – I even liked it in the old days in England, where it was known as *Build My Gallows High*."[1] I count myself among that group. Having said that, I'm willing to bet the royalties on Thomson's *"Have You Seen … ?"* that few fans remember the names of the characters played by Robert Mitchum, Jane Greer, and Kirk Douglas: Jeff Bailey, Kathie Moffat, and Whit Sterling. If we limit ourselves to films based on original scripts or obscure novels – Truffaut's *Shoot the Piano Player* – I doubt that more than one viewer in twenty recalls the characters' names even a few days after seeing a film. Most of us are equally forgetful of film scores. Fans of westerns tend to agree that the ones Anthony Mann made with James Stewart are classics, but who remembers the hero's name in *Winchester 73* or *The Far Country*? Test yourself. Here are the titles of some recent Oscar winners: *The Departed, Gladiator, American Beauty, Titanic, Driving Miss Daisy, There Will Be Blood, The Artist, Silver Linings Playbook*. Can you remember the name of even one of the leading characters? For obvious reasons I skipped *Schindler's List* and *Shakespeare in Love*. I have seen most of these at least once, but you can push me up against the usual wall and, if you're an American, put a gun to my head, and you will still get silence if you ask me to name one of the lead characters. It's as if my mind attaches two names to a character – the actor's name and the fictional name – and as soon as the film ends, the fictional name, which is a recent arrival in my database, immediately begins to fade: the synapses stay dormant when it is called. Ethan Edwards disappears into John Wayne (*The Searchers*), Roger O. Thornhill into Cary Grant (*North by Northwest*), and Daniel Plainview into Daniel Day-Lewis (*There Will Be Blood*). Even reviewers and critics refer to the character by the name of the actor: as Gabin says to Michèle Morgan or Cary Grant tells Grace Kelly or, in *8 Women*, Deneuve says to Ardant. The name in the script disappears with "The End." This is rarely the case with classical plays. If we discuss *King Lear*, the character's name dominates the discussion of the play itself; the actor's name takes over when the performance is in question – Scofield's Lear, Olivier's Othello.

I wonder if it isn't a general rule that film names are expected to fulfil their function with less aesthetic fuss (symbolism or euphony) and referential fuss than names in fiction. With rare exceptions they are not supposed to call attention to themselves as Serenus Zeitblom does in Thomas Mann's *Doctor Faustus*. If you're a scriptwriter working with a time limit, the last thing you want is an audience puzzling over the implications of a name when the story has already moved on to the next scene. I'm thinking here of Wim Wenders's *Faraway, So Close!* in which Willem Dafoe plays "Emit Flesti." By the time you figure out that the name is "Time Itself" reversed the film is half an hour along. We assume that whatever is essential about a character in a film will be communicated by appearance, action, dialogue, and the camera; the name is simply an identification badge. The only films hospitable to symbolic or phonetically memorable names are fantasies, comedies, and those based on classic novels.

Truffaut's notes show that he rarely worried about names as much as he did about titles. Working on *Stolen Kisses* he told his co-writers only what sorts of names he wanted to avoid – Martine, Caroline, Brigitte, Sylvie, Cyprienne. All these had been made popular recently by young film and music stars. Today's North American equivalents would be Britney, Taylor, and Miley. Antoine Doinel, the most important name in his body of work, he found either in the name of Renoir's secretary, Ginette Doynel, or in an anagram of Doniol-Valcroze, the editor of *Cahiers* when *The 400 Blows* was being made. Odile Jouve, the narrator of *The Woman Next Door*, got her first name from the title of a Raymond Queneau novel and her surname from Bernadette Lafont's character in *Les Mistons*. Ferrand, the director's name in *Day for Night*, probably caused the most concern because it is taken from Monferrand, his mother's maiden name. He needed it to suggest the film's autobiographical dimension. *Small Change* also shows him unable to let go of a name; this time it's his former wife's. His daughter plays a character named Madeleine Doinel: her first name is her mother's, her surname is her father's, so to speak, in the Doinel series. For the length of the film, the family is back together at least in a daughter's name. Many of the names Truffaut chooses have private associations that function as allusions to people outside the films. For the audience they function only to identify a character: in a manner of speaking, Truffaut writes a diary that we read as a novel.

A closer look at his attention to the names in *The Green Room* gives a good sense of his work on this aspect of a script based on three Henry James stories: "The Altar of the Dead," "The Friends of the Friends," and "The Beast in the Jungle." He instructs Jean Gruault, his co-writer, to "think of it as an adaptation of a play, with four or five acts. The first part is a kind of prologue, leading up to the widower's (his name escapes me) remarriage. (Consult the lists of names in James's diaries to find names that are, if not French, then at least more neutral than the original ones, which are too English."[2] Truffaut rejected all the names in James's stories: George Stransom, Mary Antrim, Acton Hague, John Marcher, and May Bartram. He replaced these with Julien Davenne, Cécilia Mandel, Madame Rambaud, Bernard Humbert, Paul Massigny. A very English story became a French one; English-sounding names were replaced by ones more compatible with a French soundscape. The name Julien Davenne is as expected in a French soundtrack as May Bartram would be in an English one.

It occurred to me a few years ago while watching *The Last Metro* that I didn't know how a native French speaker hears and interprets the names of French characters within their natural acoustic cultural space. Every language has certain names that carry culturally specific baggage. Montaigne suggests "Each nation has certain names which, I know not why, are taken in a bad sense: with us Jean, Guillaume, Benoit" ("Of Names").[3] What did Truffaut hear and understand when James Bond met Pussy Galore? Or when Tom Doniphon shot Liberty Valance? Names buzz with implications that fly past non-native speakers as quickly as clues in crossword puzzles. When in *The First Circle* Aleksandr Solzhenitsyn names one of his younger characters Lavrenti, he needs to explain to non-Soviet readers as well as later Russian generations that the boy's parents had wanted to pay tribute to Lavrenti Beria, Stalin's feared chief of security. When Beria was executed for treason after Stalin's death in 1953, a Russian boy had an onomastic crisis that he probably solved by becoming Lev and claiming he was named after Tolstoy. Proust's ear for names is clear from his changing of the name of the Countess de Guermantes from Floriane (in *Jean Santeuil*) to Oriane when promoted to Duchess in *Remembrance of Things Past*. What difference in implication, music, or semantic weight did Proust sense and does a French reader hear? Does Floriane carry the scent of an unwanted bouquet? Is Oriane more suggestive of gold and the orient, an exoticism the young narrator is responsive to? A final example – how does a Parisian hear and respond to the names in *The Last Metro*: Marion and Lucas Steiner, Bernard Granger, Arlette Guillame, Germaine Fabre, or Daxiat? The last one seems unique, what the linguists call a *hapax legomenon* or a unique usage. Are the French as positive in their response to Bernard, for instance, as Truffaut who uses the name three times and its near homonym Bertrand once? Does Arlette still call to mind Arletty and *Les Enfants du Paradis*? Are any of these names associated with a type, a class, a region, or a period? As for the Michel and Patricia in my section title, they are Michel Poiccard and Patricia Franchini, the leads in *Breathless*. In Truffaut's original treatment they are Michel and Betty. In the following quiz the left-hand column has the names of the leading characters of well-known films whose titles are listed in random order on the right. I have excluded historical films, eponymous titles and giveaways (for example, *Sylvia Scarlett, Gone with the Wind, King of Kings, Star Wars, The Man Who Shot Liberty Valance*). The answers are in the endnote.[4]

A NAME QUIZ

A. Adam and Amanda	a. *Man of the West*
B. Malcolm Crowe, Cole Sear	b. *Midnight Cowboy*
C. Charlie Allnutt	c. *The Silence of the Lambs*
D. Link Jones, Dock Tobin	d. *Stalker*
E. The Writer, the Professor	e. *Scarface*
F. Scottie Ferguson	f. *Rancho Notorious*
G. Altar Keane, Vern Haskell	g. *The African Queen*
H. Roy Neary, Claude Lacombe	h. *Vertigo*
I. Adenoid Hynkel	i. *Close Encounters of the Third Kind*
J. Alex	j. *Contempt*
K. Tony Montana	k. *The Children of Paradise*
L. Paul Javel, Jeremy Prokosch	l. *Adam's Rib*
M. Garance, Baptise	m. *Point Blank*
N. Lester Burnham	n. *American Beauty*
O. Joe Buck	o. *The Great Dictator*
P. Clarice Starling	p. *A Clockwork Orange*
Q. Walker, Chris	q. *La Notte*
R. Giovanni, Lidia	r. *The Sixth Sense*

THE GREEN ROOM (1978):
THE MAN WHO LOVED ONE WOMAN

> It's true that people sometimes do for the dead what they
> would not have done for the living.
>
> MARCEL PROUST[1]

Reading through my files recently I ran across a review in the *Times Literary Supplement* (5 November 2004) of a Parisian production of Henry James's "The Beast in the Jungle" starring Depardieu as John Marcher and "his partner" Fanny Ardant as Catherine (not May) Bartram. I must have read the review when I cut it out years ago, but I missed or more likely repressed the one detail that would have really interested and predictably unsettled me. There's something ironically appropriate about noticing precisely on the morning when I'm about to begin writing about *The Green Room* that Fanny didn't die on Truffaut's funeral pyre but, as they say, moved on. Did I expect her to make a shrine to François in her bedroom or commit herself, like Julien Davenne, to a celibate life devoted to memory and mourning? Maybe I expected (and continue to expect) this only while writing about *The Green Room*, that strangely moving anomaly – almost a ghost story – among Truffaut's films, whose hero believes that *you shouldn't move on*, that, like pigeons and Catholics, to quote Woody Allen, you can find love once and once only. Julien's attitude to love and death echoes Proust's in *Finding Time Again*: "The only painful memory is of the dead. And they rapidly decay and nothing remains, even around their tombs, save the beauty of nature, silence and pure air."[2] The film

Julien Davenne (Truffaut) and Cécilia Mandel (Nathalie Baye) in her apartment where he learns that her dead lover and the friend who had betrayed him were the same man.

is Truffaut's most personal, introspective, and problematic. It has a sacral (faux religious?) and votive quality to be found nowhere else in his work. As I wrote earlier, it is based on James's short story "The Altar of the Dead" with small additions from "The Friends of the Friends" and the late masterpiece "The Beast in the Jungle." The central figure is Julien Davenne, a veteran of the Great War who is unable to forget either the war dead or his wife Julie, who died a year after the war. We learn almost nothing about her except that she died young. Davenne makes a modest income writing obituaries of soldiers who died in the Great War. He is a melancholy man with an emotionally circumscribed life morbidly devoted to mourning those he refers to as "my dead." His commitment is so complete or definitive that he remains blind to the possibility of a new love and a new life with Cécilia Mandel (Nathalie Baye), a young woman in mourning for the great love of her life – a writer and politician named Paul Massigny – who, we later learn, had once been Davenne's best friend. To prevent his love for Julie from being forgotten or becoming merely "provisional," Julien chooses to die instead of responding to the affections of another woman. In other words, only through death can he ensure that his love for her remains as definitive as hers was and is for him. In a deft casual gesture of self-reference, which brings the film into the thematic pull of the definitive-provisional theme, the actor who posed for the several photographs of Massigny is Serge Rousseau, who makes the unforgettable manic declaration of love to Christine at the end of *Stolen Kisses*. He is also the groom shot on the steps of *The Bride Wore Black*. You might say that he's a specialist in roles that are brief, conspicuous, and necrological.

There is an anticipation of *The Green Room* in a 1970 letter in which Truffaut explains why he doesn't attend funerals: "There have been many, too many, deaths around me of people I've loved, that I took the decision, after Françoise Dorléac died, never to attend a funeral, which, as you can well imagine, does not prevent the distress I feel from casting its shadow over everything for a time and never completely fading, even as the years pass, for we live not only with the living but also with all those who have meant anything in our lives."[3] Since Truffaut indicates that he has looked into James's notebooks, he may well have known that James wrote "The Altar of the Dead" in the shadow of the deaths in 1894 of Robert Louis Stevenson and Constance Fenimore Woolson, a woman who had been in love with him and committed suicide in Venice after he failed to respond to her affections, though it's not certain that was the primary or only cause. In his early fifties James was beginning to feel like Truffaut that "we live not only with the living but also with all those who have ever meant anything in our lives." This is an accurate summary of one of the film's strongest thematic strands. It also anticipates the tragic dialectic Davenne sets in motion when he decides to devote himself to mourning his dead to the point that, like the protagonists of "The Altar of the Dead" and "The Beast in the Jungle," he remains blind to a poignant offer of love. The key figures in the first story are George Stransom (Davenne), his dead fiancée May Antrim (Julie), his widowed friend Paul Creston (Mazet), his recently dead wife Kate, and Acton Hague (Paul Massigny), the friend who betrayed him. James's original of Truffaut's Cécilia Mandel remains unnamed, one of those mysterious and suggestive omissions James saw as playing an important part in fiction, more a mystery than a Hitchcockian McGuffin. Despite her central role in Stransom's life, she remains a pronoun in the story. The onomastic gap catches our interest and probably makes us more sensitive to other names. Overall, with the exception of Stransom's, the names are less suggestive than is common in James; they don't repay the attention we give to Daisy Miller, Isabelle Archer, Olive Chancellor, Owen Wingrave, and Chad Newsome. Massigny was found by Jean Gruault in the notebooks a few pages after the entries dealing with "The Altar of the Dead" (4 March 1985) in a long list of names for future stories. According to Sandro Volpe, James probably remembered Massigny from Prosper Mérimée's death-haunted story "Le Vase Étrusque."[4] A line of dialogue not used in the film, but cited by Volpe, suggests that Truffaut knew the story. Davenne says "I admire the Etruscans: they built wooden houses to live in and cities of rock for the dead." This is the Etruscans' sole mention in Truffaut.

 The three most significant additions Truffaut makes to the Jamesian material are the films and slides of the Great War; the emphasis on Massigny and his influence on the plot; and the votive photographs of his dead that Julien hangs on the chapel wall. The war also introduces a social and historical background for the characters and their story. Without it they would still have their particular existential and universal force, but with it they gain a particular sociohistorical particularity and depth. Among the photos is a famous one of a dead French soldier suspended on a branch high in a tree that was banned in France even after the war as too demoralizing.[5] If Truffaut's presence makes the film more personal, the war acts to pull it outward toward history, its centripetal pull countering the centrifugal effect of the autobiographical. The added emphasis on Massigny helps balance the emotional claims of the relationships: Julie and Julien and Cécilia and Paul. Within the equation, the dead Paul and Julie are a ghostly couple impeding the possibility of a future relationship between Julien and Cécilia.

Davenne's eccentric view of love is the key to the film's theme. In his calculus of love, the definitive is allied with death and what psychoanalysis calls "bad mourning"; it trumps the provisional, which depends on a softer version of love than he can accept. The only possible resolution for him is a lonely *liebestod*, with the survivors having to clean up the chapel. Thom Gunn's "In Time of Plague," though concerned with AIDS, nevertheless captures something of the troubling ambivalence, more sharply defined than simple mixed feelings, of Davenne's death-bound fidelity: "My thoughts are crowded with death / and it draws so oddly on the sexual / that I am confused / confused to be attracted / by, in effect, my own annihilation."[6] Davenne reaches annihilation in his chapel amid the tall white blazing candles illuminating the photographs of his dead while Maurice Jaubert's plangent, soaring music provides a lush accompaniment. Cécilia Mandel is left holding his dying body in a *Pietà* of sorts and with the responsibility of caring for the chapel dedicated to his dead. Her question, "Who will light [a candle] for me?" remains unanswered at his death. Nathalie Baye's nearly transcendental pose throughout this simultaneously sacral and secular moment is the visual expression of the consequences of Davenne's choice. This is something that he understands even before it happens. Where Proust's narrator sees an escape of sorts through art, Julien insists that the only way to avoid the death of love is death itself.

For a man who didn't show much concern with self-denial in his life, Truffaut shows a surprising attraction to the ultimate renunciation here. James, of course, is one of the most perceptive and obsessive students of the subject: think of Isabel Archer's one long-deferred kiss with Caspar Goodwood in *Portrait of a Lady* or the contrasting choices made by Chad Newsome and Lambert Strether in *The Ambassadors*. James's George Stransom is more obviously egotistical than Davenne, whose egotism is kept in check by his job and his unexplained paternal relationship with the partly deaf boy Georges who lives with him and his housekeeper. Georges is both the son Davenne didn't have with Julie and won't have with Cécilia and a symbolic reminder of his inability to hear (and see – he wears spectacles) anything except what pertains to the past. In James's story there is an almost necrophilic dimension to Stransom's grotesque egotism that manifests itself in his wish that some of his friends die so that he might place them on his personal altar sooner than later: "There were hours at which he almost caught himself wishing that certain of his friends would now die, that he might establish with them in this manner a connexion more charming than, as it happened, it was possible to enjoy with them in life."⁷ The sinister "charming" establishes the exact Jamesian note and is damning.

Davenne is as detached as Stransom but feels guilty for having survived both his wife and fellow soldiers. Put simply, he is unable to stop grieving and to begin living again. His widowed friend Mazet has done so by remarrying soon after the death of his wife, and Cécilia seems capable of simultaneously cherishing the memory of Paul Massigny and loving Julien.

Despite the presence of Madame Rambaud and Georges in the house, Davenne's scenes are framed to emphasize his claustral isolation in its emptiness and darkness. The only fully lighted room is the housekeeper's kitchen. The lack of emotion in Davenne's pallid face – it stands in sharp contrast to Cécilia's young warm peach blush – should have warned her that he is both death-haunted and incapable of the kind of relationship she wants. The hinge of the relationship and the plot is Massigny, her dead lover and his former friend. Massigny means as much to her as Julie does to him. Yet even though he claims to have forgiven Massigny, Julien is unable to grant Cécilia's wish to include his candle among those of the other dead. As I said earlier, Georges's deafness – a nod to Truffaut's own – hints at Davenne's inability to hear others, his spectacles at his inability to really see her. They part over Massigny, whose memory divides them as decisively as Julie's. They are reunited only in the final scene in the dazzlingly candlelit chapel where the collapsing Davenne goes to join his dead. Death frames and punctuates the film: the soldiers, Julie, Mazet's first wife, Davenne's obituaries, Massigny, and finally Davenne.

The last time we see Davenne in his house he is alone, reclining on a sofa chair, almost an invalid, in the charred green room that has survived a fire caused by the candles in his shrine to Julie. We have seen its predecessor in *The 400 Blows*, where Antoine's similar shrine to Balzac catches fire. The liminal almost ghostly room, empty except for Julie's photograph, exists precariously between order and dissolution, life and death; its light is a faint chiaroscuro that seems as weak and tentative as its pale dying tenant. If we keep in mind that Davenne is a writer, then we can think of him as an Orpheus determined to join Eurydice: he realizes that he can't replace (Cécilia) or resurrect Julie (the mannequin) and that time will eventually erase her memory. His only available version of definitive love is death. Rushdie is perceptive in *The Ground beneath Her Feet* about this view of love. His narrator, the photographer Rai, distinguishes as follows between his love for the rock star Vina Aspara and that of his friend Ormus. "So I admit also that Ormus's love for Vina Apsara was greater than mine, for while I had never mourned any loss I had, after all, begun to love again. But his was a love which no other love could replace, and after Vina's three deaths he had finally entered his last celibacy, from which only the carnal embrace of death would set him free. Death was the only lover he would now accept, the only lover he would share with Vina, because that lover would reunite them forever, in the wormwood forest of the forever dead."[8]

Ormus would understand Davenne's need for a chapel with photographs of his dead. Truffaut uses the photos to reinforce the film's autobiographical dimension by relating historical individuals important to him to others with whom he had worked in film. Among the former are James, Thomas Hardy (a surprise), Oscar Wilde (another in a series of gay characters in Truffaut), Apollinaire, Prokofiev, and Proust. Among the latter we see Cocteau, Jaubert, "Simon Jardine" (Mark Peterson from *Two English Girls*), Audiberti, Moreau and her sister, the English theatre and film producer Oscar Lewenstein, and Oskar Werner, in a military uniform from *Jules and Jim*. Davenne describes Werner as "a German pilot" whose plane he helped shoot down during the war. He adds that "you must admit when you look at this photo that it's difficult to think of this man as an enemy." Most viewers would have interpreted this remark in 1978 simply as a comment directed at *Jules and Jim*. Those who knew about their problems in 1966 on the set of *Fahrenheit 451* might have seen it as a sort of settling of accounts. A more generous interpretation might see it as a message reminding Oskar of a happier time in their relationship with the suggestion that after twelve years it was time to shake hands. A less complicated memory and a long-standing thank you come with the photo of Louise de Valmorin (1902–1969), a poet and novelist who encouraged Truffaut during his early years. Fabienne

Tabard in *Stolen Kisses* owes something to her, while *The Soft Skin* mentions her television work. The most intriguing photograph is an absent one that causes a rift between Julien and Cécilia – that of Massigny who strikes me as to some extent based on Godard. Davenne tells Cécilia that they had been best friends, but that Massigny who "was good at reducing, dominating and subduing people" had betrayed him. He insists, however, that he has forgiven the betrayal and doesn't hate him. Yet until the final scene he won't allow a photograph of the man who was the most important male relationship of his life in the chapel. If I'm right that Massigny is a screen for Godard, then it may be relevant to recall Truffaut's anger (and I assume sense of betrayal) in his letters to Godard at the latter's "reducing, dominating and subduing" some of their mutual friends and at his attack on Truffaut's Oscar. Incidentally, Thomas Hardy's photograph also offers a tenuous connection to Godard: the English teacher in *Bande à part* writes his name on the blackboard. For me the connection remains a loose thread, perhaps nothing more than a teasing coincidence. While I'm playing a hunch, however, what about the possibility of a connection by way of Godard's hostility to Israel? Massigny we learn from the speech at his funeral was a member of what seems like a far-right political party, one of whose concerns was the influence of the Rothschilds (surely interwar code for "Jews") on the French economy.

The Green Room has always struck me as a curiously flat title with little thematic, symbolic, or poetic resonance. On the other hand, it gives nothing away about the movie except that there might be a green room in it. When a journalist asked "Why green?" Truffaut answered flippantly and not helpfully, "Because the other colours were taken."[9] As I wrote earlier, when it became obvious that the film would not be popular, he joked that he should have titled it "The Empty Room." He probably rejected James's title because neither of its nouns, altar or dead, is particularly appealing to an audience. In the language of the reviewers, each is a downer. One French critic wittily suggested *L'Homme qui aimait les flammes*. In the same vein, I thought of *The Man Who Loved One Woman*. Truffaut tried out the following in his notes: *The Unfinished Figure, The Mountain of Fire, Those We Haven't Forgotten, Those We Have Loved, The Last Flame, The Others, The Fête of Memory*. The earlier Proustian working titles – *La Disparue, La Fiancée disparue* – seem slightly better in that they introduce an element of mystery. Had Truffaut read Freud, he might have been tempted momentarily by *Mourning and Melancholia*.

I think of *The Green Room* as having a secure place in the very exclusive library of eccentric works with a minority appeal: it includes *Measure for Measure, Jacques le fataliste et son maître, Bouvard et Pécuchet, The Notebooks of Malte Laurids Brigge, Kangaroo, The Wild Palms, Ferdydurke, The Life and Death of Colonel Blimp, La più belle pagine di Tommaso Landolfi, Night of the Hunter, Hopscotch, Elizabeth Costello*. I recognize that it isn't among Truffaut's major work, but I would only reluctantly leave it off my list of essential films. On each viewing there is always the simple pleasure of seeing Truffaut and sensing that the film is as much about his compulsions as Davenne's (or James's). While it's running the film insists that, although Truffaut is dead, he is still alive. A film's light on a white screen always resists the inevitability of life's unconditional and irremediable darkness – when what is gone is gone. In doing that, it momentarily overcomes Davenne's melancholy and ours.

A SHORT HISTORY OF "DUMMIES": LUIS BUÑUEL, TRUFFAUT, AND OSKAR KOKOSCHKA

> It is said that in later life [Descartes] was always accompanied in his travels by a mechanical life-sized female doll which ... he himself had constructed ... He had named the doll after his illegitimate daughter, Francine, and some versions ... have it that she was so lifelike that the two were indistinguishable. Descartes and the doll were evidently inseparable, and he is said to have slept with her encased in a trunk at his side.
>
> STEPHEN GRAUKORGER[1]

—

Truffaut discussed Buñuel's *The Criminal Life of Archibaldo de la Cruz* in 1971 at Le Ciné-Club de la Victorine and touched on several of his own films without mentioning them. The talk shows Truffaut admiring a director whose films were made under the signs of ambiguity, irony, and surrealism and have little in common with his own. He begins by situating Buñuel between Bergman the pessimist who "doesn't tell us how to go on living" and Renoir the optimist who does. He describes Buñuel as a man who "finds mankind imbecilic but life diverting."[2] But he is primarily concerned with Buñuel's script, with its "ingenuity of construction, the audacious handling of time, [and] the expertise of the cinematic narrative." He concludes by distinguishing the film from those based on scripts "conceived for their literary effects [that] end up as novels written in pictures."[3] This sounds as if he's looking back at his campaign in the 1950s against French films based on literary classics. Along the way

Truffaut points to some of Buñuel's cinematic inspirations in the film: Hitchcock's *Shadow of a Doubt*, Preston Sturges's *Unfaithfully Yours*, and Chaplin's *Monsieur Verdoux*, all about men who want to kill women. Four decades later the commentary is equally interesting for what it tells us about Truffaut. First there is what might be called a synchronicity between Buñuel's film and *The Bride Wore Black*. Truffaut must have realized that the following observation about *Archibaldo* would remind many in the audience of his own film: "The day of the wedding, Archibaldo and his bride all in white, pose for a photograph. As in Hitchcock's *Foreign Correspondent*, Buñuel creates a moment of confusion between the flash of the camera and a gunshot … His bride is killed right before Archibaldo's eyes."[4] "As in Hitchcock's *Foreign Correspondent*" might easily be replaced by "As in *The Bride Wore Black*." Surely many in the audience made a mental edit. If nothing else, the sentence shows Truffaut not to have suffered from anxiety about influence. He even showed his viewers and critics where to look.

This also applies to Truffaut's interest in Buñuel's use of a life-size mannequin; though the audience couldn't have known it in 1971, it was being prepared for the mannequin's return in *The Man Who Loved Women*, *The Green Room*, and *Confidentially Yours*. Archibaldo, it is worth recalling, obtains a mannequin that resembles the woman he is infatuated with. Unfortunately for him she discovers it and leaves him. He then destroys it by melting it in a kiln. As I said, this mannequin stays with Truffaut through three films. The first is *The Man Who Loved Women* (1977). Truffaut mentions that Archibaldo notices in a dress shop window a mannequin that resembles the woman he's obsessed with. Truffaut remembered the scene when writing his script but gave it a twist. Bertrand Morane dreams that a wax mannequin of himself is being dressed in the window of a women's shop while the women he has been involved with watch from the street. The disturbing dream prefigures his funeral, the only other scene in which his women gather around him. But the proximate reason the dream troubles him is that he is being dressed by the shopowner who turned him down and the scene turns him into a passive object (a plastic doll) for her and for the women's gaze. This is a reversal of his usual relationship to women where he is the one who notices, looks, and evaluates. In the dream he is on exhibition. Among the women, although we don't know this, is Martine Barraqué, the film's editor. In a manner of speaking, once the shoot is complete, she will have the power to cut and paste Denner-Morane-Truffaut as she pleases. It's no small matter that she has been given this power by Truffaut.

In *The Green Room* (1978), Julien Davenne, is in love with a woman he cannot have – his dead wife, Julie. Desperate not to lose her completely he asks a potter to make a life-size clay substitute. When he sees it, however, he becomes violently upset and orders it destroyed. Archibaldo "kills" his "dummy" because his always frustrated desire is to kill the woman. Davenne's motive is more complex and marked by ambivalence. He wants the statue to fill the permanent gap left by Julie's death. But he simultaneously realizes that the emptiness he feels, the claustrophobic darkness within which he moves, is all that remains of his wife. Instead of filling the abyss, the statue simply intensifies his awareness of loss. No fetish, to use Buñuel's language, can really take the place of what it represents; the best it can do is call to mind what is longed for and inaccessible. This is also the case in *Confidentially Yours*. Maître Clément, the lawyer who murdered his former lover, keeps an incriminating head of a small doll resembling her in his office. Its discovery is a scene of black humour that implicates him in her murder and leads to his suicide. It's typical of Truffaut not to waste a good idea but to play with variations of it: mannequin to full-size clay figure to small head.

The mannequin was not the only detail from Buñuel's movie to stay with him. Describing the relationship in *The Criminal Life of Archibaldo de la Cruz*, Truffaut said that the "unhappy couple could live neither with nor without each other, and they chose to die together."[5] This idea resurfaces a decade later in *The Woman Next Door* as the film's thematic and emotional motive force. The sentence takes the form of "neither with you nor without you," words Madame Jouve, the film's tutelary spirit, wants to put on the lovers' tombstone even as she realizes that they can't be buried together.

I find these networks of connections fascinating because they show how centripetal and coherent Truffaut's film world is. *Day for Night* doesn't exaggerate in suggesting that the boundaries of his life are strictly defined by film. Like Ignatius of Loyola he designed a particularly rigorous spiritual discipline and followed it faithfully until his death. It wasn't happenstance that he admired Sacha Guitry for editing his last film on his deathbed.

Truffaut, however, was not the only director to remember the mannequin and to use it more than once. Buñuel himself returned to one detail when he made the better known *Tristana* in 1970. When Archibaldo drags the mannequin to the kiln, its left leg falls off in an accidental amputation. Unwilling to waste a suggestive and in the original context darkly funny image, Buñuel amputates Tristana's leg and puts it on display on her bed. This amputation may have stayed with Truffaut, especially since Deneuve played Tristana at a time when she and he were involved. An early script for *The Man Who Loved Women* has a scene involving a radio announcer with one leg. Four years later, *The Woman Next Door* is narrated by Madame Jouve, who permanently damaged her left leg in a suicide attempt. (A woman in Ophuls's *Le Plaisir* (1952) survives a similarly motivated jump.) Where Truffaut brings back the leg, Pedro Almodovar's *Live Flesh* (1997) remembers the wife and the kiln. The scene of the husband dragging the mannequin to the kiln is watched on television by the film's hero just before he is arrested. When he leaves prison, he plots to destroy the happy life of the woman responsible for his incarceration.

Bunuel's sardonic later comment on his mannequin is worth including: "I invented the dummy. Perhaps I am the precursor of the consumers of those rubber dolls sold at sex shops."[6] He also cites the tradition, so to speak, of artists who have been interested in dummies: Ramon Gomez de la Serna, Michel de Ghelderode, and Luis Garcia Berlanga, whose film *Grandeur nature* (1973) has seven. He doesn't mention my favourite, Tommaso Landolfi's unforgettable surrealistic masterpiece, the love story "Gogol's Wife," in which the so-called wife "was not a woman, nor was she a human being, nor a living creature of any kind, nor an animal or plant (as some have insinuated); she was simply a doll. Yes, a doll."[7] Buñuel insisted that he lived to make films. The raffish Landolfi told Italo Calvino that he wrote stories only to make enough money to continue gambling in San Remo's casinos.

If you are wondering what Oskar Kokoschka is doing in the title, he's there because his obsession with a mannequin anticipates and exceeds Bunuel's and Truffaut's. He is the only serious challenger to Buñuel's claim to be the king of the men who "love dummies." On 6 February 1918, the painter wrote Hermine Moos, a Munich tailor and dollmaker, to commission a life-size doll based on his former lover Alma Mahler. Her departure four years earlier had left him on the verge of despair. Very aware of what he was doing, he sought consolation in what his biographer calls a fetish. The letters and drawings to Moos specify hair, skin colours, and physical details of some intimacy not evident in Alma's photographs:

"Please give some more detail to the bust. The nipples are not to be raised, but should be a bit uneven, prominent only on account of the swell itself. The ideal model would be Hélène Fourment in that little Rubens book, the picture ['Hélène Fourment and Two of her Children'] in which she holds the one boy in her lap while the other stands. It shows all the minute forms of the breast that makes it so swellingly graceful." Understandably losing control as he warms to the idea, Kokoschka suggests that "I rather think a whole series of figures will become necessary, which you shall have to create to keep my heroine company."[8] Writing from Dresden, he warns Moos not to let anyone see the fetish because "I would die from jealousy if some man should come into contact … with this artificial woman, nude and unclothed as she is."[9] If he was this jealous of the doll, how must he have felt when he heard that not only had Alma married Gropius but that in 1917 she had begun an affair with the writer Franz Werfel? The inevitable crash came when the doll arrived in April 1919. Kokoschka, anticipating Julien Davenne by sixty years, was shocked by "the discrepancies in the proportions as against those shown in my drawings" and by various details he found repulsive – "the knees seem to be afflicted by elephantiasis."[10] When we recall the expressionist distortions of his portraits, this seems a surprising complaint. In affairs of the heart, the expressionist was an old-fashioned realist.

In the end, Kokoschka decided to make the best of a sad job and used the doll as a model. He asked a friend to spread a rumour about a mysterious woman living in his studio, took the doll to parties, and, finally, in 1920 threw a farewell champagne party for her. According to one account, the garbagemen took her away; according to another, he threw out her decapitated and reportedly bloodied body after a wild party at his studio. Next day the Police questioned him about the missing "body." Before this flawed reincarnation of Alma disappeared from his life, he transformed her into three important paintings, *The Woman in Blue* (1919), *Painter with Doll* (1920–21), and *At the Easel* (1922). Alma was finally exorcised with the entry into his life of Hulda, one of his landlord's maids, though she would reappear a half-century later in his autobiography.

Truffaut never mentions Alma or Kokoschka. The longlived painter, who died in 1980, is equally silent about him. Finally: Gogol did not have a wife and the story of Descartes's mechanical daughter is false.

THE SENTENCE THAT STICKS

Everyone who watches too many movies must have an informal list of lines that won't go away, that have slipped into the memory without the usual effort. Here are some that have settled in with me for the long haul, including one from Truffaut.

If there's anyone who has a right to his liquor, it's the victim of circumstance.
    Bruce Armstrong, *The Most Dangerous Game*

We can buy a chicken farm. There's nice money to be made in chickens.
    Paulette Godard, *The Great Dictator*

One can never protect a single human being from suffering. That is what makes one so tremendously weary.
    Naima Wifstrand, *Smiles of a Summer Night*

I used to know a girl who modelled for Renoir. You could smell the paint.
    Michel Simon, *The Train*

I think men are wonderful.
    Katharine Hepburn, *The Philadelphia Story*

He's no good, but he's what I want.
    Judith Anderson, *Laura*

Mother of mercy, is this the end of Rico?
    Edward G. Robinson, *Little Caesar*

The dead are dead! They're nothing, nothing! Nobodies!
    Pierre Arditi, *L'Amour à mort*

In love you can't bring on a substitute.
    Tony Leung, *2046*

We all have it coming.
    Clint Eastwood, *Unforgiven*

I sleep only in French perfume.
    Anita Ekberg, *La Dolce Vita*

I lived a year with Englishmen and hated all of them. And how it rained.
    Raymond Massey, *Fire over England*

Nobody escapes. Nobody really escapes.
    Burt Lancaster, *Brute Force*

Qu'est-ce que c'est dégueulasse.
    Jean Seberg, *Breathless*

Why do you think we love crowds? [in Garbo's voice]: Because everybody is alone.
    James Cagney, *Boy Meets Girl*

Kukumo. He can teach me how to survive Bezuzo.
    Richard Burton, *Exorcist II*

In the beginning was the word. Why, Papa?
    "the little man," *The Sacrifice*

Everything gets old if you do it often enough.
    Ellen Burstyn, *The Last Picture Show*

Love is for the very young.
    Kirk Douglas, *The Bad and the Beautiful*

So it shall be written. So it shall be done.
　　Yul Brynner, *The Ten Commandments*

One should always listen closely when people say good-bye.
　　Katharine Hepburn, *Stage Door*

Don't stick your nose in someone's underwear if you don't understand it.
　　Anatoli Solonitsyne, *Stalker*

No woman deserves to be loved like this. I'm not worth it.
　　Catherine Deneuve, *Mississippi Mermaid*

A guy's world comes crashing around his shoulders and all you offer him is corned beef and cabbage.
　　Mickey Rooney, *Andy Hardy Meets Debutante*

Drinking is a demanding profession, and I can't hold two jobs at once.
　　Morgan Freeman, *The Magic of Belle Isle*

He dies a hero. Had he lived, he might not have known how to grace the part.
　　Edward G. Robinson, *A Bullet for Joey*

The people in your dreams, you should call them when you're awake. It would make life simpler.
　　Juliette Binoche, *The Lovers on the Bridge*

Karczag, Peter Karczag, a real American name.
　　Hedy Lamarr, *A Lady Without Passport*

When anything I wear doesn't please Stephen, I take it off.
　　Joan Crawford, *The Women*

All she did was suck his cock and steal your money. It could have been worse.
　　Matthew McConaughey, *Killer Joe*

PAULINE KAEL'S FAREWELL TO TRUFFAUT AND GODARD

> Who wants to find out you were wrong the first time?
> Besides, most movies would bore me the second time.
> PAULINE KAEL[1]
> —

I ran across Francis Davis's *Afterglow: A Last Conversation with Pauline Kael* while looking for something else in the library. For the most part it's a lively summa, if a summa can be relatively short, of Kael's views on movies. There are no surprises and the pleasures are all retrospective. I had forgotten, for example, that she refused to see a movie more than once because she believed in the spontaneous response and didn't want to sacrifice freshness to retrospection and reflection. Some sentences could have come directly from the old reviews and probably did. After all, if we get a thought just right, why not use it again and again. "Movies became popular because they're a dating game"; "*Shoah* is exhausting because it closes your mind"; "The first two *Godfather* movies are the best movies ever made in this country."[2]

Because I checked the index first, I knew that Truffaut and Godard were on the program. In her reviews she had little enthusiasm for the later work of either. The book confirms this.

> ON TRUFFAUT: I think that the movies Truffaut made after *The Wild Child* and *The Story of Adèle H.* were like the movies he'd panned as a critic for representing "the tradition of quality." Some of the movies he disliked were actually a lot better than the later ones he made.[3]

ON GODARD: [Y]ou can't underestimate Godard's journalistic side. He was commenting on his time – "the children of Marx and Coca-Cola." *Breathless* might hold up better than some of the others, but all of his movies were like very quick skits … I don't know how to account for the fact that when he's good, he's superb, and when he isn't good, he's nothing. I can't accept the films he's just tossed off.[4]

Kael is nothing if not opinionated and critical, often to a fault, but I always enjoy reading her. Who else would venture the suggestion that there are people and critics "who seem to think that European movies are 'smarter' than ours because the characters in them speak a foreign language."[5] This reminds me of Isaiah Berlin's reported comment that the New York intellectuals were impressed by Hannah Arendt because she brought up Kant in conversation and spoke German. In a monolingual country the bilingual speaker will either be king or pariah.

I want to return to Kael's insistence that films should be seen once. Remembered in isolation and without her rhetorical authority the idea doesn't hold up, even if one values a critic's spontaneity. After all we can have the immediacy of the first response in a review, and a more considered engagement in a follow-up essay based on a second viewing. I can understand the insistence on spontaneity when it is used as a criterion in the act of creation, as it is in Romantic theories of art. Think of the emphasis in D.H. Lawrence's theory of the poem of the present or Jackson Pollock's action painting. But the critic is not an artist. Vladimir Nabokov's and Iris Murdoch's view that we must read a novel at least twice is simply right. One reading can't possibly spot all the details contributing to the moral and aesthetic complexity of a work. And then there's the problem of irony. The full implications of Jane Austen's or Thomas Mann's irony aren't available until the end of the novel by which point we have often forgotten, if we noticed, the relevant earlier sentences or scenes that set up the irony. A second reading foregrounds the relevant material as our awareness of irony helps us reconstitute a character or scene into a larger and more complex frame of meaning. Think of the early scenes in *Death in Venice* when we read them the second time around. Watching a film we forget or misremember details – or if it's a mystery, clues – names, and bits of dialogue. There's also the simple fact that a film will change for us because we have been changed by age. *Jules and Jim* is a different film for a twenty-year-old watching with a girlfriend, a forty-year-old married man with children, and a sixty-five-year-old "smiling public man" (Yeats) watching it alone. Bazin insisted on a second viewing as a necessary reality check because it compels us to ask, "Did I get it right?" I recently reread nearly three hundred reviews I published and broadcast between 1985 and 2005, when I stopped reviewing. The ones that caught my attention were the ones where I got it wrong. There should be a code of ethics, a rule about how to behave in such a situation. Do you write the author an apology? Do you write a letter with a belated retraction? Should you offer to take the author and his significant other for dinner at a restaurant of his choice? The reliable Stanley Kauffmann doesn't help me with this but he agrees about the need to see a film at least twice: "If a film has genuine worth, it's more than one film. It changes with further viewings. The second time you see it, it's larger. This time you aren't 'distracted' by the story, by discovering what happens next. You can concentrate on the qualities that made you want to see it again, usually acting or felicities of vision or both. (Third and later viewings – of especially fine films – have an even stranger effect: as you learn more about them, you simultaneously feel you're seeing them for the first time.)"[6] All viewings after the first endow us with a quasi-divine perspective. Like the Stoic gods, who might be omniscient but not omnipotent, we know what is going to happen and watch the events carefully but are detached from them. Still, while no longer surprised by what is happening and by what will happen, we often find ourselves irrationally hoping for a different ending. When I found out that Truffaut had shot three different endings for *Shoot the Piano Player* I hoped against hope that one of them showed Charlie and Léna walking away through the snow together. Damn it, they deserve happiness, and I dislike walking away from that film as unconsoled as Charlie. But, then, if I did get the ending I want, I wouldn't believe it. It's a lose-lose situation.

PAUL SCHRADER'S TEARS

> The significance of tears and sadness for one's world view.
> The tearful aspect of the world.
> MIKHAIL BAKHTIN[1]

Schrader touches on tears when he mentions that he often finds himself crying in the last movement of an Ozu film. Truffaut admitted that he always cried when watching Abel Gance's *Lost Paradise*, a sumptuous melodrama he saw in 1940. It is the first film he recalls seeing, and he saw it several times. My eyes tend to mist over with Ozu during scenes of self-sacrifice, parting, and loneliness, when we sense that the characters will remain unconsoled. But I should confess that I have cried at everything from the late recognition scenes in *The Adventures of Robin Hood* and *The Natural* to the death scenes in *Love Story* and *Terms of Endearment* and the separation of the father (Max von Sydow) and son in *Pelle the Conqueror*. In other words both at movies and films "The tears stream down my cheeks from my unblinking eyes. What makes me weep so?"[2] I find some consolation and company in the fact that J.M. Coetzee, the contemporary novelist with the most restrained emotional register, admits he only partly understands why he cries whenever he reads the chapter in *The Brothers Karamazov* "in which Ivan hands back his ticket of admission to the universe God has created … It is not as if I am in sympathy with Ivan's rather vengeful views. Contrary to him, I believe that the greatest of all contributions to political ethics was made by Jesus when he urged the injured and offended among us to turn the other cheek, thereby breaking the cycle of revenge and reprisal. So why does Ivan make me cry in spite of myself." He answers that "It is the voice of Ivan, as realized by

Dostoevsky, not his reasoning that sweeps me along."[3] Unlike Coetzee, I don't cry over Ivan, but I do when Dmitri hits a man in front of his son. Dostoevsky is also responsible, at least indirectly, for Geoff Dyer's tears at a key scene in Tarkovsky's Dostoevskian *Stalker*, a film I admire, but at which I have yet to weep.

If my tears are any indication, Truffaut's saddest scenes focus on women crying: Christine (Claude Jade) crying when dressed as a geisha in *Bed and Board*; Cécilia Mandel (Nathalie Baye) crying as she lights the candle for the dead Julien at the end of *The Green Room*; and Mathilde's (Fanny Ardant) eyes, shining black pools filling with tears as she shoots Depardieu before shooting herself. This is one of those screen moments where my eyes moist over even as I remember Dee Clark singing "A man ain't supposed to cry."

THE LAST METRO (1980): FRANÇOIS TRUFFAUT-LÉVY

[Truffaut] always felt like a Jew.
CLAUDE DE GIVRAY[1]

—

Truffaut's discovery in autumn 1968 that his birth father was a Jew intensified his sense of estrangement from his mother's family, the Monferrands, and from French society in general but had little effect on his daily life. After 1968 he began making annual financial contributions in support of Israel, something that, had Godard known about it, would have probably brought the friendship to an even earlier end since he was a very public supporter of the Palestinian cause. Truffaut began to occasionally puzzle interviewers and friends with comments like "We're all German Jews."[2] A different example occurs in an interview about *The Wild Child*, a profoundly autobiographical film in which Truffaut is to some extent both Doctor Itard and Victor the wild boy. In the following comment Truffaut discusses the scene in which Itard unjustly punishes Victor to see whether the boy can distinguish between justice and injustice, fairness and unfairness. He then goes off on an unexpected tangent: "here is another example of the same situation which is also incredible: it is the true story of a Jew during the war waiting to be deported. He has one daughter. He adores her. When he knows that his arrest is just a question of days, he becomes very severe, hard, unjust toward the little girl as a way of making her miss him less when he will be taken away. For me, that's the height of heroism ... One day, perhaps I will make a film about it."[3] I find this passage remarkable each time I read it. I imagine myself interviewing Truffaut and listening to this and wondering how to make a transition with my next question to somehow nudge him into revealing how he made the daring leap from the scene in the film to the one from the period of the war.

Truffaut never made the film he imagines, though some version of it – a convoy on its way to a camp – had been on his mind since the 1960s. With the exception of Cécilia Mandel, whose family name might be Jewish, there are no Jewish characters in his films until *The Last Metro*. Though he had long been thinking about a film set during the Occupation, I doubt it would have taken the form it did if he had not found out about Roland Lévy. He told an interviewer that he delayed making it because of the appearance of Max Ophuls's *The Sorrow and the Pity* (1969), Louis Malle's *Lacombe, Lucien* (1975), and Joseph Losey's *Mr Klein* (1976). Nowhere does he mention *Ici et Ailleurs* (*Here and Elsewhere*, 1973–76), Godard's controversial anti-Zionist film about Jews and Palestinians which suggests that the Jews stand in relation to the Palestinians as the Nazis did to Europe's Jews. It also compares Golda Meir and Hitler. Given the controversy that accompanied its appearance, Truffaut's silence is surprising. Having broken with Godard in 1973, did he think there was nothing more to say? Did his habitual discretion counsel avoiding an argument in public? Most probably there was still a residual loyalty to an old friend whom he never criticized in public, not even after they stopped speaking. Whatever the reason, Truffaut never mentions the film. On the other hand, even though *The Last Metro* neither mentions nor alludes to Godard's film, I can't avoid thinking that it is on some level an answer to its provocation. Neither Truffaut nor Godard's biographers and critics have suggested the connection.

Truffaut justified making *The Last Metro* with the suggestion that it "is interesting, I suppose, because of its small details. It's almost as if seen by a child because the things that struck me at the time are woven into the film."[4] The Occupation and the war appear as they impinge on people's everyday lives. Soldiers, blackouts, deportations, censorship, and the resistance are present but they are felt indirectly through their effect on the black market, clothes, employment, food, curfews, entertainment, necessary documents, and love affairs. This emphasis brings the film close to Fellini's *Amarcord* and Skvorecky's *The Swell Season*, which offer similarly focused views from within or below of wartime small towns in Italy and Czechoslovakia. In Paris, Rimini, and Náchod, if you weren't a Jew you could have an endurable war, something not possible in Berlin, Kiev, or Warsaw.

Though Truffaut points to several sources for the script, he doesn't mention the most obvious, Renoir's *Carola*, a play about an actress who helps conceal a Resistance fighter in a Paris theatre. An English version, starring Leslie Caron and directed by Norman Stone, was filmed for television in 1973. Like Truffaut, Renoir shows the wartime French to be occasionally more eager than the Germans in their pursuit of Jews and resisters. Carola is attracted both to the young French fugitive and to German General von Claudius, with whom she has a prewar history. The General is that troubling figure in Second World War movies, the good German. The issue isn't whether there were any – think of Władysław Szpilman's memoir *The Pianist* – but that they were so few as not to be representative. To put the emphasis on one, as Renoir does, is to risk distorting our sense of the past.

In Truffaut and Schiffman's script, the man under threat becomes Lucas Steiner (Heinz Bennent), a distinguished director now hiding in the basement of the Théâtre Montmartre while his wife runs it. Marion (Deneuve) is another of Truffaut's strong and independent women, with the added dimension that she has a significant social responsibility and a lover. She could say, as Sartre did, that she had never felt as free as during the Occupation. The film's ending offers an unexpectedly non-Truffauldian resolution of the lovers' triangle: facing the audience at the end of a curiously flat postwar play, Marion stands radiant and smiling between her husband and lover (Depardieu) – every adulterer's dream. That all three are complicit and content is emphasised in the closing credits: each is seen separately in an iris surrounded by a red screen. It's a shot that recalls the ending of Renoir's *French Cancan*. If you're looking for Truffaut, he's in all three: he's the director, the lover, and the wife.

While the Jewish theme separates *The Last Metro* from Truffaut's other films, his various signatures or his visual system can be seen throughout. A large model of the Eiffel Tower is prominent in Marion's office, and the tower itself is in the background in a late shot. The happy triangle looks back antithetically to other less happy trios. The newspaper presses have been seen in *Love on the Run* and *The Man Who Loved Women*. Some of the words spoken during the lovemaking between Marion and her lover and Marion and her husband have been rehearsed in *Jules and Jim* and will reappear a year later in *The Woman Next Door*. When Bernard tells Marion that love is both a joy and a torment, Truffaut is looking back to *Mississippi Mermaid*, where Deneuve first heard them playing a different

"Marion," and again forward to *The Woman Next Door*. After Truffaut's death, Deneuve will hear the words again when she speaks them to her daughter in François Ozon's *8 Women* ("Seeing you ... so close brings me both joy and suffering"). The scene's emotional reach ramifies when Ozon shows the partly hidden Fanny Ardant overhearing the sentence – spoken by Deneuve, Truffaut's former lover – and slowly giving way to tears: she had last heard the words nineteen years earlier in *The Woman Next Door*. One filmic connection to Truffaut is in three of the photos on Marion's wall borrowed from *The Green Room*. As well, the actors memorizing and reciting their lines are kinsmen of the memorizers in *Fahrenheit 451* and live in an equally oppressive society. There is something in the motif of silence-reading-memorization that won't let him go.

This rich tessera of related motifs always gives me a slightly irrational pleasure, as if I'm seeing and hearing an internal dialogue among the films available only to the initiated, those of us who have lived with them for a long time. I like observing Truffaut enfolding the various films one into another in ways similar to Balzac's in *The Human Comedy*, Proust's in *Remembrance of Things Past*, or Powell's in *A Dance to the Music of Time*. Each creates a complex multifarious world held together by voices, style, characters, and countless repeated details of tone, object, colour, form, verbal echo, music, names, and themes, not to mention coincidences as incredible as those that happen in everyday life. Truffaut's recurrences are directed at those who follow him film by film captivated by his advances and recapitulations in the development of his vision. The individual films are responsive commentaries on one another, restatements of fundamental concerns, problems, and themes. Think of *The Mischief Makers*, *The 400 Blows*, *The Wild Child*, and *Small Change* as a single unit of interconnected films about the lives of children. The projected *La Petite Voleuse* would have been the fifth act in the cycle. Another unit is made up of *Day for Night*, *The Last Metro*, and the planned film about a group of itinerant French actors travelling in North Africa. *The Story of Adèle H.* can be read in tangent with *The Man Who Loved Women* as another narrative of an absolute, obsessive love rooted in a failed relationship with a demanding parent. And finally, *The Mischief Makers*, *The Bride Wore Black*, and *Such a Gorgeous Kid like Me* play different riffs on the situation of a woman having to deal with several males. The deep resemblance among the films in each of these groups doesn't prevent them from being different in kind, tone, emotional colouring, and plot.

If Truffaut repeats himself within a slender sheaf of issues, he does so like a poet or painter who during a particularly intense period of creativity works compulsively around a handful of images, characters, and themes. Think of certain periods in the careers of Rilke, Yeats, both Renoirs, Rothko, and Scorsese. Truffaut addressed the issue of repetition directly during a television interview when promoting *The Last Metro*. He said "I've made twenty films and sadly we must reinvent ourselves, and we do that by copying our own past work … If I'm going to make more than twenty films, I can only do it by mixing up the old ones. C'est la vie."[5] There's some truth here, but there's more to the issue than he offers in the soundbite. Surely the question of repeating himself was also a serious worry, especially in light of the protean Godard's ability to ignore boundaries and remake himself every few years by taking his camera in a new direction. *The Green Room* had been Truffaut's attempt to find a source for a script outside his own life. The failure to find an audience may have been as serious a setback as that of *Shoot the Piano Player*. He had begun sensing that repetition, in some form, was inevitable and that, contra Kierkegaard, a repetition is not always a surprise. The question had to be posed not as "Will I repeat myself?" but "Since repetition is inevitable for someone making films past his fiftieth birthday, what sort of repetition will it be?" The notebooks and scripts in progress indicate some possible directions. I will return to these.

The one development I am sure of is that had Truffaut lived he would have done some finetuning in the form of "a director's cut" of several of the films. With *The Last Metro*, for instance, I think he would have given serious consideration to restoring some scenes cut primarily because of concerns about the film's length. He had already done a director's cut with *Two English Girls*. *The Last Metro* DVD has additional scenes including an emotionally subtle one between Marion and Valentin, an old and elegant writer who has come to her office to discuss a film script, *The Angels of Mercy*, he had left with her earlier. Obviously fond of him, she tells him that she's too busy with theatre to think of a return to film. When she invites him to dinner, he declines courteously, citing his departure next morning for the mountains where, gravely ill, he says he is going for his health. When she tries to kiss him goodbye, he gently and regretfully tells her that it would be dangerous. I assume he has tuberculosis, but Truffaut leaves open the possibility that he's Jewish and it would be a risk for her to kiss a Jew in public, especially one not wearing a star.

Instead he strokes her cheek à la Doinel. The scene is emotionally muted; the actors' complex feelings are communicated with their eyes, gentle gestures, courtesies, and nuances of usage and tone. Without Marion using these words we know that she is feeling concern, anxiety, sadness, and remorse. The scene is finely played; it is unhurried, unforced, and deftly paced. Valentin has only a few minutes of screentime but in dress (a camel-hair coat, a knotted scarf), manner, and tone he embodies a passing culture and era. Marion feels more than just respect for his talent. The editors indicate in the DVD interview that Valentin is "based at least in part on the eminent playwright Jean Giraudoux who co-scripted Bresson's first feature, *The Angels of Sin* (1943), a film about nuns. It is alluded to in the second play performed within *The Last Metro*, 'The Angels of Mercy.'" He died in 1944.

SUBTITLES AND VOICES

... worse than dubbing or the substitution that dubbing implies
is one's general awareness of a substitution, of a fake.
JORGE LUIS BORGES[2]

—

Stanley Kaufmann mentions that even though he can't follow dialogue in French he prefers subtitles to dubbing because he likes the sound of an actor's voice in the original language. No two languages sound alike. Each has its register, tonality, timbre, pitch, pace, and music. It was along these lines that Jorge Luis Borges objected as long ago as 1945 that "the arbitrary implant of another voice and another language" is always a mistake because "the voice of Hepburn or Garbo is not accidental but, for the world, one of their defining features. Similarly, it is worth remembering that gestures are different in English and Spanish."[2] The languages of Kurosawa's *The Seven Samurai* and Tarkovsky's *Andrei Roublev* create their own music that expresses both the characters and their cultures. Characters, in a film even more than in a novel, have their own speech rhythms and favoured words. Each voice is part of a sonic palette important for itself and for the way it relates to the voices of others. The verbal dance between Moreau and Werner disappears when they are dubbed, even if each of the bilingual actors does the dubbing. Powell and Pressburger's *The Life and Death of Colonel Blimp* is as English as Deborah Kerr and Roger Livesay or Elgar's *The Dream of Gerontius* – but only in English. This linguistic specificity is particularly true with deeply literary films like *Jules and Jim* and *Two English Girls* in which much of the script is taken from the text. Truffaut's direct borrowing from Roché suggests that he thinks the words are perfect and admirable as written; they should not be tampered with. He agrees with Welles that dialogue is a kind of music, even a dance of words to the music of the film's time. Although he doesn't use these terms, we might think of a monologue as a sonata, a dialogue as a duet, a scene with four people as a quartet, and the sound of a crowd – the ball in Sergei Bondarchuk's *War and Peace*, the train station in *North by Northwest* – as a symphony or oratorio. Dubbing would erase this aurally constitutive aspect of the film. Subtitles, by contrast, allow the original soundtrack to have at least a chance of being a sort of oral pentimento, a meaningful white noise that lets the audience reading the subtitles sense simultaneously what the words sound like when allowed to sing. If nothing else we can hear what the character really sounds like when Hepburn says "I think men are wonderful" or when Wayne growls "A man's got to do what a man's got to do."

Here are some voices whose music I would not want to lose: Mathieu Amalric, Fernando Rey, James Stewart (only an asthmatic gasp away from stuttering), John Wayne's Amarone, Hepburn, Mercedes McCambridge's menacing drone, Kathleen Turner's update on Bacall, George Sanders's condescending purr, Monroe's orgiastic squeal, Cary Grant (unplaceable), Nick Nolte's slurry, Walter Matthau's grate, Woody's whine, Wallace Beery (what the sidewalk feels like at the end of the day), Claude Rains's claret, Max von Sydow (how God would sound if he were Swedish), Sharon Stone, Trevor Howard, Alec Guinness, Bruno Ganz ("Ganz doesn't talk, he croons"),[3] Gérard Depardieu, Deborah Kerr, Jean Gabin, Robert Ryan, James Mason (like a spider web), Eugene Pallette's hoarsely laryngeal rasp, Barbara Stanwyck, Bette Davis (as manic as a polygraph), Delphine Seyrig (a gin martini), John Gielgud (a Platonic model for all flutes), Mastroianni (how I want to sound in Italian), Peter Lorre's whine from the planet Weimar, Groucho's lurching quack, Glenda Jackson's androgynous rasp, Debra Winger ("Do you want to?"), Charles Bickford, Judy Davis, Helena Bonham-Carter.

ROBERTO ROSSELLINI (1906–1977): THE ITALIAN GODFATHER

> A great father, like Adam, [Rossellini] created us all.
> FEDERICO FELLINI[1]

Truffaut was fortunate in his mentors – Bazin, Cocteau, Rossellini, and, at a distance, Renoir. Rossellini's insistence on the director's freedom to shoot films on a small budget, without a fixed script and about contemporary topics anticipated similar emphases among the New Wave. Truffaut couldn't have made *The 400 Blows* without the example of his new realism in films like *Germany Year Zero*. Perhaps most important was the fact that the radically independent and often irresponsible Rossellini was an auteur before the *Cahiers* critics made it one of their foundational terms. Truffaut repeatedly acknowledged through the 1950s the connection between Rossellini's films and the events in the French film world. You can hear his over-the-top lover's enthusiasm – his criticism rarely has a middle range of response – in his review of *Voyage in Italy* (1953). The film follows a married couple – Bergman and George Sanders – on a tense vacation during which they question their marriage. If you trust the young Truffaut, this is the greatest film since *Citizen Kane*. "What first strikes you is the novelty, the audacity … This movie resembles those that will be made ten years from now, when film-makers the world over will give up imitating the novel in favour of the filmed confession and the essay ... At times, points of emotion come to liberate the heart oppressed by a continuous dramatic tension that acts 'physically' on the spectators. *Voyage in Italy* is not like anything ever done in cinema."[2] Truffaut is twenty-two when he writes this, but he has been thinking about film for nearly a decade. He senses Rossellini's difference and realizes that simply calling him an Italian neorealist won't capture the uniqueness of his films or draw French audiences to them.

But if you know their biographies you may suspect that Truffaut also finds Rossellini fascinating, even irresistible, because of his zest for life and women, especially actresses and prostitutes. The always discreet Truffaut never refers to the older man's women directly, but they are there in a coded form in the references to his "ardent" nature and Italian zeal for life. In other words, Rossellini lived openly the sort of life that Truffaut would later keep secret from almost everyone. The Italian, by contrast, was a graduate of the kiss-and-tell school of Italian *machismo* and enjoyed telling a friend why he had no choice but to be unfaithful to Bergman – she didn't enjoy fellatio. The visits to his favourite prostitutes continued during the marriage. The most touching and unexpected connection between the two filmmakers occurs during the last year of their lives. After surgery for a brain tumour, when Truffaut was too weak to live alone and Fanny was away working, Madeleine took him in. Only when his condition made professional care necessary was he moved to Paris's American Hospital. Rossellini doesn't quite move in with his first wife, the always faithful Marcelina, but a year before his death in 1977 of a heart attack, he moves into an apartment directly across the street from hers. She continued to think of herself as Signora Rossellini and, when needed, looked after and cooked for her "husband." Tag Gallagher, his sympathetic biographer, offers a touching summary of the relationship during the last year.

> In September 1976 he moved into an apartment that Marcelina had found for him directly across from her own, Via Caroncini 43 ... Marcelina kept Baruff [the dog] and fed Roberto too. He had always loved her cooking: eggs fried, then cut like noodles with tomato, basil and butter; or cod fried then baked with white wine and tomato sauce, black olives and oregano. His happiness came first for her. She had not disapproved of Silvia [D'Amico, his latest love].

"How important it was for him to have had that love at that age" she said. She had been having a longtime relationship herself but cut it off the moment he told her needed her and asked her to. In her mind his other women had always been *scappatelle* (escapades) and her other men *flirt sportivi*; she was Roberto's wife. She was never willing, however, to resume marital relations after their separation.³

Truffaut took from Rossellini what he needed to become himself. He knew, however, that the Italian was an inimitable life force and that he could not sustain or survive a career as chaotic. Like others in the New Wave he learned a great deal from him, but in the end his films owe less to him than do Godard's, with their experimentation, emphasis on the importance of documentary, didactic intention, and almost aleatory poetics. For instance, the chapter-like form of *Vivre sa vie* (1962) owes much to *Francesco, Giullare di Dio* (1950). Rossellini might have understood and even grudgingly approved Godard's challenging *Histoire(s) du cinéma* (1998). After all, several of his own projects have the same "a man's reach should exceed his grasp" quality. That Truffaut sensed the Rossellini-Godard connection is suggested in a 1965 letter to Helen Scott: "[Roberto] was, just as Jean-Luc is, quicker than anyone else, more alive, more intelligent, more enterprising and, of necessity, more quickly disillusioned with the cinema ... Today his activity consists in obtaining enormous sums of money from the great financial powers of Europe ... If Roberto wasn't the man he is – sincere and brilliant – one might describe it all as a huge confidence trick, a mammoth deal or else the biggest swindle of the century, but it isn't so."⁴ The last four words don't quite convince. There were too many advances even when Truffaut worked with Rossellini in the mid-1950s that resulted in nothing more than a brief outline or treatment. It's also difficult to overlook the past tense in the first sentence.

Other than *The 400 Blows*, *Shoot the Piano Player*, *The Wild Child*, and *Small Change*, few of Truffaut's films would have interested Rossellini. Truffaut's two most obvious debts to him are Antoine's shrine to Balzac (*Germany Year Zero*) and the spinning game Claude and the sisters play in *Two English Girls* (*Francesco, Giullare di Dio*). Thomson deftly and memorably captures the difference between them in his description of the Italian as "less a filmmaker than someone who observed the world through film."⁵

THE WOMAN NEXT DOOR (1981): "NEITHER WITH YOU NOR WITHOUT YOU"

> True love makes the thought of death frequent, easy, without terrors; it becomes merely a standard of comparison, the price one would pay for many things.
>
> STENDHAL[1]
>
> ―

I sometimes think of *The Woman Next Door* as primarily aimed at anyone ever left by a lover, as Truffaut had been by Deneuve, and no matter how much time has passed or what has happened in his or her life has remained convinced, against all the evidence, like the hero of *Silver Linings Playbook*, that the lover will return. Every ring of the telephone and every letter is a moment of hopeless and unrequited hope. Whether you live alone or have a new love, you carry the toxic mixture of hope and despair in secret: not just the self divided, but also the self divided against itself. There is a quality of self-abasement and self-disgust in awaiting the impossible. It's dramatized in *The Story of Adèle H.* and it forms the background to its companion film, once titled *The Story of Mathilde B.* Perhaps the most searing commentary on both films is Jacques Brel's "Mathilde." In Brel's song of tough love the male singer responds to the return of a woman his saner self had hoped had gone forever, while another weaker part longed for her return. The first verse is directed at his mother and his friends warning them of the danger of Mathilde's presence; the second verse announces his return to Mathilde and "hell." The "enfer" colours everything. Its effect is as unsettling as the line in Brel's better-known hit

"Ne me quitte pas," in which the man begs the woman to let him be "the shadow of your dog" in an attempt to keep her from leaving. A woman's version would be Nina Simone's "Don't Explain." It's not an accident that "Ne me quitte pas" is among the songs Mathilde Bauchard (Ardant) praises to her lover Bernard Coudray (Depardieu) for telling the truth about love – or at least love as she sees it from the bottom of the well. Her chosen songs deal with betrayal, abandonment, and despair. Some are permeated by an inescapable self-abasement which at least lets one know that things can't get much worse. Like *The Story of Adèle H.*, the film offers only two possible endings, each inflected by despair: breakdown or death, with the latter, as Stendhal suggests, setting "a standard of comparison" by which all other options are measured.

As almost always I can find an antecedent in Shakespeare, though it applies more directly to Adèle's situation than to Mathilde's. It's the scene in *A Midsummer Night's Dream* in which Helena pleads with Demetrius, don't leave me.

> I am your spaniel; and, Demetrius,
> The more you beat me, I will fawn on you.
> Use me but as your spaniel, spurn me, strike me,
> Neglect me, lose me; only give me leave,
> Unworthy as I am, to follow you.
> What worser place can I beg in your love –
> And yet a place of high respect with me –
> Than to be used as you use your dog? (II, i, 203–10)

What's worse, to be someone's "dog" or "the shadow of your dog"?

The delicately named Elizabeth Butterfly mentions in *François Truffaut: Le Journal d'Alphonse* that among the reasons Truffaut made *The Woman Next Door* was the desire to use the phrase "ni avec toi, ni sans toi" ("neither with you nor without you"). Unfortunately he wasn't able to work it into the film until Schiffman suggested an epilogue spoken by Madame Jouve, that wounded survivor of definitive love.

One of the aspects of the film I increasingly admire is that even as it focuses on Mathilde and Bernard's downward spiral, it also pays sensitive attention to the middle range of affections that we tend to take for granted in our lives outside the movie theatre. Both married couples are

Fanny Ardant as Mathilde Bauchard in *The Woman Next Door* (1981). She would also star in Truffaut's last film, *Confidentially Yours* (1983).

shown doing the things that ordinary couples do most of the time: eating meals, playing with children, meeting friends and neighbours, and planning their future. Truffaut also shows each couple dealing with the fallout of the affair. Arlette Coudray's pregnancy with the couple's second child adds a poignancy similar to what we feel when Sabine is on the screen with the adults in *Jules and Jim*. What does Sabine make of her mother's changing sleeping arrangements?

FANNY MARGUERITE JUDITH ARDANT

> We watched with Norman Mozzato a Truffaut film with a wonderful actress, Fanny Ardant. The film is average, but the actors are excellent. Frankly, with actors such as Jean-Louis Trintignant and Fanny Ardant, you can only make a good film.
> ANDREI TARKOVSKY[1]
> —

Like the names Laetitia le Coq (the late Joanne Dru) and Cécile de France, Fanny's name seems at first too suggestively evocative and too symbolically suggestive to be wasted on a real person. There would have been a fine symmetry had she made her debut in *Confidentially Yours*. Our first view of her would have been in the opening scene sashaying down a street in Nice followed by a frisky white terrier; we would have been unable to resist the spring in her walk, her smile, and her charm. Coming at the camera she has the rhythm and lilt of a model, what Eric Rohmer would have described as a walk with a "certain behavioral grace, close to that of the dance."[2] But the slightly knowing and almost sly smile – *You know I'm irresistible* – exudes the same sort of aura Hayworth has when she struts onto the stage in *Gilda* and into immortality. Truffaut noticed Ardant on television in 1979 in a show that gave him both his actress and almost his title, *Les Dames de la côte*.

Of her films after his death, I think he would have enjoyed her especially in two. Her ravenous, vulpine sexy Queen of Scotland in *Elizabeth*

(Shekhar Kapur, 1998) would have held him, though differently from the self-protective and scheming wife in *Colonel Chabert* (Yves Angelou, 1994). Based on one of Balzac's best short novels, Angelou's film is the story of a soldier presumed dead in Napoleon's Russian campaign who returns to a wife who has married above her and is unwilling to recognize him. This is one of Depardieu's best roles; it shows him brave, stubborn, resilient, befuddled, betrayed, bedraggled, understanding, broken, perdurable, and stoic. The completely convincing historical melodrama is Balzac's, but the chilled control surrounding the discussions of love and betrayal are Stendhalian. It's a film I imagine Truffaut making, though I have no complaints about Angelou's version. Still, perhaps the film's success owes something to Ardant and Depardieu's recall of *The Woman Next Door*. I wonder if Rivette was looking over his shoulder at the film when he made the very different *La Duchesse de Langeais* (2008) with Depardieu's late son Guillaume as the Balzacian lead. Rivette's is really the kind of story Stendhal, a master of unconsummated or interrupted love, might have written. *De l'Amour*, his sometimes tediously serpentine account of a frustrating courtship, is a bemused commentary on the inevitable failure of passionate love. Fanny and Gérard return less memorably as nineteenth-century lovers in *Balzac* (1999), a film that reminds us that "le cinéma du papa" is as alive, perhaps more so, than the cinema of the auteur. Moreau, as Balzac's unloving mother, is there to remind us that far away and long ago in a world not quite forgotten one could have gone to see films like *La Notte*, *Jules and Jim*, and *Diary of a Chambermaid* if disinclined to watch old puff pastry like this.

The desire for a rhetorical ending made me forget, but only for a moment, Fanny Ardant's memorable brief appearances in Paolo Sorrentino's very different triumphs, *Il Divo* (2008) and *La Grande Bellezza* (2013).

FRANÇOIS AND SAM: SOME FAVOURITE FILMS

This isn't just about the best films ever made or the historically most important. It's also about ones that gave pleasure.

François Truffaut: *Zéro de conduite* (Vigo), *L'Atalante* (Vigo), *Germany Year Zero* (Rossellini), *Citizen Kane* (Welles), *Paradis perdu* (Gance), *Le Roman d'un tricheur* (Guitry), *The Magnificent Ambersons* (Welles), *Les Enfants terribles* (Melville), *Le Journal d'un curé de campagne* (Bresson), *Les Visiteurs du soir* (Carne), *Le Corbeau* (Clouzot), *À Bout de souffle* (Godard), *La Règle du jeu* (Renoir), *La Grande Illusion* (Renoir), *The Passion of Joan of Arc* (Dreyer), *The Naked Dawn* (Ulmer), *Les Dames de Bois de Boulogne* (Bresson), *Fanny and Alexander* (Bergman), *Rear Window* (Hitchcock), *Lola Montès* (Ophuls), *Johnny Guitar* (Ray).

Sam Solecki: *Point Blank* (Boorman), *The Adventures of Robin Hood* (Curtiz), *Wings of Desire* (Wenders), *The Godfather I and II* (Copolla), *Out of the Past* (Tourneur), *The Searchers* (Ford), *Children of Paradise* (Carné), *Ulzana's Raid* (Aldrich), *Love and Death* (Allen), *Cinema Paradiso* (Tornatore, short version), *8 1/2* (Fellini), *The Bicycle Thieves* (De Sica), *War and Peace* (Bondarchuk), *Elisa Vida Mia* (Saura), *Pelle the Conqueror* (August), *Smiles of a Summer Night* (Bergman), *Blade Runner* (Scott), *La Grande Illusion* (Renoir), *Nostalghia* (Tarkovsky), *The Girl on the Bridge* (Leconte), *La Belle Noiseuse* (Rivette), *Black Narcissus* (Powell), *The Umbrellas of Cherbourg* (Demy), *Lawrence of Arabia* (Lean), *The Long Goodbye* (Altman), *La Grande Bellezza* (Sorrentino), *Invasion of the Body Snatchers* (Siegel).

A GODARD DREAM
(26 JUNE 2011)

> I don't understand his work [À la Recherche du temps perdu], but that's my fault not his.
> ANATOLE FRANCE[1]

The shadows tell me that it is very early evening, and the way people are dressed suggests late summer. The walkers on the street closed off to traffic are at first like the sombre figures in Munch's *The Scream*. I know at once that I'm somewhere in Europe and look around for signs that will tell me which country. I see Godard and myself from behind walking down the street talking about Truffaut. He smokes a cigar, is almost expansive and, for him, garrulous though he manages to be simultaneously distant. He is in his prime, and so am I. He admits that he behaved badly to Truffaut, that he was blinded by his zeal to change the world with film and politics. He says that he thinks it's obvious from his foreword to Truffaut's letters that he wishes the break had never happened. I trot along by his side like a happy and anxious terrier (the white one in *Confidentially Yours*), worrying that I'll run out of questions or forget some of what he's saying. There's also the chance, given the crowds sauntering around us on a warm evening on what I now recognize as Bern's most famous street – my father and I walked here in 1982 – that I will lose him or he will take off with someone else. (My lifelong anxiety about being left out.) I'm also uneasy about perhaps betraying Truffaut by being so friendly with Godard – even feeling honoured by being seen with him (*Who is that with Godard?*).

Maybe I should have contacted Chabrol or Rohmer or Schiffman? What I'm really going through is the same set of interconnected mixed feelings I have whenever I'm with someone whose work I admire. In this case there is the added problem that I'm beginning to feel guilty for finding that I'm beginning to like the "Anti-Truffaut."

As he talks, the streetlights suddenly go on around the pillars surmounted by the famous coloured bears. I notice that it has gotten duskier, that many of the other strollers have left the streets for the cafés, and that Godard and I are in what seems like a tunnel or cone of dimming light, almost an iris. I hear a curious sort of shuffling susurrus and realize that there are small groups of people scurrying along together in the shadows, even huddling close to the shops, as in a black and white Bruno Schulz drawing, because there is a pack of mongrel dogs wandering the now more deserted streets. Godard notices my anxiety – when I was ten I had been attacked by a German shepherd – and tells me "Don't worry. I know how to deal with dogs." (This is getting close to my old dreams of being rescued by my father or some father surrogates.) True to his word, with a smile that makes him look like Terry Eagleton, he somehow calms them by doing a shamanistic gesture with his hands and arms and manages to make them mill around us tamely. And then, almost too quickly for me to understand how it happens, he starts in fast-forward throwing them two or more at a time up into the air like a juggler. I say, "How did you do that?" and he laughs and replies, "Oh, it's just something I picked up when I was in South America." The dogs float, almost flow in slow motion, like the astronauts in *2001: A Space Odyssey*, with the surprised look of puppies on their faces: when I look up I see a cascade of yelping mongrels falling from a surreal canine cornucopia. Next to me Godard's arms are manic, but his face is smiling and radiant, at peace. It is obvious that he is in complete control and very happy in his work. The remaining evening strollers stare in wonder and admiration. They begin to laugh with relief and pleasure. Then they applaud and call out "Well done, Jean-Luc, well done." He nods in acknowledgment. Then he turns to me and says, "I told you I could do it, didn't I. You know, I can also walk on my hands." And he does and then jumps up, rubs his palms together, and smiles irresistibly. The applause continues even as the scene darkens and I begin to awake.

Later in the day I trace the dogs to Michael Ondaatje's *Running in the Family*, the oneiric scene in which the father walks out of the jungle:

"In one hand he holds five ropes; dangling from the end of each is a black dog. None of the five are touching the ground. He is holding his arm outstretched, holding them with one arm as if he has supernatural strength. Terrible noises are coming from him and from the dogs as if there is a conversation between them that is subterranean, volcanic. All their tongues hanging out."[2]

The dream is a reminder that, although I prefer Truffaut's films, Godard is a genius. In the dream, as in life, he does things no one else can do: he subdues and juggles the mongrel dogs, brings violence and chaos under control. He can do with ease things unimagined by others, even or especially things others wouldn't consider doing. He borrows his credo from Piet Mondrian, "always further."[3] There's a subtle link to Shakespeare by way of Ondaatje's daring use of *King Lear* in *Running in the Family*. In 1987, five years after Ondaatje's fictional memoir, Godard filmed his own *King Lear*. For a brief insane moment it looked as if Norman Mailer would star and his daughter would play Cordelia. The dream suggests that Godard is as great as Shakespeare and as greatly flawed as Lear. Lear, you may recall, had three dogs, Tray, Blanch, and Sweetheart. What happens to them?

LE JOURNAL D'ALPHONSE: A DOINEL SEQUEL

> What a wonderful child. He's really fantastic! ...
> He'll be the writer I wanted to be – Victor Hugo or nothing!
> ANTOINE DOINEL, BED AND BOARD
> —

Nineteenth-century novelists weren't the first to understand that most people find fictional characters as real as themselves. The New York fans of Dickens's *The Old Curiosity Shop* who called out to an arriving English ship "Does Little Nell live?" were expressing a profound fact about our reading experience: the novelist has the power to bring a character to such a pitch of life that she has an almost palpable presence for us. The disappointment of fans of *Downton Abbey* at the unexpected death of Matthew Crawley is a recent reminder of our emotional investment in someone who doesn't exist. Natasha Rostov, Jude Frawley, Hans Castorp, Holden Caulfield, and Harry Potter are more than fictional simulacra to those who have entered imaginatively and affectively into their worlds. The regret we feel each time we finish a cherished novel or see "The End" on the screen indicate as much. Writers and filmmakers understand this each time they risk an epilogue or sequel. The epilogue has a sort of indeterminate liminal status as a bridge between the novel proper and the reader's world. Like Demerol it helps us adjust to the morphine we can no longer have. Like a school reunion the epilogue tells us what happened to the characters after the novel's end. The effect is almost always ambiguously satisfying because most of us probably feel queasy knowing that the rules have been slightly bent – think back to *Murder at Pemberley*. I mentioned earlier a good recent example of a reader taking the rules into his own hands in order to gain the satisfaction he wants from novels and films – the lunatic in Mankell's *The Troubled Man* who "spent forty years reading the classics and changing the endings when he thought they were too tragic." There can't be many of us, even those committed to the autonomy of the work of art, who don't find this appealing at some guilty level. Imagine Natasha Rostov and Prince Andrei Bolkonsky having a second chance, Bazarov outliving his parents as every son should, and Jude Fawley marrying a woman who makes him happy. In a body of work as death-haunted as Truffaut's, the insane revisionist impulse would make revolutionary changes in the erotic dynamic and in Truffaut's theory of love.

Prequels and sequels work even harder to satisfy our desire to spend more time with a character (or actor). Think of John Wayne in John Ford's cavalry trilogy or Sigourney Weaver's Ripley in the *Alien* films. More familiar and more reassuring are crime novels with a recurring hero (Raymond Chandler's) or even with a recurring cast of characters (as in Robert B. Parker, Sjowall and Wahloo, Colin Dexter). I can't be the only person who had tears in his eyes at the end of the last Inspector Morse novel, the plangently titled *The Remorseful Day*. The death of John Thaw, television's Morse, a few years later, was a dark day as well. I still keep his photo on the refrigerator next to one of Jerry Orbach, Detective Lennie Briscoe in *Law and Order*. There is no indication that when Truffaut made *The 400 Blows* he intended it as the first instalment in a series of feature films dealing with the life of Antoine Doinel, though he had played with the idea of a series of shorts. *Antoine and Colette*, the second, was made in response to a request for a short episode for a group work titled *Love at Twenty* (1962). *Bed and Board* (1970) and *Love on the Run* (1979) might not have been made if more of the non-Doinel films had been hits. All of which makes Elizabeth Butterfly's discovery in 2004 in the Truffaut Archives of a nine-page typescript titled *Le Journal d'Alphonse* particularly unexpected. Truffaut had been working on it as recently as 1982, though it isn't mentioned in his published letters or the biography.

The typescript opens with Alphonse's voiceover describing a situation similar to that found in Max Ophuls's *La Ronde*: "Paris, le 12 Juillet 1982. Marion aime Patrick. Patrick sort avec Julie, mais il aime Aline. Aline sort avec moi; moi, j'aime Marion qui sort avec Paul, un jeune homme au pair, pâle, venu d'Angleterre par bateau." ("Paris, 12 July 1982. Marion loves Patrick. Patrick goes out with Julie, but he loves Aline. Aline goes out with me; me, I love Marion, who goes out with Paul, a pale young au pair, who came by boat from England.")[1] Everyone is in love with the wrong person. The rest of the brief scenario narrows the complication down to the triangle Alphonse-Marion-Patrick, though there is not enough material to determine whether that would be the film's focus.

Alphonse, the son of Antoine and Christine, resembles Truffaut in not knowing how to swim, not liking the company of men after seven, and in his admiration for Paul Léautaud, a taste both share with Antoine. He resembles his father, as Butterfly points out, in completing "his emotional education alone."[2] But unlike Antoine his "existence follows a straight line"; in a handwritten marginal note, Truffaut adds "Antoine, is completely different."[3] In other words, Antoine's influence on his son has been at best partial. Still, there are enough similarities to leave the impression that, writing about Alphonse, Truffaut is simultaneously writing about Antoine, himself, and Léaud. It is never an accident when Truffaut repeats a name in his body of work. There is only one other Alphonse in the films, the immature Doinel-like actor in *Day for Night* played by Léaud. I have the hunch that Truffaut found himself wondering whether he could bring Doinel back after *Love on the Run*, a film with which he was dissatisfied. He found two possibilities – the already mentioned *La Petite Voleuse* and *Le Journal d'Alphonse*. The first retells Antoine's childhood as the story of a girl (her connection to Truffaut is a camera). The second has a wealth of associations and a great deal of material assimilated from the earlier films. An early scene shows Alphonse jumping into the Seine to impress a girlfriend; later on we see him working as a delivery boy for a florist; Marion steals Léautaud's *Journals* for him; and Aline takes him to a record booth to listen to a favourite song. The only scene sounding a new note occurs in a hospital room where Christine and Alphonse talk as he recovers from a suicide attempt. It isn't the suicide attempt that surprises but Christine's moving realistic appraisal of relationships in general that may reflect Truffaut's with Madeleine, Catherine, and Fanny. "You know, Alphonse, contrary to what your father maintains, life is not a novel. Each person is a couple that never stops arguing. You break vases, you smash dishes, you tell yourself stupid things, you hate yourself, you despise yourself, but you always finish by making up. Then you understand that slitting your throat is not part of the game … Life is hard, Alphonse, but it's beautiful since one hangs on to it so hard."⁴ The situation of an older woman educating a younger man in a mature tone about love recalls Delphine Seyrig's visit to Antoine's room in *Stolen Kisses*. The last sentence recasts her comment to Antoine that her father once said, "People are wonderful."

Except for this fine scene, the short script leaves me uneasy because it shows Truffaut too dependent on earlier films. There is a point at which self-quotation seems like a too comfortable repetition without significant variation and self-analysis. I still enjoy the feeling of being an insider recognizing every nudge and wink to the initiated, but, as sometimes with Woody Allen, the surprise of the new is missing. Perhaps repetition at some point, even with variation, carries with it an inevitable diminution of interest, intensity, and affect? Think of Sir Walter Scott's novels, Francis Bacon's paintings, late Renoir. Think of "A man's gotta do what a man's gotta do" as it works its way from *The Grapes of Wrath* (1940) to its perfection in *Red River* (1948) to *Hondo* (1953), where it loses its metre and its punch and deflates into banality with "A man oughta do what he thinks is right."

IN HIS OWN WORDS II

There are no optimists or pessimists …
There are only sad idiots and happy idiots.[1]

There are no great men, there are only men,
and as far as politics are concerned
I tend to prefer those who behave like cleaning women:
punctuality, modesty, liveliness, equilibrium, the fight
against dust, for cleanliness is daily, carries no prestige,
is indispensable and unremitting.[2]

There are partings which are like deaths.[3]

When I shoot a film, I don't know if the result will give the
impression of a normal film made by a fool or of a crazy
film made by a normal man, but I am convinced that
writing a book or making a film we are the abnormal who
address a speech to normal people.[4]

TRUFFAUT'S AFTERLIFE: *AMÉLIE* (2001)

I tend to forget occasionally that of Truffaut's twenty-one films eight are comedies and that Léaud is a talented comic actor. Truffaut's criticism has perceptive essays and reviews of Chaplin, Lubitsch, Hawks, Cukor, Wilder, Tati, Fellini, and Allen. In "A Certain Tendency" he suggests that "comedy is the most difficult of genres, that which asks the most work, the most talent and also the most humility."[1] Even a tragic film like *Jules and Jim* tips its hat to Chaplin and Mack Sennett. It's therefore appropriate that Jean-Pierre Jeunet's *Amélie*, the most successful, if supposedly unintentional, *hommage* to Truffaut is a feel-good comedy set in Montmartre. As to whether the film is indebted to Truffaut (Jeunet says it isn't), I'm going to follow D.H. Lawrence's well-known advice, "Never trust the artist. Trust the tale."[2] Audrey Tautou plays a magical young girl-woman from a sheltered background who works as a waitress in a café. Innocent and knowing, passive and decisive, she slowly becomes a sort of avenging angel – at one point she dresses as Zorro – dedicated to making some deserving people happier while mildly but rightfully chastising the unkind. Threaded through the several subplots is her interest in an eccentric young man named Nino who collects torn-up photographs people throw away outside an automatic photostall.

All's well that ends well, and all ends well in the film as Amélie and Nino meet, make love, and ride his moped through Montmartre in one of several scenes echoing Truffaut, in this instance *Jules and Jim*, a film

Amélie watches in her one visit to the cinema. Before we see Truffaut's film we hear Georges Delerue's now-classic score as Catherine, dressed as "Thomas," races with the two men. Jeunet then cuts to a much later postwar scene in which Catherine and Jim kiss. His film, like Truffaut's, is about the centrality of love in our lives. Another link to Truffaut is the presence of Claire Maurer, Antoine's mother in *The 400 Blows*, whom Truffaut considered at an early stage for the role of Séverine in *Day for Night*. As she explains to a client in her café, she is also a victim of love: working in a circus, she fell off her horse immediately after her lover told her he was leaving. The accident left her with a shortened leg and a permanent limp. This must be an echo of Madame Jouve's similar love affair and the "fall" from an apartment balcony that leaves her permanently dependant on a crutch. The love plot hangs on the torn photograph of Amélie that Nino finds under the photo booth. The source here is *Love on the Run*, in which Antoine explains to his girlfriend Sabine that he first became interested in her when he picked up the pieces of her photograph torn and thrown away by a man who had just had an angry conversation with someone on the phone. I've always taken this as Truffaut's look back to the Tramp's torn photo of Georgia in *The Gold Rush*. There are also some less obvious traces like the shots of the Eiffel Tower and Sacré-Coeur; the older man who hasn't left his apartment in twenty-five years (*Bed and Board*); the cat approaching a bowl of milk (*The Soft Skin, Day for Night, The Woman Next Door*); and the reference to the rue Trudaine, around the corner from Truffaut's childhood home on rue de Navarin and almost a pun on his name. If these are all accidental synchronicities, then Jeunet's unconscious must have been putting in a great deal of overtime during the making of the film.

Truffaut might have been uneasy with the film's magic or hyper realism and the degree to which its eye-opening colour depends on digital tinting, but I suspect that he would have been charmed by Tautou's talent and *gamine* beauty, the film's humour, the sympathy for the subject, and Jeunet's disarming comment in an interview that "Amélie, c'est moi." He would also have noticed the echo of Guitry's *Le Destin fabuleux de Désirée Clary* in the full title *Le Destin fabuleux d'Amélie Poulin*. He liked women, he liked love stories, and he liked to laugh. He also liked Montmartre, and *Amélie*, like *The 400 Blows* and Melville's *Bob the Gambler*, is one of the most memorable evocations of the neighbourhood. In fact, Montmartre is so prominent in the film that you might call it a character.

To my disappointment, Jeunet has said that he finds New Wave films boring and that he got the idea for the torn photographs from a friend who collects them. And he doesn't mention Truffaut in the promotional interviews. If a film contradicts its director, believe the film.

ANTOINE DE BAECQUE'S
TWO IN THE WAVE (2010)

> [My two former friends] have been making bourgeois garbage and I have been making revolutionary garbage.
>
> JEAN–LUC GODARD[1]

We all have films that we're happy to see if for no other reason than because some actor or actress we like is in them. The film studios count on this. Carol Reed's *Trapeze* (1956) is not a film I would recommend, and yet I watch it often because I like Burt Lancaster enough to forget Tony Curtis and Gina Lollobrigida. It's the sort of movie I never discuss with anyone unless they share my infatuation. Among the actors whom I will watch in almost anything are the following: Michel Piccoli, Ava Gardner, Fernando Rey, Claude Rains, Nathalie Baye, Arletty, James Mason, Bruno Ganz, Robert Ryan, Hanna Schygulla, Max von Sydow, Erland Josephson, Michael Lonsdale, Sharon Stone, Mathieu Amalric, Christine Lahti, and John Wayne. In some cases I would have some difficulty explaining why I feel a flow of emotion toward the screen (Erland Josephson, Claude Rains, Arletty). In others the connection is obvious: Wayne and von Sydow remind me of my father; Mason resembles my Uncle Karl, a soldier in the last good war. Sharon Stone came into favour when I noticed that she resembles the departed Elle. There's much of my ex-wife in Claude Jade. I have always agreed with Kael that we go to movies for sex, but I think she might also have included subtler shades of feeling – unspoken and sometimes not completely understood affections for and attractions to friends, strangers, and lovers. The older I get the more I sense that these other aspects of attachment, affection and love are at play in watching a movie. For instance, there's the complex sense of gratitude I feel when a new film like *The Grand Budapest Hotel* or *The Great Beauty* gives me pleasures I had not expected despite good reviews. We bond with films as we bond with people. Afterward I can almost imagine the void that would be there without these characters and films – a void that wouldn't be possible, so to speak, without their existence. What would my life be like without the films I listed above as lifelong favourites? Films I watch over and over with, for the most part, undiminished pleasure and gratitude.

I watch de Baecque's *Two in the Wave* periodically for the obvious reason that I like seeing Truffaut, and he is on screen here for at least half the documentary. The film is a pendant to de Baecque's remarkably thorough, though for understandable reasons incomplete, biographies of Truffaut and Godard. It has two narratives: (1) the Truffaut-Godard friendship and (2) their relationship to Léaud. De Baecque's film adds nothing new to the record about either, but he offers a useful summary for those not aware of the close contact between the two fathers of the New Wave in the early years, Godard and Truffaut's overlapping importance in Léaud's career, and the extent to which some early New Wave films quote each other. Perhaps the two most revealing moments are Truffaut's promotional puff for Godard's *Deux ou Trois Choses que je sais d'elle* (1966) and the previously mentioned scene describing Godard and Anne-Marie Miéville's response to Truffaut's death. In the former, Truffaut comments that "[Godard] is not the only director for whom filming is like breathing, but he's the one who breathes best. He is rapid like Rossellini, witty like Sacha Guitry, musical like Orson Welles, simple like Maurice Pagnol, wounded like Nicholas Ray, effective like Hitchcock, profound like Bergman, and insolent like nobody else."[2] This may be a puff but it is nevertheless perceptive, generous and memorable. "Wounded" and "insolent" are as apposite as "rapid" and "witty." It says more about Godard than some essays on his work. It's worth repeating that Godard's most interesting comments about Truffaut come several years after the latter's death and are *not* specifically about his films. In *Histoire(s) du Cinéma* he refers to Truffaut as one of his "friends." And in the documentary he says – it's worth repeating – that when she heard about Truffaut's death Miéville said to him 'Now that he's dead, nobody will protect you since he was the only one of the New Wave who was accepted by and tried, in a way, to join the establishment.'" The question "How did he protect you?" goes unanswered. Miéville's comment is perceptive if a bit self-serving in its tacit judgment on Truffaut as the conformist protecting Godard the revolutionary. If Godard and Miéville judged him for his collaboration with the establishment, Truffaut questioned Godard's willingness to sacrifice film and friendship for radical politics. One can see the beginning of the fraying of the relationship in the footage shot at Cannes during the troubled May of 1968. Both men address those attending the Festival to persuade them to close it since the country is in turmoil. Truffaut's talk is measured and emotionally restrained. Godard, by contrast, harangues the audience for not being radical enough in its politics and for not having been in the vanguard of the demonstrations; in other words, for not being as radical as he thinks he is. Watching him I have the impression he thinks he's Lenin addressing the crowds during the early days of the Revolution. Standing to the side, Truffaut is visibly uncomfortable with Godard's assault. De Baecque wisely lets the footage speak for itself.

The film has the gaps that are inevitable in any work dealing with living and recently dead figures. Madeleine Morgenstern and Fanny Ardant are absent, as is Léaud, who is one of the film's essential figures. Still, there is the undoubted pleasure of seeing and hearing Truffaut on screen. It is like receiving a letter with some previously unseen photographs from the past. Like Julien Davenne, I'll take whatever I can get. *Le Temps retrouvé*.

UNFINISHED BUSINESS:
FILMS TRUFFAUT DIDN'T MAKE II

> Do the books that writers don't write matter?
> JULIAN BARNES[1]
> —

> Old artists are entitled to caricature themselves.
> JOHN UPDIKE[2]
> —

Old age is a universal problem but it carries an additional twist for the artist whose inspiration is chiefly autobiographical. How many times can a director return to the same characters, themes, and plots? Could Truffaut have returned to Antoine Doinel for a sequel about middle age? Could he imagine a love story about lovers in their fifties? What about a Jep Gambarella – from *The Great Beauty* – in Paris? John Updike, born in 1932 like Truffaut, faced a similar problem and despite a prolific and inventive late phase (he died in 2009) there was a significant decline in his fiction after *Rabbit at Rest* (1990), the fourth and final instalment of his Rabbit Angstrom tetralogy. And since Updike's style never changed, one can't argue for an interesting "late style." Truffaut's late period would have been complicated by social and cultural factors beyond his control: by 1986 most French people were watching movies on television; between 1980 and 1989 theatre admissions had dropped from 200 to 118 million; and by the latter year, only 34 percent of the films playing in French cinemas were French. Looking at the ominous decline, Charles Drazin suggests that "the 1980s was the decade in which the old kind of cinema that people went to see in darkened halls finally crumbled as a major form of entertainment."[3]

From early in his career Truffaut usually had three or four projects in preparation simultaneously as a form of protection against the sort of dry spell he had experienced twice during the 1960s when he found himself without work on hand either because of production delays or because a script wasn't ready. This was also true during the last decade of his life. Among projects mentioned without elaboration are the following: *Julien and Marguerite*, a story of incest during the reign of Henry IV; *The Little King*; *Journal of a First Love*; *The Man Who Strangled Women* (this must be a take on *Monsieur Verdoux*); *Nightfall*; *The Journal of a Madman*; *Project Dracula*; *The Dialogue of the Carmelites* (a curious choice for a man without a religious cell in his body); and *The Leather Nose*. Most of these are mentioned in passing and are not heard of again. He seems to have taken more seriously material based on Paul Léautaud, *The Little Thief*, *00/14* – a film about the turn of the century – and *The Magic Company*, the story of a small troupe of actors touring Senegal which, with *Day for Night* and *The Last Metro*, would complete a trilogy about acting. He also mentions a film for television based on *The Count of Monte Cristo*. The novel has been filmed at least once a decade in my lifetime, and I can't imagine its popularity waning. In my imagination, and without any concession to the passage of time, I cast Truffaut's version as follows: Fanny as Mercédès Herrera-Mondego, Léaud as her son, Jean-Luc as the treacherous Fernand Mondego, and, as you've guessed, Truffaut as Edmond Dantès. I understand that the casting is impossible, but that's how it plays out in my mind. Even granting that the scenario is a stretch, it's no more so than the rumour Tarkovsky claims to have heard that the Russian poet Yevgeny Yevtushenko had been invited to Hollywood to play D'Artagnan in a new version of *The Three Musketeers*.[4]

If some of the projects indicate Truffaut wasn't quite done with his past, others suggest that he also looked in new directions. In hopeful moments, I sometimes imagine his late phase as resembling Woody Allen's: some predictable and even tired films indicating a drying up of inspiration interspersed with surprises like *Match Point*, *Vicky Cristina Barcelona*, and *Midnight in Paris*. Had Truffaut lived into his sixties and seventies, we might have had at least a dozen more films including a documentary about the New Wave and perhaps more acting in films by others. I try to believe that there's enough here for a distinctive late period with a late style. What I don't see is Truffaut surrendering to the temptation of what Kael calls "the self-destructive fulfillment" of a monumental folly like *Intolerance, Duel in the Sun, Apocalypse Now,* or *1900*, in which a director goes "goes mad on the potentialities of movies."[5] He didn't have that gene. Even his big films like *The Last Metro* feel intimate, small.

Truffaut's grave in Montmartre Cemetery on an overcast February day. Maurice Jaubert, whose music Truffaut used in several films, lies nearby, as does Stendhal.

THE GRAVE
IN MONTMARTRE

I'm in Paris with G. in February 2003 and remember that the sixth is Truffaut's birthday. So on a chilly sunny morning I set off on foot from our apartment in the Marais toward his grave in Montmartre. On the way, I wander in his old neighbourhood around Place de Clichy and find the apartment he lived in as a child. I resist the momentary temptation to ring the bell at 33 rue de Navarin just around the corner from one of Léautaud's childhood homes and not far from where Moreau was born on 23 January 1928. A darker presence in Clichy during Truffaut's youth, though he couldn't have known it then, was the doctor-novelist Louis-Ferdinand Destouches (Céline), author of *The Voyage to the End of the Night* (1932), a novel I have never been able to finish despite several determined starts, and a number of anti-Semitic tracts like *Bagatelles pour un massacre* calling for the extermination of French Jews.

Truffaut's grave is easy to find. Like Ozu's, it is marked by a black marble slab: François Truffaut 1932–1984. Truffaut's is flat. Ozu's is a cube with only his name and the Chinese character for "Nothingness." You can see it in Wenders's documentary *Tokyo-Ga* (1985). Among the several bouquets, one catches my eye because the varied flowers are tied with a wide golden ribbon that is inscribed. I take a closer look and realize that it is a fan letter, as simple and moving in translation as in the original: "Dear François, Happy Birthday from all your fans on rue de Navarin." I step back and take a photograph. Looking around in all directions, almost a 360 degree pan shot, I remember Madeleine Morgenstern saying that Truffaut wanted to be buried where he could see the great Gaumont movie theatre from his grave. Unfortunately the famous cinema, like much of Truffaut's world, is gone. It opened in 1911 and closed on 31 March 1972. At its peak it could seat 6,000. This was reduced to 2,800 in 1966 to accommodate Cinerama. The retreat had begun.

On the way out I notice Stendhal's grave. There is a glass vase with one red rose in it. I ask the caretaker about it. He says the French government provides the flowers at the graves of distinguished figures. When I mention that I'm a Polish-Canadian, he points further down the row and says that even Juliusz Słowacki, the great Polish Romantic poet, gets a rose. He lived in Paris from 1831 until his death in 1849, the same year as Chopin's. Stendhal said he wrote for the future: "I am taking a ticket in a lottery of which the great prize consists in this: to be read in 1935."[1] The rose reminds passersby that he won his bet. Léautaud visited the grave often. On 29 March 1901 he wrote in his journal, "Went to see again Stendhal's tomb in Montmartre Cemetery to thank him for *Lucien Leuwen*."[2] When a publisher suggested in 1903 he write a book about the author he revered, he answered "I love him too much ... I would bungle it."[3] If we all had his integrity, books would regain the aura they once possessed and the publishing season would be much shorter. Antoine's shrine to Balzac suggests that Truffaut turned to him more often than to his older contemporary from Grenoble. He makes few references to Stendhal, but the ones he does are telling. In a letter to Deneuve he says that he imagines Belmondo in *Mississippi Mermaid* "alive and fragile like a Stendhal hero, and you the blond siren whose chant would have inspired Giraudoux."[4] One of the "book-men" is shown memorizing *La Vie d'Henri Brulard*. And there is an important reference in the review of Joseph Mankiewicz's *The Barefoot Contessa*. "When the moviegoers on the Champs-Elysées snicker as a man admits physical impotence to a woman, it says a great deal about the public's responsibility for the banality and vulgarity of the average screenplay. It is one more proof that the time has not come for adapting Stendhal's *Armance*. In *The Red and the Black*, Claude Autant-Lara did not dare film Mathilde holding the severed head of Julien Sorel on her lap. Mankiewicz is more Stendhalian. The Countess's last try to have a baby by her chauffeur so that she can offer it to her husband would be in character for Mathilde de la Môle."[5] This is also the review which calls the palindromic Ava "Hollywood's most exquisitely beautiful actress." Ava was thirty-two in 1954 and on the cusp of her dark and shimmering beauty.

Before leaving Montmartre, I return to the flower seller by the entrance, buy a yellow rose, and walk back to leave it on the grave. A few blocks from the cemetery, I turn the corner and find myself standing at the entrance to the Lycée d'Enseignment Commercial: François Truffaut. What an unexpected monument to a famous filmmaker who had been a juvenile delinquent and had never held an everyday job of the kind that the students in the Lycée train for. Still, he did attend the school that stood there during his childhood. And the French remember these things.

LAST WORDS

MARIE DUBOIS: When he was dying – I think it was the last time I saw him – I arrived at his place and said, "I can't kiss you hello because you're tired and I have a cold." He said, "My dear old lady, what's become of us?" He knew that I had multiple sclerosis and that he was dying.[1]

NESTOR ALMENDROS: My life is split: before and after the death of François Truffaut … The funeral seemed like a film because of all the cemeteries in Truffaut's films.[2]

JEAN-PIERRE LÉAUD: I owe everything to François … I will add that François is the man I loved most in the world.[3]

FRANÇOIS TRUFFAUT: This is why I am the happiest of men: I realize my dreams and am paid for that, I am a filmmaker. To make a film is to make life better, to arrange it in a certain way, to prolong the games of childhood, to make an object which is at once a new game and a vase into which one places, as if it were a matter of a bouquet of flowers, ideas that one feels now or forever. Our best film is perhaps the one in which we succeed in expressing, intentionally or not, both our ideas about life and our ideas about film.[4]

NOTES

Epigraphs on page 1: Baudelaire, 363; Fanny Ardant, *The Observer*; *The Faber Book of French Cinema*, 369.

WHY TRUFFAUT?
1. Truffaut, *Le Cinéma selon François Truffaut*, 442.
2. Quoted in Drazin, *The Faber Book of French Cinema*, 330.
3. Brody, *Everything Is Cinema*, 50.
4. Truffaut, *The Films in My Life*, 289.
5. See Truffaut's "La Savate et la Finance, ou deux ou trois choses que je sais de lui," "Préface" to *Deux ou Trois Choses que je sais d'elle*, *L'Avant-Scène Cinéma*, no. 70, May 1967, in *Truffaut by Truffaut*, 201.
6. de Baecque, *Godard*, 655; the exchange is repeated in *Two in the Wave*.
7. de Baecque, *Godard*, 336.
8. Bazin, *Orson Welles*, 20.
9. Badiou, *Cinema*, 19.
10. Chandler, "Fearless Malevich," 18.
11. Badiou, *Cinema*, 59.
12. Sterritt, *Jean-Luc Godard Interviews*, ix.
13. Hoberman, 94.
14. de Baecque and Guigue, *Le Dictionnaire Truffaut*, 158.
15. *L'Express*, "François T." in Bergan, *François Truffaut Interviews*, 122.

16 Camus, 236. "Petits choses au hazard" is translated by Justin O'Brien as "hodge-podge."
17 Burke, *The Rhetoric of Literary Form*, 23.
18 Truffaut, *La Nuit Américaine et le Journal de tournage de Fahrenheit 451*, 172.
19 Dyer, *Zona*, 19. Dyer gives his source as Peter Dogget's *There's a Riot Going On* (Edinburgh: Canongate, 2007), 211.
20 Davis, *Afterglow: A Last Conversation with Pauline Kael*, 73–4.
21 Sarris, *Confessions of a Cultist*, 187.
22 Brody, *Everything Is Cinema*, 180. Eric Neuhoff puts it as follows: "He has nothing to say, but he says it well; that is perhaps the definition of style" (*Lettre ouverte à François Truffaut*, 78).
23 Braunberger, *Cinémamémoire*, 168.
24 Truffaut, *Le Plaisir des yeux*, 39.
25 Scammell, "The CIA's 'Zhivago,'" 40.
26 Truffaut, *Truffaut by Truffaut*, 200.
27 Kael, *Kiss Kiss Bang Bang*, 184.
28 Sontag, *As Consciousness Is Harnessed to Flesh*, 9.
29 Coetzee, *Diary of a Bad Year*, 7.
30 *Children of Paradise*, 433.
31 A dissenting view is offered by Michelangelo Antonioni in an interview with Charles Thomas Samuels: "I think his films are like rivers, lovely to see, to bathe in, extraordinarily refreshing and pleasant. Then the water flows and is gone … His images are as powerful as those of Resnais or Godard, but his stories are frivolous. I suppose that's what I object to." (Charles Thomas Samuels, "Michelangelo Antonioni," 94.) Truffaut's view of Antonioni is reciprocally unenthusiastic: "He bores me; he's so solemn and humorless. And I don't like the way he deals with women, because instead of talking about them as a man would, he talks about them as though he had been told their secrets …" (Sanche de Gramont, "Life Style of Homo Cinematicus," 42).

IN HIS OWN WORDS I

1 Truffaut, *Truffaut by Truffaut*, 105.
2 Truffaut, *Le Cinéma selon François Truffaut*, 141.
3 Truffaut, *The Films in My Life*, 138.
4 Truffaut, *Le Cinéma selon François Truffaut*, 189.

5 Ibid., 141.
6 Spoken by Camille Bliss, the heroine of *Such a Gorgeous Kid like Me*. The script, by Truffaut and Jean-Luc Dabadie, is based on Henry Farrell's novel of the same title.

ROLAND LÉVY AND ROLAND TRUFFAUT

1 Truffaut *Correspondence 1945–1984*, 387.
2 de Baecque, *Godard*, 656.
3 Ondaatje, *Running in the Family*, 152.
4 de Baecque and Guigue, *Le Dictionnaire Truffaut*, 206.

EARLY FILMS: FRANÇOIS AND SAM

1 Truffaut, "Truffaut's Last Interview," 2.
2 de Baecque and Toubiana, *Truffaut*, 22.
3 Bazin, *French Cinema of the Occupation and Resistance*, 22.
4 Calvino, *The Road to San Giovanni*, 41.
5 Kennan, *The Kennan Diaries*, 21.
6 Gide, *Journals 1889–1949*, 102.

THE GODFATHER: ANDRÉ BAZIN (1918–1958)

1 Braunberger, *Cinémamémoire*, 143.
2 Camus, *Notebooks 1942–1951*, 105.
3 Truffaut, "A Certain Tendency," 9.
4 Truffaut, *The Films in My Life*, 55.
5 Bazin, *The Cinema of Cruelty*, xvi. That Truffaut liked, perhaps even loved, Renoir can be felt even in his passing comment on Renoir's novel *Le Capitaine Georges*: He describes it as "simple, raw, funny, touching, absolutely alive like his films, like himself" (*La Nuit Américaine et le Journal de tournage de Fahrenheit 451*, 197).
6 Bazin, *What Is Cinema? II*, v.
7 Bazin, *French Cinema of the Occupation and Resistance*, 6.
8 Truffaut, *Truffaut by Truffaut*, 19.
9 Mounier was also highly regarded by the young Pierre Elliott Trudeau.
10 Bazin, *French Cinema of the Occupation and Resistance*, 31.
11 Sarris, *Confessions of a Cultist*, 363.
12 *What Is Cinema?: II*, vi.

1 JANUARY 1954: "A CERTAIN TENDENCY IN FRENCH CINEMA"

1. de Baecque, *Godard*, 37.
2. Quoted by Andrew Sarris, *Confessions of a Cultist*, 1970, 360.
3. "A Certain Tendency," 10.
4. Truffaut, "Truffaut's Last Interview," 3.
5. Drazin, *The Faber Book of French Cinema*, 102. An indication of the extent of the New Wave's influence is the following comment by Abbas Kiarostami: "Perhaps you won't believe me if I tell you that the movement started in French cinema by the New Wave was followed day-by-day in Iran … Before, I believed that cinema belonged to superstars, to studios and spectacular sets. With the New Wave, I saw myself and my neighbours in films." *Cahiers du Cinéma,* January 1999, 96.

SOME TITLES FOR *THE 400 BLOWS* (1959)

1. Quoted in T.W. Adorno, *Notes on Literature 2*, 3.
2. *Antoine Runs Away, The 400 Blows, The Four Thursdays, The Children of Paradise, The Forgotten Children, Vagrancy, The Thursday Tramps, Down with Back to School, The Little Idlers, The Bad Geniuses, The Little Idiots, The Little Rebels, The Wild Ducks, The Little Thugs, The Primary Schoolchildren, Street Games, Little Soldiers.*
3. Chandler, *The Raymond Chandler Papers*, 75, 191.
4. Truffaut, *Correspondence 1945–1984*, 43.
5. Proust, *À la Recherche du temps perdu: II*, 923.

MAKING FILMS TOGETHER: *A LETTER TO THE CAST AND CREW OF THE LAST METRO* (21 JANUARY 1980)

1. Nathalie Baye, "Nathalie Baye: 'Joelle, The Continuity Girl,'" *Day for Night* DVD.
2. Brody, 499. Groucho Marx plays Firefly, a scapegrace appointed leader of the small country Freedonia in *Duck Soup*.
3. Truffaut, *Truffaut by Truffaut*, 173.
4. Russell, *Matisse: Father and Son*, 303.
5. Dyer, *Zona*, 106.
6. Burlaev, "Interview with Nikolai Burlaev," *Stalker* DVD.

***THE 400 BLOWS*: A LIFE ON FILM**

1. Drazin, 84.
2. Truffaut, *Truffaut by Truffaut*, 59.

3 Eliot, "Hamlet," 145.
4 Mankell, *The Troubled Man*, 114.
5 Charles Thomas Samuels, "François Truffaut," 65.
6 de Baecque and Toubiana, *Truffaut*, 139.
7 de Baecque and Toubiana, *François Truffaut*, 536.
8 Ibid., 142.
9 Ibid., 143. The letter was written 19 October 1963.

JEAN-PIERRE LÉAUD WITH TRUFFAUT, GODARD, AND BERNARDO BERTOLUCCI

1 Mars-Jones, *Noriko Smiling*, 167.
2 Thomson, *The New Biographical Dictionary of Film*, 505.
3 Ungari, *Bertolucci by Bertolucci*, 89.
4 Ibid., 238–9.
5 Léaud, *Elle* (18 October 2004): 107.
6 Ibid., 110.

ROBERT LACHENAY (1930–2005): THE BEST FRIEND AND THE ANCILLARY LIFE

1 Auden later changed the title "Not All the Candidates Pass" to the "The Watchers."
2 de Baecque and Toubiana, *Truffaut*, 391.
3 Balzac, *The Wrong Side of Paris*, 50–1.

SACHA GUITRY (1885–1957): *LE ROMAN D'UN TRICHEUR* (1936) AND *THE 400 BLOWS*

1 Guitry, *Le Cinéma et moi*, 20.
2 de Baecque and Toubiana, *François Truffaut*, 47.
3 Truffaut, *The Films in My Life*, 219.

SHOOT THE PIANO PLAYER (1960): ALL YOU NEED IS LOVE

1 Turnell, *The Novel in France*, 140.
2 Quoted in Brody, *Everything Is Cinema*, 140.
3 Truffaut, *Le Cinéma selon François Truffaut*, 112.
4 Kael, "Shoot the Piano Player," 76.
5 Ibid., 77.
6 Ibid., 78.
7 Ibid., 134–5.

8   Goodis, *Down There*, 663.
9   Ibid., 717.

TRUFFAUT IN HIS LETTERS
1   Truffaut, *Le Cinéma selon François Truffaut*, 437.
2   Almendros "Interview with Nestor Almendros," *The Last Metro* DVD.
3   Truffaut, *Correspondence 1945–1984*, 426.
4   Ibid., 259.
5   Ibid., 213.
6   Turk, *Children of Paradise*, 408–9.
7   Truffaut, *Correspondence 1945–1984*, 390.
8   Ibid., ix–x.
9   Brody, *Godard*, 656.

JULES AND JIM (1961): WHEN WE SPEAK OF FREEDOM AND LOVE AND DEATH
1   Beattie, *New York Stories*, 116.
2   Salter and Phelps, *Memorable Days*, 18.
3   Pater, *The Renaissance*, 158.
4   Macdonald, *Dwight Macdonald on Movies*, 378.
5   Bergan, *Jean Renoir*, 342–3.
6   Truffaut, *Le Cinéma selon François Truffaut*, 106.

ERIC ROHMER'S *LA COLLECTIONNEUSE* (1967) AND *JULES AND JIM*
1   Quoted by Neuhoff, *Lettre ouverte à François Truffaut*, 127.
2   Truffaut, *Correspondence 1945–1984*, 428.

JULIAN BARNES'S *TALKING IT OVER* (1991) AND *JULES AND JIM*
1   Rudolf Freiburg, "'Novels Come out of Life, Not out of Theories': An Interview with Julian Barnes," 31.

SALMAN RUSHDIE'S *THE GROUND BENEATH HER FEET* (1999) AND *JULES AND JIM*
1   Rushdie, *The Ground beneath Her Feet*, 51.
2   Ibid., 74.
3   Ibid., 294.
4   Ibid., 557–8.

TRUFFAUT IN AND OUT OF HIS TIME
1 Schickel, *D.W. Griffith*, 185.
2 Truffaut, *Le Cinéma selon François Truffaut*, 401.
3 Truffaut, *Le Plaisir des yeux*, 34.
4 Truffaut, *Le Cinéma selon François Truffaut*, 239.

CARLOS SAURA ON *THE SOFT SKIN* (1964), OBLIQUELY
1 Brody, "Movies," *The New Yorker*, 14 March 2011, 12.

THE AUTEUR AND THE EMPTY ROOM
1 Mars-Jones, 188.
2 Saura, "Interview with Carlos Saura," *Cria Cuervos* DVD.
3 Ibid.
4 Schiffman, "Au Coeur de la méthode," 82.

MEETING JEANNE MOREAU IN VENICE
1 *Lettre ouverte à François Truffaut*, 125–6. Odilon Redon recorded a similar encounter with Delacroix, four years before the great painter's death, in 1859: "He was of medium height, thin and highly strung. We spied on him all evening in the middle of the crowd and till we left at the same time as he did. We followed him. He crossed Paris alone, his head bent, moving like a cat on the best pavements. A notice saying 'pictures' drew his attention; he went up to it, read it, went on, apparently in a dream, wrapped in some inner thought. He crossed the town till he reached the door of an apartment in rue La Rochefoucauld which he lived in no longer. Perhaps that was mere habit. He moved quietly on, still self-absorbed, till he came to the small rue Furstenburg, the silent street he then lived in" (Timothy Wilson-Smith, *Delacroix: A Life*, 18–19). The Delacroix museum is at the last address.
2 *The Moviegoer*, 19–21.

FAHRENHEIT 451 AND TRUFFAUT'S ENGLISH
1 Truffaut, *Correspondence, 1945–1984*, 528.
2 Ibid., 351.
3 Truffaut, *La Nuit Américaine et Le Journal de tournage de Fahrenheit 451*, 168.
4 Robb, *Victor Hugo*, 324.
5 Proust, *Selected Letters I, 1880–1903*, 290.

THE BRIDE WORE BLACK (1967)
1 Bazin, *Orson Welles*, 20.
2 Ibid., 22.
3 Truffaut, *The Films in My Life*, 314–15.
4 Meyers, *John Huston*, 84.
5 Auzel, *François Truffaut: Les Mille et Une Nuits Américaines*, 83.

STOLEN KISSES (1968): A DEBT TO MARCEL PROUST OR ANATOLE FRANCE
1 Truffaut, *The Adventures of Antoine Doinel*, 187–8.
2 Proust, *Selected Letters III, 1910–1917*, 185.

DAVID THOMSON'S *MISSISSIPPI MERMAID* (1969)
1 Thomson, *Have You Seen ... ?"* 801.
2 Ingram and Duncan, *François Truffaut: The Complete Films*, 127.

FAHRENHEIT 451 (1966), WEEK-END (1967), AND THE WILD CHILD (1969): A DIALOGUE?
1 Coutard, "Interview with Raoul Coutard," *Week-end* DVD.
2 Benjamin, "Theses on the Philosophy of History," in *Illuminations*, 256.
3 Vico, *The New Science*, 381.

MAURICE PIALAT'S WILD CHILD: *L'ENFANCE NUE* (1968)
1 Truffaut, *Truffaut au travail*, 128.
2 de Baecque and Toubiana, *Truffaut*, 262.

WOODY ALLEN'S *DECONSTRUCTING HARRY* (1997) AND ANTOINE DOINEL
1 Truffaut, *Le Plaisir des yeux*, 51.
2 Ibid.

"FRANÇOIS, MY BOY" AND "MR HITCHCOCK"
1 Truffaut, *Truffaut by Truffaut*, 200.
2 Bazin, *The Cinema of Cruelty*, 112.
3 Truffaut, *Hitchcock*, 13.
4 Truffaut, *The Films in My Life*, 82.
5 Truffaut, *Hitchcock*, 25.

6 McGilligan, *Alfred Hitchcock*, 3.
7 Truffaut, *Hitchcock*, 346–7.

THE ENDING OF *TWO ENGLISH GIRLS* (1971)

1 Joseph Blottner, *Faulkner: A Biography, II,* 978. While making *Two or Three Things I Know about Her* and *Made in USA* Godard considered, though it's not clear how seriously, releasing them as one film with an alternating-scene form based on *Wild Palms.* Varda had already done something like this in 1955 with *La Pointe courte.* Jean Seberg quotes from *Wild Palms* in *Breathless.* The novel had been published in France by Gallimard in 1952 as *Les Palmiers sauvages.*
2 de Baecque and Toubiana, *Truffaut,* 282.
3 Ibid., 282.
4 Ibid., 416.
5 Roché, *Les Deux Anglaises et le continent,* 345.
6 Ibid., 349.
7 Ibid., 320.

TWO ENGLISH GIRLS, AGORA (2009), AND SEEING RED ON THE SCREEN

1 Truffaut, *Le Cinéma selon François* Truffaut, 280.
2 Greer, *The Female Eunuch,* 51.

TRUFFAUT, GODARD, AND *TIMBRES*

1 I know a source exists for this quotation, but I can't find it in my files.
2 Powell, *A Life in Movies,* 94–5.

TRUFFAUT'S AFTERLIFE: *THE DIVING BELL AND THE BUTTERFLY* (2007)

1 Thomson, *"Have You Seen ... ?"* 227.

JOHNNY GUITAR (1954): BAD FAITH IN TRUFFAUT AND DAVID THOMSON

1 Bergan, *Jean Renoir,* 119.
2 Thomson, *"Have You Seen ... ?"* 423.
3 Truffaut, *The Films in My Life,* 141–3.
4 Truffaut, *Correspondence 1945–1984,* 281.
5 Truffaut, *Truffaut by Truffaut,* 293.
6 Truffaut, *The Films in My Life,* 143.

A TITLE QUIZ
1 A/e; B/h; C/f; D/g; E/a; F/c; G/d; H/b.

CREATIVITY AND ACCIDENTS
1 Renoir-Rivette Interview: *Elena and Her Men* DVD.
2 Gilot, *Life with Picasso*, 152.
3 Bray, "G for Grand," 33.
4 Almendros, "Interview with Nestor Almendros," *The Last Metro* DVD.
5 Rohmer, *The Taste for Beauty*, 190.

DAY FOR NIGHT (1973): THE FAMILY MOVIE
1 Bisset, "*Day for Night*: A Conversation with Jacqueline Bisset," *Day for Night* DVD.
2 Truffaut, *Correspondence 1945–1984*, 384.

8 1/2 (1963), DAY FOR NIGHT (1973), STARDUST MEMORIES (1980), NINE (2009)
1 Truffaut, *Correspondence*, 220.

PAULINE KAEL, WIM WENDERS, AND TRUFFAUT
1 Wenders, *On Film*, 443.
2 Ibid., 323.
3 Ibid., 47.
4 Ibid., 64.
5 Cocteau, "Lecture [1932]," *Blood of the Poet* DVD.
6 Wenders, *On Film*, 174.
7 Truffaut, *Le Plaisir des yeux*, 39.
8 Talbot, "Home Movies," 57.
9 Powell, *Million-Dollar Movie*, 556.

TRUFFAUT, ADAM ZAGAJEWSKI, AND THE FATE OF SPIRIT
1 Zagajewski, *Poetry*, 50.

TRUFFAUT AND PAUL LÉAUTAUD (1872–1956)
1 Neuhoff, *Lettre Ouverte à François Truffaut*, 34.
2 Harding, *Lost Illusions*, 66.
3 de Baecque and Guigue, *Le Dictionnaire Truffaut*, 265.

4 Harding, *Lost Illusions*, 152.
5 Ibid., 138.
6 Proust, *Selected Letters II, 1904–1909*, 242.
7 Léautaud, *Journal littéraire*, 560.

MONTMARTRE AND "CERTIFICATION"
1 Claude Beylie and Alain Carbonnier, "Celluloid and Stone," 75.
2 Percy, *The Moviegoer*, 55.

THE STORY OF ADÈLE H. (1975): TRUFFAUT'S FEMINISM
1 Adair, "Adèle H.," 98.
2 Keesey, 20-1.
3 Guille, *Adèle Hugo*, 44–5.
4 Ibid., 45.
5 Robb, *Victor Hugo*, 475.

TRUFFAUT AND DENEUVE IN *THE STORY OF ADÈLE H.*
1 Truffaut, *The Story of Adèle H.* (novelization), 9.
2 Kael, *Reeling*, 57.

SMALL CHANGE (1976) AND RENOIR'S *THE RIVER* (1951)
1 Bazin, *Orson Welles*, 66.
2 Truffaut, *Small Change: A Film Novel*, 10.
3 Rohmer, *The Taste for Beauty*, 60.
4 Bergan, *Jean Renoir*, xv.
5 Ibid., xviii.
6 Truffaut, *Le Plaisir des yeux*, 265-6.

AN AGED MAN IS BUT A PALTRY THING
1 Davies, *Fifth Business*, 202–3.
2 Updike, *My Father's Tears*, 32.
3 Kundera, *Ignorance*, 189–90.

INGMAR BERGMAN, *CAVALEUR*
1 Faulkner, *Mosquitoes*, 206.
2 Truffaut, *The Films in My Life*, 255.

THE MAN WHO LOVED WOMEN (1977): TRUFFAUT AND DON JUAN

1 Truffaut, *Truffaut au travail*, 258. The lines were cut from the final script of *Love on the Run*.
2 Camus, *The Myth of Sisyphus*, 69–77.
3 Camus, *Notebooks 1942–1951*, 255.
4 Ibid., 113–14.
5 Copleston, *A History of Philosophy*, VII, 112–15.
6 Samuel Beckett, *Letters of Samuel Beckett* II: *1941–1956*, 187.

LESLIE CARON

1 de Baecque and Guigue, *Le Dictionnaire Truffaut*, 75.
2 de Baecque and Toubiana, *Truffaut*, 256.
3 Ibid., 393.

SUZANNE SCHIFFMAN (1929–2001)

1 Schiffman, "Au Coeur de la méthode," 82.
2 Ibid., 80.
3 Ibid.
4 Ibid., 82.
5 Ibid.

TRUFARD AND GODFAUT: RESEMBLANCES

1 Truffaut, *Le Cinéma selon François Truffaut*, 179.

BALTHUS (1908–2001)

1 Truffaut, *Correspondence 1945–1984*, 183–4.

FILM NAMES: WHO REMEMBERS MICHEL POICCARD AND PATRICIA FRANCHINI?

1 Thomson, *"Have You Seen ... ?"* 636.
2 Truffaut, *Correspondence 1945–1984*, 405.
3 Montaigne, *The Complete Works of Montaigne*, 201.
4 A/l; B/r; C/g; D/a; E/d; F/h; G/f; H/i; I/o; J/p; K/e; L/j; M/k; N/n; O/b; P/c; Q/m; R/q.

THE GREEN ROOM (1978): THE MAN WHO LOVED ONE WOMAN

1 Proust, *The Guermantes Way, Remembrance of Things Past II*, 526.
2 Proust, *Finding Time Again*, 182.

3 Truffaut, *Correspondence 1945–1984*, 345.
4 Volpe, "*Sur des Thèmes de Henry James*," 101.
5 Erich Maria Remarque's *All Quiet on the Western Front* has an earlier "version" of this scene when Paul and his fellow soldiers notice as they walk through a devastated wood that "In the branches dead men are hanging. A naked soldier is squatting in the fork of a tree, he still has his helmet on, otherwise he is entirely unclad. There is only half of him sitting up there, the top half, the legs are missing" (178).
6 Gunn, *The Man with Night Sweats*, 1992.
7 James, *Stories of the Supernatural*, 367.
8 Ibid., 563.
9 *L'Express*, "François Truffaut," 124.

A SHORT HISTORY OF "DUMMIES": BUÑUEL, TRUFFAUT, AND OSKAR KOKOSCHKA

1 Graukorger, *Descartes: An Intellectual Biography*, 1.
2 Truffaut, *The Films in My Life*, 261.
3 Ibid., 267–8.
4 Ibid., 266.
5 Ibid., 265.
6 Buñuel, *My Last Sigh*, 120.
7 Landolfi, *Words in Motion*, 49.
8 Keegan, *The Eye of God*, 111.
9 Ibid., 114.
10 Ibid., 115.

PAULINE KAEL'S FAREWELL TO TRUFFAUT AND GODARD

1 Quoted in Lopate, *Totally, Tenderly, Tragically*, 248.
2 Davis, *Afterglow: A Last Conversation with Pauline Kael*, 35, 43, 79.
3 Ibid., 72.
4 Ibid., 73–4.
5 Ibid., 24.
6 Braudy, *A World on Film*, 3.

PAUL SCHRADER'S TEARS

1 Bakhtin, *Speech Genres and Other Late Essays*, 140.
2 Beckett, *Molloy, Malone Dies, The Unnamable*, 333.
3 Coetzee, *Diary of a Bad Year*, 223–5.

THE LAST METRO (1980): FRANÇOIS TRUFFAUT-LÉVY

1 de Baecque and Toubiana, *Truffaut*, 247.
2 Ibid., 246. *Truffaut*.
3 Truffaut, *Le Cinéma selon François Truffaut*, 257.
4 Annette Insdorf, "How Truffaut's *The Last Metro* Reflects Occupied Paris," 143.
5 Truffaut Interview: *The Last Metro* DVD. See Mirella Joan Affron's *The Last Metro: François Truffaut Director* for more about the historical and cultural background.

SUBTITLES AND VOICES

1 Borges, *Selected Non-Fictions*, 263.
2 Ibid., 262. See also Chiara Barzini's "Read My Lips."
3 Kael, *When the Lights Go Down*, 313.

ROBERTO ROSSELLINI (1906–1977): THE ITALIAN GODFATHER

1 Scorsese, *My Voyage to Italy* DVD.
2 Gallagher, *The Adventures of Roberto Rossellini*, 450.
3 Ibid., 677.
4 Truffaut, *Correspondence 1945–1984*, 278.
5 Thomson, *The New Biographical Dictionary of Film*, 757.

THE WOMAN NEXT DOOR (1981): "NEITHER WITH YOU NOR WITHOUT YOU"

1 Stendhal, *Love*, 255.

FANNY MARGUERITE JUDITH ARDANT

1 Tarkovsky, *Journal 1970–1986*, 301.
2 Adair, "Rohmer's *Percival*," 45.

A GODARD DREAM (26 JUNE 2011)

1 Painter, *Marcel Proust: II*, 287.
2 Ondaatje, *Running in the Family*, 181–2.
3 Golding, *Paths to the Absolute*, 45.

LE JOURNAL D'ALPHONSE: A DOINEL SEQUEL

1 Butterfly, *Le Journal d'Alphonse*, 111.
2 Ibid., 32.

3 Ibid., 17.
4 Ibid., 126.

IN HIS OWN WORDS II
1 Ibid., 429.
2 de Baecque and Toubiana, *Truffaut*, 316.
3 Truffaut, *The Films in My Life*, 284.
4 Truffaut, *La Nuit Américaine et le Journal de tournage de Fahrenheit 451*, 235.

TRUFFAUT'S AFTERLIFE: *AMÉLIE* (2001)
1 Truffaut, "A Certain Tendency of French Cinema," 10.
2 D.H. Lawrence, *Studies in Classic American Literature*, 8.

ANTOINE DE BAECQUE'S *TWO IN THE WAVE* (2010)
1 Penelope Gilliatt, "The Urgent Whisper," 79. I assume that one of the "erstwhile friends" is Truffaut. The other? Chabrol? Rohmer?
2 de Baecque, *Godard*, 336.

UNFINISHED BUSINESS: FILMS TRUFFAUT DIDN'T MAKE II
1 Barnes, *Flaubert's Parrot*, 115.
2 Updike, *Just Looking*, 82.
3 Drazin, *The Faber Book of French Cinema*, 369. The statistics are Drazin's.
4 Tarkovsky, *Journal 1970–1986*, 369.
5 Kael, *When the Lights Go Down*, 323–4.

A GRAVE IN MONTMARTRE
1 Stendhal, *The Life of Henri Brulard*, 206.
2 Léautaud, *Journal littéraire*, 24.
3 Ibid., 50.
4 de Baecque and Toubiana, *Truffaut*, 253–4.
5 Truffaut, *The Films in My Life*, 131.

LAST WORDS
1 Marie Dubois, "Interview with Marie Dubois," *Shoot the Piano Player* DVD. Marie Dubois died on 15 October 2014.
2 Almendros, "Interview with Nestor Almendros," *The Last Metro* DVD.
3 de Baecque and Guigue, *Le Dictionnaire Truffaut*, 236.
4 Truffaut, *Le Plaisir des yeux*, 271.

BIBLIOGRAPHY

BOOKS BY TRUFFAUT

[All of Truffaut's films are available on DVD and in the earlier VCR format, as are almost all the films and movies mentioned or discussed.]

The Adventures of Antoine Doinel. Translated by Helen G. Scott. New York: Simon and Schuster, 1971.
"Breathless: Truffaut Treatment for." *Breathless* Criterion DVD Handbook. No Date.
"Certain Tendency of French Cinema, A." jdcopp.blogspot.ca/2007/01/francois-truffaut-certain-tendency.html.
Le Cinéma selon François Truffaut. Edited by Anne Gillain. Paris: Flammarion, 1988.
Correspondence 1945–1984. Edited by Gilles Jacob and Claude de Givray. Translated by Gilbert Adair. New York: Farrar, Straus and Giroux, 1989.
The Films in My Life. Translated by Leonard Mayhew. New York: Simon and Schuster, 1978.
The 400 Blows. Edited by David Denby. New York: Grove Press, 1969.
Hitchcock. With the collaboration of Helen Scott. New York: Simon and Schuster, 1985.
Jules and Jim. Translated by Patrick Evans. Introduction by François Truffaut. London: Marion Boyars, 1993.
La Nuit Américaine et le Journal de tournage de Fahrenheit 451. Paris: Seghers, 1974.
L'Homme qui aimait les femmes: cinéroman. Paris: Éditions J'ai Lu, 1977.

Le Plaisir des yeux. Paris: Flammarion, 1987.

Small Change: A Film Novel. Edited by Helen Scott. Translated by Anselm Hollo. New York: Grove Press, 1976.

The Story of Adèle H. Edited by Helen Scott. Dialogue by Jan Dawson. New York: Grove Press, 1976.

Truffaut au travail. Edited by Carole Berre. Paris: Cahiers du Cinéma, 2004.

Truffaut by Truffaut. Edited by Dominique Rabourdin. Translated by Robert Erich Wolf. New York: Harry N. Abrams. 1987.

"Truffaut's Last Interview." www.newyorker.com/online/blogs/movies/2020/08/françois-truffaut-last-interviews.

BOOKS ABOUT TRUFFAUT, FILM, AND OTHER MATTERS

Adair, Gilbert. "Adèle H." In *François Truffaut Interviews*, edited by Ronald Bergan, 97–101. Jackson: University Press of Mississippi, 2008.

– "Rohmer's Percival." In *Eric Rohmer: Interviews*, edited by Fiona Handyside, 41–9. Jackson: University Press of Mississippi, 2013.

Adorno, T.W. *Notes on Literature*. 2 vols. Translated by Shierry Weber Nicholson. New York: Columbia University Press, 1991.

Almendros, Nestor. *Man with a Camera*. Translated by Rachel Phillips Belash. New York: Farrar, Straus and Giroux, 1984.

– "Interview with Nestor Almendros." *The Last Metro* DVD.

Andrew, Dudley and Anne Gillain. "It's Time for Truffaut: An Interview with Arnaud Desplechin." *Cineaste* 1 (Winter 2012): 4–10.

Affron, Mirella Jona and E. Rubinstein. *The Last Metro: François Truffaut Director*. New Brunswick, New Jersey: Rutgers University Press, 1985.

Aumont, Jean-Pierre. *Sun and Shadow*. Translated by Bruce Benderson. Foreword by François Truffaut. New York: W.W. Norton, 1977.

Auzel, Dominique. *François Truffaut: Les Mille et Une Nuits Américaines*. Paris: Henri Veyrier, 1990.

Baecque, Antoine de, and Serge Toubiana. *François Truffaut*. Paris: Gallimard, 1996.

– *Truffaut*. Translated by Catherine Temerson. New York: Alfred A. Knopf, 1999.

– *Godard: Biographie*. Paris: Grasset, 2010.

– and Arnaud Guigue, eds. *Le Dictionnaire Truffaut*: Paris: Éditions de la Martinière 2004.

Bakhtin, Mikhail. *Speech Genres & Other Late Essays*. Translated by Vern W. McGee. Austin: University of Texas Press, 1986.

Balthus. *Vanished Splendors: A Memoir*. Translated by Benjamin Ivry. Introduction by Joyce Carol Oates. New York: Ecco, 2002.

Balzac, Honoré de. *The Wrong Side of Paris*. Translated by Jordan Stump. New York: Modern Library, 2005.

Barnes, Julian. *Flaubert's Parrot*. London: Jonathan Cape, 1984.

– "Night for Day." *New York Review of Books* (11 October 1990): 14–16.

– *Talking It Over*. London: Jonathan Cape, 1991.

Barzini, Chiara. "Read My Lips." *Harper's* (May, 2012): 74–8.

Baudelaire, Charles. *Selected Writings on Art and Literature*. Translated with an Introduction by P.E. Charvet. London: Penguin Books, 1972.

Baye, Nathalie. "Nathalie Baye: 'Joelle, the Continuity Girl.'" *Day for Night* DVD.

Bazin, André. *The Cinema of Cruelty: From Buñuel to Hitchcock*. Edited with an introduction by François Truffaut. Translated by Tiffany Fliss. New York: Seaver Books, 1982.

– *French Cinema of the Occupation and Resistance*. Edited with an introduction by François Truffaut. Translated by Stanley Hochman. New York: Frederick Ungar, 1981.

– *Orson Welles: A Critical View*. Translated by Jonathan Rosenbaum. Foreword by François Truffaut. New York: Harper and Row, 1978.

– *What Is Cinema?* Vol. II. Translated by Hugh Gray. Foreword by François Truffaut. Berkeley: University of California Press, 1971.

Beattie, Ann. *The New Yorker Stories*. New York: Scribner, 2010.

Beckett, Samuel. *The Letters of Samuel Beckett,* Vol. I: 1929–1940. Edited by George Craig, Martha Dow Fehsenfeld, Dan Gunn, Lois More Overbeck. Cambridge: Cambridge University Press, 2009.

– *The Letters of Samuel Beckett*, Vol. II: 1941–1956. Edited by George Craig, Martha Dow Fehsenfeld, Dan Gunn, Lois More Overbeck. Cambridge: Cambridge University Press, 2011.

– *Molloy, Malone Dies, The Unnamable*. New York: Alfred A. Knopf, 1997.

Benjamin, Walter. *Illuminations*. Edited with an introduction by Hannah Arendt. Translated by Harry Zohn. New York: Schocken Books, 1969.

Bergala, Alain, Marc Chevrie, Serge Toubiana, eds. *Le Roman de François Truffaut*. Paris: Cahiers du Cinéma – Éditions de l'Étoile, 1985.

Bergan, Ronald. *Jean Renoir: Projections of Paradise*. New York: Alfred A. Knopf, 1983.

– ed. *François Truffaut Interviews*. Jackson: University Press of Mississippi, 2008.

Beylie, Claude and Alain Carbonnier. "Celluloid and Stone." In *Eric Rohmer: Interviews*, edited by Fiona Handiside, 72–81. Jackson: University Press of Mississippi, 2013.

Bickerton, Emilie. *A Short History of Cahiers du Cinéma*. London: Verso Books, 2011.

Bisset, Jacqueline. "*Day for Night*: A Conversation with Jacqueline Bisset." *Day for Night* DVD.

Blottner, Joseph. *Faulkner: a Biography*. 2 vols. New York: Random House, 1974.

Borges, Jorge Luis. *Selected Non-Fictions*. Edited by Eliot Weinberger. New York: Viking, 1999.

Bornstein, George. "Say It with Music." *Times Literary Supplement* (15 June 2012): 9.

Bradbury, Ray. *Fahrenheit 451*. New York: HarperCollins, 2011.

Braudy, Leo, ed. *Focus on Shoot the Piano Player*. Englewood Cliffs, NJ: Prentice-Hall, 1972.

– *The World in a Frame: What We See in Films*. Garden City: Anchor Press / Doubleday, 1976.

Braunberger, Pierre. *Cinémamémoire*. "Préface" by Jean-Luc Godard. Paris: Centre National de la Cinématographie, 1987.

Bray, Christopher. "G for Grand." *Times Literary Supplement* (26 September 2008): 33.

Brody, Richard. *Everything is Cinema: The Working Life of Jean-Luc Godard*. New York: Henry Holt and Company, 2008.

– "The Soft Skin." *The New Yorker* (14 March 2011): 12–13.

Buñuel, Luis. *My Last Sigh*. Translated by Abigail Israel. New York: Alfred A. Knopf, 1983.

Burke, Kenneth. *The Philosophy of Literary Form: Studies in Symbolic Action*. Baton Rouge: Louisiana State University Press, 1967.

Burlaev, Nikolai. "Interview with Nikolai Burlaev." *Stalker* DVD.

Butterfly, Elizabeth. *François Truffaut: Le Journal d'Alphonse*. Paris: Gallimard, 2004.

Calvino, Italo. *The Road to San Giovanni*. Translated by Tim Parks. Toronto: Vintage Canada, 1995.

Camus, Albert. *The Myth of Sisyphus and Other Essays*. Translated by Justin O'Brien. New York: Vintage Books, 1991.

– *Notebooks 1942–1951*. Translated by Justin O'Brien. New York: Harcourt Brace Jovanovich, 1965.

Cardullo, Bert, ed. *Michelangelo Antonioni Interviews*. Jackson: University Press of Mississippi, 2008.
Cavell, Stanley. *The World Viewed: Reflections on the Ontology of Film*. New York: Viking Press, 1971.
Chandler, Raymond. *The Raymond Chandler Papers*. Edited by Tom Hiney and Frank MacShane. New York: Atlantic Monthly Press, 1994.
Chandler, Robert. "Fearless Malevich." *New York Review of Books* (9 October 2014): 18–20.
Chutkow, Paul. *Depardieu: a Biography*. New York: Alfred A. Knopf, 1994.
Cocteau, Jean. "Lecture [1932]." *The Blood of the Poet* DVD.
Coetzee, J.M. *Diary of a Bad Year*. London: Harvill Secker, 2007.
Copleston, Frederick. *A History of Philosophy, Vol. VII: Modern Philosophy II*. Garden City, NY: Image Books, 1963.
Coutard, Raoul. "Interview with Raoul Coutard." *Week-end* DVD.
Crisp, C.G. *François Truffaut*. New York: Praeger, 1972.
Crittenden, Roger. *La Nuit Américaine (Day for Night)*. London: BFI, 1998.
Davenport, Guy. *A Balthus Notebook*. New York: Ecco, 1989.
Davies, Robertson. *Fifth Business*. New York: Viking Press, 1970.
Davis, Francis. *Afterglow: A Last Conversation with Pauline Kael*. Cambridge, MA: Da Capo Press, 2002.
Dixon, Wheeler Winston. *The Early Film Criticism of François Truffaut*. Bloomington: Indiana University Press, 1993.
Dow, Leslie Smith. *Adèle Hugo: La Misérable*. Frederiction: Goose Lane Press, 1993.
Drazin, Charles. *The Faber Book of French Cinema*. London: Faber and Faber, 2011.
Dyer, Geoff. *Zona: A Book about a Film about a Journey to a Room*. London: Canongate, 2012.
Eisenschitz, Bernard. *Nicholas Ray: An American Journey*. London: Faber and Faber, 1993.
Eliot, T.S. *Selected Essays*. London: Faber and Faber, 1969.
Faulkner, William. *Mosquitoes*. New York: Boni & Liveright, 1927.
– *The Wild Palms*. New York: Vintage Books, 1990.
Freiburg, Rudolf. "'Novels Come out of Life, Not out of Theories': An Interview with Julian Barnes." In *Conversations with Julian Barnes*, edited by Vanessa Guignery and Ryan Roberts, 31–52. Jackson: University Press of Mississippi, 2009.

Friedkin, William. *The Friedkin Connection: A Memoir*. New York: Harper, 2013.
Gallagher, Tag. *The Adventures of Roberto Rossellini*. New York: Da Capo Press, 1998.
Gide, André. *Journals 1889-1949*. Translated, selected and edited by Justin O'Brien. Harmondsworth: Penguin, 1956.
Gilliatt, Penelope. "The Urgent Whisper." In *Jean-Luc Godard Interviews*, edited by David Sterritt, 69-84.
Gilot, Françoise and Carlton Lake. *Life with Picasso*. New York: McGraw-Hill, 1964.
Golding, John. *Paths to the Absolute: Mondrian, Malevich, Kandinsky, Pollock, Newman, Rothko and Still*. Princeton: Princeton University Press, 2000.
Goodis, David. *Down There*. In *Crime Novels: American Noir of the 1950s*. Edited by Robert Polito. New York: Library of America, 1997.
Gramont, Sanche de. "Life Style of Homo Cinematicus." In *François Truffaut Interviews*, edited by Ronald Bergan, 32-47. Jackson: University Press of Mississippi, 2008.
Graukorger, Stephen. *Descartes: An Intellectual Biography*. Oxford: Oxford University Press, 1995.
Greer, Germaine. *The Female Eunuch*. London: Paladin, 1971
Grey, Marianne. *La Moreau*. New York: Donald I. Fine Books, 1994.
Guignery, Vanessa and Ryan Roberts, eds. *Conversations with Julian Barnes*. Jackson: University Press of Mississippi, 2009.
Guitry, Sacha. *If Memory Serves: Memoirs of Sacha Guitry*. Translated by Lewis Galantière. New York: Doubleday, Doran and Co., 1936.
– *Le Cinéma et moi*. Edited by André Bernard and Claude Gauteur. "Préface" by François Truffaut. Paris: Éditions Ramsay, 1977.
Gunn, Thom. *The Man with Night Sweats*. London: Faber and Faber, 1992.
Handyside, Fiona, ed. *Eric Rohmer: Interviews*. Jackson: University Press of Mississippi, 2013.
Harding, James. *Lost Illusions: Paul Léautaud and His World*. London: George Allen & Unwin, 1974.
Hoberman, J. "Godard the Obscure." *Harper's* (October 2008): 88-94.
Hugo, Adèle. *Le Journal d'Adèle Hugo*, 4 vols. Introduction and notes by Frances Vernon Guille. Paris: Lettres Modernes, 1968.
Ince, Karen, ed. *Five Directors: Auteurism from Assayas to Ozon*. Manchester: Manchester University Press, 2008.
Ingram, Robert and Paul Duncan, eds. *François Truffaut: The Complete Films*. Köln: Taschen, 2004.
Insdorf, Annette. *François Truffaut*. Cambridge: Cambridge University Press, 1994.

– "How Truffaut's *The Last Metro* Reflects Occupied Paris." In *François Truffaut Interviews*, edited by Ronald Bergan, 142–6. Jackson: Unversity Press of Mississippi, 2008.

James, Henry. *Stories of the Supernatural*. Edited by Leon Edel. New York: Taplinger Publishing Company, 1970.

Kael, Pauline. *Hooked*. New York: E.P. Dutton, 1989.

– *Kiss Kiss Bang Bang*. Boston: Little Brown, 1970.

– *Reeling*. Boston: Little, Brown, 1976.

– "Shoot the Piano Player." In Leo Braudy, *Focus on Shoot the Piano Player*, 77–82.

– *When the Lights Go Down*. New York: Holt Rinehart and Winston, 1980.

Kauffmann, Stanley. *Regarding Film*. Baltimore: Johns Hopkins Press, 2001.

– *A World on Film*. New York: Harper & Row, 1966.

Keegan, Susanne. *The Eye of God: A Life of Oskar Kokoschka*. London: Bloomsbury, 1999.

Keesey, Douglas. *Catherine Breillat*. Manchester: Manchester University Press, 2009.

Kennan, George F. *The Kennan Diaries*. Edited by Frank Costigliola. New York: W.W. Norton, 2014.

Landolfi, Tommaso. *Words in Motion and Other Stories*. Translated by Katherine Jason. Introduction by Italo Calvino. New York: Viking, 1986.

Lawrence, D.H. *Studies in Classic American Literature*. Harmondsworth: Penguin, 1971.

Léaud, Jean-Pierre. "Mes 400 Coups." *Elle* (18 October 2004): 108–10.

Léautaud, Paul. *Journal littéraire*, 19 vols. Paris: Mercure de France, 1954–66.

– *Journal littéraire*. Choix par Pascal Pia et Maurice Guyot. Paris: Mercure de France, 1968.

– *Le Petit Ami*. Paris: Mercure de France, 1987.

L'Express. "François T." In *François Truffaut Interviews*, edited by Ronald Bergan, 114–27. Jackson: University Press of Mississippi, 2008.

Lopate, Philip. *Totally, Tenderly, Tragically: Essays and Criticism from a Lifelong Affair with the Movies*. New York: Anchor/Doubleday, 1998.

Macdonald, Dwight. *Dwight Macdonald on Movies*. New York: Prentice-Hall, 1969.

Mankell, Henning. *The Troubled Man*. Toronto: Vintage Canada, 2011.

Makaryk, Irena R., ed. *Encyclopedia on Contemporary Literary Theory*. Toronto: University of Toronto Press, 1993.

Mars-Jones, Adam. *Noriko Smiling*. London: Notting Hill, 2011.

McCabe Colin. *Godard: A Portrait of the Artist at Seventy*. New York: Farrar, Straus and Giroux, 2003.

McCarthy, Todd. *Howard Hawks: The Grey Fox of Hollywood*. New York: Grove Press, 1997.

McGilligan, Patrick. *Alfred Hitchcock: A Life in Darkness and Light*. New York: Regan Books, 2003.

Meyers, Jeffrey. *John Huston: Courage and Art*. New York: Crown Archetype, 2011.

Monaco, James. *The New Wave: Truffaut, Godard, Chabrol, Rohmer, Rivette*. New York: Oxford University Press, 1981.

Montaigne, Michel de. *The Complete Works of Montaigne*. Translated by Donald N. Frame. Stanford: Stanford University Press, 1980.

Neuhoff, Eric. *Lettre ouverte à François Truffaut*. Paris: Albin Michel, 1987.

Ondaatje, Michael. *Running in the Family*. Toronto: McClelland & Stewart, 1982.

– *The Conversations: Walter Murch and the Art of Editing Film*. Toronto: Vintage Canada, 2002.

Painter, George. *Marcel Proust*. 2 vols. New York: Vintage, 1978.

Pater, Walter. *The Renaissance: Studies in Art and Poetry*. Introduction by Louis Kronenberger. New York: New American Library, 1959.

Percy, Walker. *The Moviegoer*. New York: Avon, 1982.

Pons, Maurice. *Virginales*. Paris: René Julliard, 1955.

Porcile, François. *Maurice Jaubert: Musicien populaire ou maudit?* Paris: Les Éditeurs Français Réunis, 1971.

Powell, Michael. *A Life in Movies: An Autobiography*. London: Heinemann, 1986.

– *Million-Dollar Movie*. London: Heinemann, 1992.

Proust, Marcel. *À la Recherche du temps perdu*. Paris: Bibliothèque de la Pléiade, 1954.

– *Finding Time Again*. Translated by Ian Patterson. London: Penguin, 2002.

– *Remembrance of Things Past II*. Translated by C.K. Scott Moncrieff and Terence Kilmartin. New York: Random House, 1981.

– *Selected Letters, Vol. I, 1880–1903*. Edited by Philip Kolb. Translated by Ralph Mannheim. New York: Doubleday, 1983.

– *Selected Letters, Vol. II, 1904–1909*. Edited by Philip Kolb. Translated by Terence Kilmartin. London: Collins, 1991.

– *Selected Letters, Vol. III, 1910–1917*. Edited by Philip Kolb. Translated by Ralph Mannheim. Chicago: University of Chicago Press, 1983.

– *Time Regained*. Translated by Andreas Mayor. London: Chatto & Windus, 1972.

Remarque, Erich Maria. *All Quiet on the Western Front*. New York: Little Brown and Company, 1929.

Renoir, Jean. *My Life and My Films*. Translated by Norman Denny. New York: Atheneum, 1974.

Richie, Donald. *Ozu*. Los Angeles: University of California Press, 1974.

Robb, Graham. *Victor Hugo*. London: Picador, 1997.

Roché, Henri-Pierre. *Jules and Jim*. Translated by Patrick Evans. Introduction by François Truffaut. London: Marion Boyars, 1993.

– *Jules et Jim*. Paris: Gallimard, 1953.

– *Deux Anglaises et le continent*. Paris: Gallimard, 1956.

Rohmer, Eric. *The Taste for Beauty*. Translated by Carol Volk. Cambridge: Cambridge University Press, 1989.

Romney, Jonathan. "Interview with Fanny Ardant." *The Observer* (15 June 2014). www.richardhartley.com/2014//06/fanny-ardant-tears-are-like-diamonds-you-cant-waste-them/.

Ross, Alex. *The Rest Is Noise: Listening to the Twentieth Century*. New York: Picador, 2007.

Rushdie, Salman. *The Ground beneath Her Feet*. New York: Alfred A. Knopf, 2004.

– *Joseph Anton*. New York: Alfred A. Knopf, 2012.

Russell, John. *Matisse: Father and Son*. New York: Harry N. Abrams, 1999.

Salter, James and Robert Phelps. *Memorable Days: The Selected Letters of James Salter and Robert Phelps*. Edited by John McIntyre. Foreword by Michael Dirda. Berkeley: Counterpoint, 2010.

Samuels, Charles Thomas. "François Truffaut." In *François Truffaut Interviews*, edited by Ronald Bergan, 55–74. Jackson: University Press of Mississippi, 2008.

– "Michelangelo Antonioni." In *Michelangelo Antonioni Interviews*, edited by Bert Cardullo, 79–103. Jackson: University Press of Mississippi, 2008.

Sarris, Andrew. *Confessions of a Cultist: On the Cinema 1955–1969*. New York: Simon and Schuster, 1970.

Saura, Carlos. "Interview with Carlos Saura." *Cria Cuervos* DVD.

Scammell, Michael. "The CIA's 'Zhivago.'" *The New York Review of Books* (10 July 2014): 39–41.

Schickel, Richard. *D.W. Griffith: An American Life*. New York: Simon and Schuster, 1984.

Schiffman, Suzanne. "Au Coeur de la méthode." In *Le Roman de François Truffaut*, edited by Alan Bergala, 77–82. Paris: Cahiers du Cinéma – Éditions de l'Étoile, 1985.

– "Interview with Suzanne Schiffman." *Shoot the Piano Player* DVD.

Scorsese, Martin. *My Voyage to Italy* DVD.
Sjöwall, Maj, and Per Wahlöö. *The Abominable Man*. Translated by Thomas Teal. New York: Vintage, 1972.
Sontag, Susan. *As Consciousness Is Harnessed to Flesh*. Edited by David Rieff. New York: Farrar, Straus and Giroux, 2012.
Steegmuller, Francis. *Cocteau: A Biography*. Boston: Little, Brown and Company. 1970.
Stendhal. *The Life of Henry Brulard*. Translated by Jean Stewart and B.C.J.G. Knight. Harmondsworth: Penguin, 1973.
– *Love*. Translated by Gilbert and Susanne Sale. London: Penguin, 1988.
Sterritt, David ed. *Jean-Luc Godard Interviews*. Jackson: University Press of Mississippi, 1998.
Talbot, Margaret. "Home Movies: Alexander Payne, High Plains Auteur." *New Yorker* (28 October 2013): 50–9.
Tarkovsky, Andrei. *Journal 1970–1986*. Translated from the Russian by Anne Kichilova with Charles H. de Brantes. Paris: Cahiers du Cinéma, 1993.
Tavernier, Bernard. "Interview" *Elena and Her Men* DVD.
Thomson, David. *"Have You Seen ... ?"* New York: Alfred A. Knopf, 2008.
– *The New Biographical Dictionary of Film*. New York: Alfred A. Knopf, 2002.
– *Suspects*. London: Secker and Warburg, 1985.
– "When Is a Movie Great?" *Harper's Magazine* (July 2011): 35–9.
Turk, Edward Baron. *Child of Paradise: Marcel Carné and the Golden Age of French Cinema*. Cambridge: Harvard University Press, 1989.
Turnell, Martin. *The Novel in France*. New York: Vintage, 1951
Ungari, Enzo (with Donald Ranvaud). *Bertolucci by Bertolucci*. Translated by Donald Ranvaud. London: Plexus, 1987.
Updike, John. *Just Looking: Essays on Art*. New York: Alfred A. Knopf, 1989.
– *My Father's Tears and Other Stories*. New York: Alfred A. Knopf, 2009.
Vico, Giambattista. *The New Science of Giambattista Vico*. Translated by Thomas Goddard Bergin and Max Harold Fisch. Ithaca: Cornell University Press, 1970.
Volpe, Sandro. "Sur des Thèmes de Henry James: François Truffaut, Jean Gruault et *La Chambre verte*." In *Narrare / Rappresentare*, edited by Francesca Torchi, 101–14. Bologna: CLUEB, 2003.
Wenders, Wim. *On Film*. Translated by Michael Hofmann. London: Faber and Faber, 2001.

Wilson-Smith, Timothy. *Delacroix: A Life.* London: Constable, 1992.
Wood, Michael. *Film: A Very Short Introduction.* New York: Oxford University Press, 2012.
Zagajewski, Adam. "Dangerous Considerations: A Notebook." *Poetry* (October 2007): 44–55.

INDEX

Adjani, Isabelle, 202–5
Agora, 161–2
Akhmatova, Anna: on *Doctor Zhivago*, 19
Aldrich, Robert, 170
Allen, Woody, 50, 116, 199, 241; *Annie Hall*, 144; Antoine Doinel and *Deconstructing Harry*, 144–5
Almendros, Nestor, 51, 90, 104, 157, 174, 207, 302
Althusser, Louis, 112
Amalric, Mathieu, 166
Amélie, 289–91
Amènabar, Alejandro, 162
Anderson, Wes, 12, 144; and Truffaut, 180–2
Angelou, Yves: *Colonel Chabert*, 279
Antonioni, Michelangelo, 12, 304n31
Ardant, Fanny, 24, 91, 192–3, 274–9; and *Il Divo* and *La Grande Bellezza*, 279
Arletty, 85, 109, 164, 239
L'Arroseur arosé, 42
Assayas, Olivier, 12, 62, 67; *Irma Vep* and *Day for Night*, 66–7

Astaire, Fred, 226
Auden, W.H., 69
Audiberti, Jacques, 87, 247
Aurenche, Jean, 36
Auteuil, Daniel, 14

Bach, Johann Sebastian, 43
The Bad and the Beautiful, 176
Badiou, Alain, 12–13
Baecque, Antoine de, 16, 65; Godard and Truffaut in *Two in the Wave*, 292–4
Bakhtin, Mikhail, 261
Balthus, 19, 85; *Le Passage du commerce Saint-André des Arts*, 234–5
Balzac, Honoré de, 49, 56, 84, 87, 107, 109, 266; allusions in Truffaut's films, 158; friendship in *The Wrong Side of Paris*, 70
Bardot, Brigitte, 9, 45
Barnes, Julian, 107–8, 295
Barthes, Roland, 12, 15, 122
Bartholdy, Frédéric, 23
Battleship Potemkin, 139

Bauby, Jean-Dominique, 166
Baumbach, Noah, 25, 58, 191–3, 199
Baye, Nathalie, 58, 177, 244–5
Bazin, André, 5–6, 9, 31–5, 37, 38, 82, 86, 113, 211, 260
Bazin, Janine, 34
Beattie, Ann, 95
Beauvois, Xavier, 58
Becker, Jacques, 37
Bellow, Saul: *More Die of Heartbreak*, 204
Bergan, Ronald, 101
Bergman, Ingmar, 12, 105, 157, 217–18; *Summer with Monika* and Truffaut, 56
Bergman, Ingrid, 271
Bertolucci, Bernardo, 62, 65–6; on *The Conformist*, 65; on *Last Tango in Paris*, 64–5
Bibesco, Antoine, 127
Bisset, Jacqueline, 176–9
Blain, Gérard, 41
Blier, Bernard, 164
The Blob, 30
Bolaño, Roberto, 109
Bondarchuk, Sergei, 270
Bonnello, Bertrand: *The Pornographer*, 67
Bonnie and Clyde, 46, 162
Bory, Jean-Louis, 105
Borzage, Frank: *The Mortal Storm* and *Shoot the Piano Player*, 81
Bost, Pierre, 36
Boulez, Pierre, 91
Bradbury, Ray: *Fahrenheit 451*, 126, 139–41; "The Picasso Summer" and Truffaut, 46

Brandt, Bill, 40, 146
Braque, Georges, 235
Braunberger, Pierre, 24, 31, 45; on Godard, Resnais and Truffaut, 18
Breillat Catherine, 12, 37, 62, 201; and *36 fillette*, 66, 147
Brel, Jacques, 164, 274–5
Bresson, Robert, 26, 33, 37, 189
Brialy, Jean-Claude, 156
Brody, Richard, 16, 65
Buñuel, Luis: *The Criminal Life of Archibaldo de la Cruz*, 251–3; *That Obscure Object of Desire*, *Tristana*, *Viridiana*, 162
Burke, Kenneth, 15
Butor, Michel, 15

Cahiers du Cinéma, 31–41, 152, 232, 271
Camus, Albert, 31; *Don Juan* and *The Myth of Sisyphus*, 221–2; on writing, 15
Carax, Leos, 12, 136
Carillo, Leo, 28
Carné, Marcel, 13, 20, 91; *Les Enfants du Paradis*, 25, 239; *Les Visiteurs de Soir*, 33
Cartier-Bresson, Henri, 40, 234
Caron, Leslie, 94, 226–8
Carson, Anne, 210
Cavalcanti, Alberto, 39
Céline, Louis-Ferdinand, 299
Chabrol, Claude, 9, 157, 200; with Truffaut and Hitchcock, 150
Chandler, Raymond, 49
Chaplin, Charlie, 9, 23, 32, 251, 290
Chevalier, Maurice, 164
Chiarini, Luigi, 10

Chirac, Jacques, 87
Christopher, Michael: *Original Sin* and *Mississippi Mermaid*, 137
Clair, René, 39
Clark, Dee, 262
Clift, Montgomery, 62
Cluzot, Henri: *The Crow*, 25
Cocker, Joe, 78
Cocteau, Jean, 32, 62, 164; on black and white film, 186
Coetzee, on *The Brothers Karamazov*; 261 J.M.: on old age, 20
Constant, Benjamin: on love in *Adolphe*, 86
Constantine, Eddie, 124
Cotten, Joseph, 42
Cottilard, Marion, 183
Coutard, Raoul, 77, 138
Crawford, Joan, 169, 227
Cukor, George, 157

Dadd, Richard: "The Fairy Feller's Master-Stroke," 235
Darrieux, Danielle, 133
Davies, Robertson: on faith and old age in *Fifth Business*, 214
The Day the Earth Stood Still, 30
Day-Lewis, Daniel, 183–4
Dean, James, 41
de Beauvoir, Simone: *La Cerémonie des adieux*, 228
de Gaulle, Charles, 87
de Givray, Claude, 263
Delacroix, Eugène, 204, 309
Delannoy, Jean, 38; *La Symphonie Pastorale* and *Shoot the Piano Player*, 80–1

de la Tour, Georges, 202
de Laurentis, Dino, 45
Delerue, Georges, 85, 173
DeMille, Cecil B.: *Samson and Delilah*, 29; and Jeanie Macpherson, 229
Demongeot, Catherine, 82
Demy, Jacques, 131–3, 214
Denby, David, 20
Deneuve, Catherine, 45, 51, 91, 94, 131–3, 160, 206–8; Truffaut on her beauty, 227
Depardieu, Gérard, 24, 50, 274–7
Derain, André, 234
Derrida, Jacques, 112
Desailly, Jean, 81, 114
De Sica, Vittorio, 157
Desplechin, Arnaud: *A Christmas Tale*, 216
Dickens, Charles, 109, 284; *David Copperfield* in *Fahrenheit 451*, 124
Le Dictionnaire Truffaut, 226, 230
Dietrich, Marlene, 85
Dorléac, Françoise, 94, 131–3
Dostoevsky, Fyodor, 262
Douglas, Kirk, 236
Dow, Leslie Ann, 203
Downing, Fred, 120
Drazin, Charles, 20
Dreyer, Carl: *The Passion of Joan of Arc*, 19
Dubois, Marie, 79; on last meeting with Truffaut, 302
Dumas, Alexander, 296
Duras, Marguerite, 112
Duvivier, Julien, 44
Dyer, Geoff, 14, 262; on Tarkovsky, 52

Eastwood, Clint, 36
Edwards, Blake, 10
Eliot, T.S.: on *Hamlet*, 56
Éluard, Paul, 124
Êustache, Jean, 62, 191

Fassbinder, Rainer Werner, 112; filming *Beware of a Holy Whore*, 176
Faulkner, William, 38, 156, 205, 217; *The Wild Palms*, 249
Faure-Poirée, Colline, 24
Fellini, Federico, 12, 183–4, 264, 271
Finney, Albert, 46, 209–10
Flaubert, Gustave, 94, 97, 249; *A Sentimental Education* and *The Story of Adèle H.*, 203
Fonda, Jane, 45
Forbidden Planet, 30
Ford, John, 139, 157
Foucault, Michel, 12, 112
France, Anatole, 134–5, 281
Frasier, 220
Frye, Northrop, 120
Fuller, Samuel, 38

Gabin, Jean, 164, 176–7
Gallant, Mavis, 194
Gance, Abel, 20, 88
Gardner, Ava, 109
Gass, William, 210
Genet, Jean, 82, 87
Gibbs, Nancy, 120
Gibson, Mel, 30
Gide, André, 80; on childhood reading, 30
Giordana, Marco Tullio: *The Best of Youth*, 214

Giraudoux, Jean, 87, 268
Gish, Lillian, 165
Godard, Jean-Luc, 9–19, 24, 46, 50, 59, 62, 92, 108, 113, 133, 199, 212, 263, 281–3; on friends, 93; and Piet Mondrian, 283; and Rossellini, 273; as Socrates, 93; on Truffaut as critic, 36
Godard, Jean-Luc (films): *Breathless*, 19, 82–3, 105, 117, 177, 258; *Les Carabiniers*, 117; *La Chinoise*, 66, 82; *Deux ou Trois Choses que je sais d'elle*, 293; *Histoire(s) du cinéma*, 93, 273, 293; *Ici et Ailleurs* and *The Last Metro*, 264; *Made in USA*, 16; *Masculin-Féminin*, 63–4, 140; *Pierrot le fou*, 158; *Sympathy for the Devil*, 18; *Vivre sa vie*, 273; *Weekend*, 63, 138–41
Goldwyn, Samuel, 36
Goodis, David, and *Shoot the Piano Player*, 16, 75, 79
Goodman, Benny, 146
Gösta Berling, 139
Graukorger, Stephen, 250
Greer, Germaine, 162
Greer, Jane, 236
Grey, Zane, 28
Griffith, D.W., 165
Gruault, Jean, 156, 196; and *The Green Room*, 238, 244
Guille, Frances Vernor, 206
Guitry, Sacha, 72–4, 88, 136; *The Story of a Cheat*, 25

Haneke, Michael, 166
Harding, James, on Paul Léautaud, 197
Hardy, Thomas, 247

Hawks, Howard, 38
Hayworth, Rita, 109, 192, 278
Heller, Joseph, 110
Hemingway, Ernest, 86
Herzog, Werner, 20, 112
Hessel, Helen: and *Jules and Jim*, 100
Hitchcock, Alfred, 10, 13, 50, 251; compared to Renoir, 32; and Truffaut, 148–52
Hitler, Adolf, 28; and Chaplin, 32
Hobbes, Thomas, *Leviathan*, 138
Hopkins, Miriam, 95
Hugo, Victor, 24, 106, 127, 202
Hundertwasser, Fritz, 234
Huston, John: *The Maltese Falcon*, 38

Intolerance, 29
Invasion of the Body Snatchers (Don Siegel), 30

Jade, Claude, 94
James, Henry, 24, 49; "The Altar of the Dead," "The Beast in the Jungle," "The Friends of the Friends," and *The Green Room*, 238, 241–9
Jameson, Fredric, 37
Jaubert, Maurice, 33, 202, 298
The Jazz Singer, 29
Jeopardy, 220
Johnny Guitar, 139, 168–70
Joyce, James, 110

Kael, Pauline, 20, 38, 179, 297; on "Don Juanism" in film, 207; on *Shoot the Piano Player*, 76–9; on Truffaut, 185–9; on Truffaut and Godard, 258–60

Karina, Anna, 19, 161
Kauffman, Stanley, 260
Kaurismäki, Aki, 62
Kechiche, Abdellatif: *La Vie d'Adèle* (*Blue Is the Warmest Colour*) and *The Story of Adèle H.*, 208
Keesey, Douglas, 38
Kelly, Gene, 226
Kennan, George, F., 28–9
Kerr, Deborah, 29
Kiarostami, Abbas, 61, 306n5
Kierkegaard, Søren, 79, 121, 190, 223; in Walker Percy's *The Moviegoer*, 123
Kokoschka, Oskar, 253–4
Korczak, Janusz, 87
Krupa, Gene, 146
Kundera, Milan: *Ignorance*, 215; *Immortality*, 222
Kurosawa, Akira, 269

Lacan, Jacques, 112, 209
Lachenay, Pierre, 81
Lachenay, Robert, 69–71
Lafont, Bernadette, 41–3
Lamarr, Hedy, 29, 257
The Land of the Pharaohs, 30
Lang, Fritz, 38
Lawrence, D.H., 15, 57, 94, 97, 98, 215, 249, 259, 289
Léaud, Jean-Pierre, 6, 62–8; on Truffaut, 302
Léautaud, Paul, 113, 194–8, 286
Leconte, Patrice, 12; and *The Girl on the Bridge*, 146–7
Lelouch, Claude, 11, 133
Léotard, Philippe, 194
Le Roy, Mervyn: *Quo Vadis?*, 29

Index | 335

Lessing, Gotthold Ephraim, 48
Lévy, Roland, 23–5
Linklater, Richard, 61
Litvin, Liliane, 44, 208
Lonsdale, Michael, 128
Losey, Joseph: *Mr Klein*, 264
Lubitsch, Ernst, 73

Macdonald, Dwight, 37, 97
Mahler, Alma, 253–4
Mahoney, Jock, 28
Mailer, Norman, 283
Malle, Louis, 9, 129; *Lacombe, Lucien*, 264
Malson, Lucien, 142
Mankell, Henning: *The Troubled Man*, 57, 285
Mann, Anthony, 236
Mann, Thomas: *Doctor Faustus*, 237, 259
Mansfield, Jayne, 133
Márquez, Gabriel García, 109; old age in *Love in the Time of Cholera*, 214–15
Mars-Jones, Adam, 62
Matisse, Henri, 16, 234
Mature, Victor, 29
May, Karl, 28
McCabe, Colin, 16, 65
McCambridge, Mercedes, 169
Méliès, George, 164
Melville, Jean-Pierre, 37, 199; *Bob the Gambler* and *Shoot the Piano Player*, 75
Mérimée, Prosper: "Le Vase Étrusque," 244
Messiaen, Pierre, 91
Michelangelo, Buonarroti, 16

Miéville, Anne-Marie: on Godard and Truffaut, 10, 294
Milestone, Lewis, 88
Miller, Claude, 46
Mimieux, Yvette, 46
Mitchum, Robert, 236
Montand, Yves, 164
Monteiro, João César, 224–5
Moreau, Jeanne, 42, 87, 91, 94, 195; and Malle's *The Lovers*, 129; in Venice, 119–23
Morgan, Michelle, 81
Morgenstern, Madeleine, 24, 71, 94, 160, 228, 294
Morse, Inspector, 285
Mounier, Emmanuel, 33
Mozart, Wolfgang Amadeus: *Don Giovanni*, 223
Munch, Edvard, 175, 281
Murdoch, Iris, 259

Nabokov, Vladimir, 224, 259
Neill, A.S., 87
Neuhoff, Eric, 14, 194; on seeing Truffaut, 119–20
Nine, 183–4
Nureyev, Rudolf, 235
Nussbaum, Martha, 19

O'Hara, Maureen, 172
Ondaatje, Michael, 15, 25; and Godard, 281–3; *Running in the Family* and Truffaut, 25
Ophuls, Max: and *Le Journal d'Alphonse*, 285; *Le Plaisir* and *The Woman Next Door*, 253 *La Ronde* and *Shoot the Piano Player*, 78
Orbach, Jerry, 285

Ozon, François, 12, 193, 266
Ozu, Yasujiro, 19, 174, 188, 261; his grave, 299

Pabst, G.W., 87
Painter, George, 228
Paradis, Vanessa, 146
Pascal, Blaise, 19
Pasolini, Pier Paolo, 62
Pater, Walter, 96
Pawlikowski, Pawel, 189
Payne, Alexander: on black and white films, 186
Penn, Arthur, 91, 133
Percy, Walker: "certification," 199; and *The Moviegoer* and despair, 121
Perl, Jed, 15
Piaf, Edith, 164
Pialat, Maurice, 54; *L'Enfance nue* and Truffaut, 142–3
Picasso, Pablo, 16, 46, 47
Piccoli, Michel, 133
Piero della Francesca, 234
Plevano, Rosa Maria, 120
Plummer, Christopher, 120
Pollock, Jackson, 259
Pompidou, Georges, 87
Pons, Maurice, 41
Powell, Anthony, 99, 266
Powell, Michael, 165, 269; on black and white films, 188
Preminger, Otto, 50, 86
Prévert, Jacques, 87
Proust, Marcel, 48–9, 97, 228, 239, 241, 266; on learning English, 127; on Paul Léautaud, 197
Purdy, Al, 15
Pynchon, Thomas, 109

Rawls, John, 213
Ray, Nicholas, 168–9
Ray, Robert T., 172
Reagan, Ronald, 87
Redon, Odilon, 309n1
Remarque, Erich Maria, 315n5
Renaldo, Duncan: and *The Cisco Kid*, 28
Renaud, Jules, *Poil de carotte*, 40
Renoir, Jean, 20, 45, 50, 79, 81, 112, 168, 172, 188; and Bazin, 32; *Boudu Saved from Drowning* and Truffaut, 68; *French Cancan*, 45, 176–9, 265; on *The Lower Depths*, 52; *The Night at the Crossroads*, 168; *The Rules of the Game*, 25; and stamps, 164
Rerberg, Georgi, 52
Resnais, Alain, 9, 18, 20; and *Hiroshima, mon amour*, 105; *Vous n'avez encore rien vu*, 20
Rivette, Jacques, 9; censoring of *La Religieuse*, 126; *La Duchesse de Langeais*, 279; *Hurlevant*, 231; nudity in *La Belle Noiseuse*, 227
The Road to Morocco, 28
Robb, Graham, 203
Roché, Henri-Pierre, 70, 97, 155–6, 161, 221
Rodin, Auguste, 158
Rohmer, Eric, 9, 44, 175, 199, 212, 278; on adaptations, 38; *La Collectioneuse* and *Jules and Jim*, 104–6
Ronin, 128
Rooney, Mickey, 68
Rossellini, Marcelina, 272
Rossellini, Roberto, 32, 44–5, 148, 172, 271–3
Ruiz, Raul, 62

Rushdie, Salman, 109–11, 247

Salter, James, 96
Sanders, George, 29, 271
Sarris, Andrew, 37
Sartre, Jean-Paul, 9, 37, 54, 89, 228
Saura, Carlos, 61, 114–15; on *Los Golfos*, 118; failure of *La Noche Oscura* and *El Dorado*, 117
Schiffman, Suzanne, 5–6, 229–31; "Au Coeur de la méthode" and Truffaut, 229; on Truffaut's approach to film, 118
Schnabel, Julian: *The Diving Bell and the Butterfly*, 116–17, 166
Schneider, Romy, 164
Schrader, Paul, 261
Scorsese, Martin, 12, 30, 36, 112; *Raging Bull* and black and white films, 188
Scott, Helen, 24; role in *Bed and Board*, 230; with Truffaut and Hitchcock, 150
Scott, Randolph, 28
The Searchers, 139
Shakespeare, William, 25, 167, 225, 275, 283
Signoret, Simone, 164
Simone, Nina, 275
Sinatra, Frank, 170
Singing in the Rain, 176
Skolimowski, Jerzy, 62
Skvorecky, Josef, 15, 264
Socrates, 93
Soderbergh, Steven, 36
Solzhenitsyn, Alexandr: *The First Circle*, 239
Sontag, Susan, 20
Sorrentino, Paolo, 12, 295
The Sorrow and the Pity, 264
Soulages, Pierre, 146
Stauffer, Ruby, 120
Stein, Gertrude, 209–10
Stendhal, 11, 37, 75, 85, 87, 112, 274, 300
Stevenson, Robert Louis, 126, 243
Stone, Oliver, 36
Sturges, Preston, 251
Sullavan, Margaret, 81
Szpilman, Wladyslaw, 265

Tarantino, Quentin, 12
Tarkovsky, Andrei, 52, 61, 112, 157, 262, 269; on Truffaut's films, 278
Tavernier, Bernard, 168
Taylor, Rod, 91
Thomson, David, 20, 62; on *The Diving Bell and the Butterfly*, 166; on *Mississippi Mermaid*, 136–7
Tolstoy, Leo: *War and Peace*, 48, 92, 285
Tornatore, Giuseppe: *Cinema Paradiso*, 57
Trenet, Charles, 87
Truffaut, François (articles and books): "Année d'enfance assassinée," 213; "A Certain Tendency in French Cinema," 36–40, 92; *Hitchcock*, 148–52; "La Savate et la Finance, ou deux ou trois choses que sais d'elle," 303n5
Truffaut, François (films): *Bed and Board*, 86, 290; *The Bride Wore Black*, 84, 128–9; *Confidentially Yours*, 16, 155, 211, 252; *Day for*

Night, 34, 67, 73, 91, 92, 176–9, 180–2, 183–4, 252, 286, 290; *Fahrenheit 451*, 84, 124–7, 138–41, 173, 247; *400 Blows*, 53–61, 73, 93, 105, 147, 166, 285, 290; *The Green Room*, 34, 102, 173, 241–9, 251–2, 266; *Jules and Jim*, 73, 95–103, 107–8, 109–11, 147, 157, 247, 289; *The Last Metro*, 39, 101, 153, 263–8; *Love on the Run*, 24, 153, 285; *The Man Who Loved Women*, 99, 100, 147, 153–4, 221–7; *The Mischief Makers*, 39, 41–3, 73, 212; *Mississippi Mermaid*, 79, 136–7, 186; *Shoot the Piano Player*, 39, 73, 75–81, 186, 260; *Small Change*, 34, 111, 186, 211–13; *The Soft Skin*, 81, 114–15, 140, 290; *Stolen Kisses*, 100–1, 135–6; *The Story of Adèle H.*, 99, 102, 147, 201–5, 206–8, 209–10, 258; *Such a Gorgeous Kid Like Me*, 84, 99, 102; *Two English Girls*, 73, 97, 101, 153–4, 156–60, 161–2, 266; *The Wild Child*, 34, 80, 86, 138–41, 164, 258; *The Woman Next Door*, 42, 73, 101, 102, 132, 161, 174, 227, 274–7, 290

Truffaut, François (life), 5–21, 23–40, 53–61, 69–71, 84–9, 90–4, 206, 232–3; on Bergman's female characters, 217–18; on Bunuel, 250–3; on Carné's *Terrain vague*, 91; on children, "Année d'enfance assassinéee," 213; and contemporary thought, 112; on the director's "delayed insight" into own work, 207; and English, 125; on Eric Rohmer, 105–6; on Godard's politics, 93; on Hitchcock, 148–52; *Le Journal d'Alphonse*, 275, 284–7; on Nicholas Ray, 168–70; on nudity in film, 129; on Proust, 135–6; typewriters, 153–5; unfinished projects, 295–7

Truffaut, Janine, 23, 58–61, 92
Truffaut, Roland, 23–4, 58–61
Turk, Edward, Baron, 20

Ulysses, 145
Updike, John, 295; old age in "Free," 215
Uris, Leon, 110

Vadim, Roger: *And God Created Woman*, 45
Valli, Alida, 41
Van Gogh, Vincent, 94, 234
Varda, Agnes, 9
Ventura, Lino, 164
Vico, Giambattista, 140
Vidal, Gore, 120
Vigo, Jean, 20, 48, 54, 143
Visconti, Luchino, 133
von Sternberg, Joseph, 50, 86
von Trotta, Margarethe, 112, 166

Wajda, Andrzej, 87
Wayne, John, 28
Weisz, Rachel, 162
Welles, Orson, 10, 86, 172; compared to Herman Goering, 10
Wenders, Wim, 112, 185–9, 299; on black and white films, 186
Werner, Oskar, 173
Wiesel, Elie, 45
The Wild Bunch, 162

Wilde, Oscar, 247
Woolf, Virginia, 94
Woolson, Constance Fenimore, 243
Wyler, William: *Dodsworth* and *Jules and Jim*, 100

Zagajewski, Adam, 190